ENGLISH

ELGIN HIGH SCHOOL

Bloom's Literary Themes

∽✕∾

Alienation
Death and Dying
Human Sexuality
Rebirth and Renewal
The American Dream
The Grotesque
The Hero's Journey
The Labyrinth

Bloom's Literary Themes

THE HERO'S JOURNEY

Edited and with an introduction by
Harold Bloom
Sterling Professor of the Humanities
Yale University

Volume Editor
Blake Hobby

BLOOM'S
LITERARY CRITICISM
An imprint of Infobase Publishing

Bloom's Literary Themes: The Hero's Journey

Bloom's Literary Criticism
An imprint of Infobase Publishing
132 West 31st Street
New York NY 10001

Library of Congress Cataloging-in-Publication Data

The hero's journey / edited and with an introduction by Harold Bloom ; volume editor, Blake Hobby.
   p. cm. — (Bloom's literary themes)
 Includes bibliographical references and index.
 ISBN 978-0-7910-9803-5 (acid-free paper) 1. Heroes in literature. 2. Travel in literature. I. Bloom, Harold. II. Hobby, Blake.
 PN56.5.H45H47 2009
 809'.93352—dc22
                    2008042983

Text design by Kerry Casey
Cover design by Takeshi Takahashi

Printed in the United States of America

IBT FOF 10 9 8 7 6 5 4 3 2

This book is printed on acid-free paper.

~ Contents ~

Series Introduction by Harold Bloom: Themes and Metaphors

1. TOPOS AND TROPE

What we now call a theme or topic or subject initially was named a *topos*, ancient Greek for "place." Literary *topoi* are commonplaces, but also arguments or assertions. A topos can be regarded as literal when opposed to a trope or turning which is figurative and which can be a metaphor or some related departure from the literal: ironies, synecdoches (part for whole), metonymies (representations by contiguity) or hyperboles (overstatements). Themes and metaphors engender one another in all significant literary compositions.

As a theoretician of the relation between the matter and the rhetoric of high literature, I tend to define metaphor as a figure of desire rather than a figure of knowledge. We welcome literary metaphor because it enables fictions to persuade us of beautiful untrue things, as Oscar Wilde phrased it. Literary *topoi* can be regarded as places where we store information, in order to amplify the themes that interest us.

This series of volumes, *Bloom's Literary Themes*, offers students and general readers helpful essays on such perpetually crucial topics as the Hero's Journey, the Labyrinth, the Sublime, Death and Dying, the Taboo, the Trickster, and many more. These subjects are chosen for their prevalence yet also for their centrality. They express the whole concern of human existence now in the twenty-first century of the Common Era. Some of the topics would have seemed odd at another time, another land: the American Dream, Enslavement and Emancipation, Civil Disobedience.

I suspect though that our current preoccupations would have existed always and everywhere, under other names. Tropes change across the centuries: the irony of one age is rarely the irony of another. But the themes of great literature, though immensely varied, undergo transmemberment and show up barely disguised in different contexts. The power of imaginative literature relies upon three constants: aesthetic splendor, cognitive power, wisdom. These are not bound by societal constraints or resentments, and ultimately are universals, and so not culture-bound. Shakespeare, except for the world's scriptures, is the one universal author, whether he is read and played in Bulgaria or Indonesia or wherever. His supremacy at creating human beings breaks through even the barrier of language and puts everyone on his stage. This means that the matter of his work has migrated everywhere, reinforcing the common places we all inhabit in his themes.

2. Contest as both Theme and Trope

Great writing or the Sublime rarely emanates directly from themes since all authors are mediated by forerunners and by contemporary rivals. Nietzsche enhanced our awareness of the agonistic foundations of ancient Greek literature and culture, from Hesiod's contest with Homer on to the Hellenistic critic Longinus in his treatise *On the Sublime*. Even Shakespeare had to begin by overcoming Christopher Marlowe, only a few months his senior. William Faulkner stemmed from the Polish-English novelist Joseph Conrad and our best living author of prose fiction, Philip Roth, is inconceivable without his descent from the major Jewish literary phenomenon of the twentieth century, Franz Kafka of Prague, who wrote the most lucid German since Goethe.

The contest with past achievement is the hidden theme of all major canonical literature in Western tradition. Literary influence is both an overwhelming metaphor for literature itself, and a common topic for all criticism, whether or not the critic knows her immersion in the incessant flood.

Every theme in this series touches upon a contest with anteriority, whether with the presence of death, the hero's quest, the overcoming of taboos, or all of the other concerns, volume by volume. From Monteverdi through Bach to Stravinsky, or from the Italian Renaissance through the agon of Matisse and Picasso, the history of all the arts demonstrates the same patterns as literature's thematic struggle with itself. Our country's great original art, jazz, is illuminated by what the great creators called "cutting contests," from Louis Armstrong and

Duke Ellington on to the emergence of Charlie Parker's Bop or revisionist jazz.

A literary theme, however authentic, would come to nothing without rhetorical eloquence or mastery of metaphor. But to experience the study of the common places of invention is an apt training in the apprehension of aesthetic value in poetry and in prose.

Volume Introduction by Harold Bloom

The High Romantic internalization of quest-romance sent the poet-as-hero upon an inward journey still central to Western literature. Ancestral paradigm of such a trek to the interior is the Shakespearean tragic hero Hamlet and his even darker successor Macbeth. Hamlet, the hero of Western consciousness, voyages to the bourn of death's undiscovered country while Macbeth drives himself into the heart of his own darkness.

Most conspicuous of Romantic poet heroes, George Gordon, Lord Byron, made his final journey to Greece in order to lead an army of brigands in rebellion against the Turks. His best friend Shelley, an incessant revolutionary, was a more metaphysical quester, starting with *Alastor: The Spirit of Solitude* and ending with a Sublime death-fragment, *The Triumph of Life*.

Shelley's lifelong disciple, the superb dramatic monologist Robert Browning, wrote the starkest of hero-journeys in *Childe Roland to the Dark Tower Came* where the quester, after a life spent training for the sight, fails to recognize the Dark Tower and ends in defiance, dauntlessly repeating Shelley's "trumpet of a prophecy."

The American revision of the poet-hero's journey has Walt Whitman's *Leaves of Grass* as its Scripture. *Song of Myself* begins as a joyous quest for the authentic "knit of identity" and starts a Great Decade of poetry that culminates in the majestic elegy *When Liliacs Last in the Dooryard Bloom'd*. The American poet-hero's journey ends in a transcendence of death, a new mode of apotheosis in which Whitman marries the visionary fourfold of Night, Death, the Mother, and the Sea.

American Romanticism's triumph and sorrow inform our greatest poet since Whitman and Emily Dickinson, the seer of *White*

Buildings, The Bridge, and "The Broken Tower"—Hart Crane, the Orphic splendor of our own imaginative tradition. *The Bridge,* which disputes with *Song of Myself* and *Moby-Dick* the honor of being *the* American epic, portrays a poet-hero's journey from dawn to dusk on a New York City day. Journeying both to his own and his nation's past, Crane follows the hero's trajectory from childhood through poetic incarnation and on to a descent into Avernos in "The Tunnel," an unmatchable demonic vision of the New York subway. In the epic's final chant, "Atlantis," the poet celebrates the vision of a lost mythic America. Surpassingly, *The Bridge* "lends a myth to God," who certainly seems to need it.

THE AENEID
(VIRGIL)

"Aeneas"
by T. R. Glover,
in *Virgil* (1904)

INTRODUCTION

As repositories of myth, Homer's *Iliad* and Virgil's *Aeneid* express how two vast civilizations—one Hellenic, the other Roman—understand themselves, seek to preserve the past, and envision a future based upon a structured social order seeking justice. The self-sacrificing heroes of each of these epics, Achilles and Aeneas, complete perilous journeys, vying for control amid warring foes and intervening gods. They battle for the founding of the social order and undertake mythic journeys that demand perseverance amid strife. During their epic struggles, key values emerge. These highly imaginative tales, set in a distant past, were intended to offer instructive stories for those seeking to survive and gain wisdom. Ultimately, both mythic worlds preserve the past, speak to the present, and define values for the future. By comparing Greek and Roman epic, both of which contain larger-than-life figures that meet moral obligations through strife, early twentieth-century critic

---

Glover, T.R. "Aeneas." *Virgil*. Seventh Edition. New York and London: Barnes & Noble, Methuen & Co., 1969 (First printed in 1904). 208–32.

T.R. Glover argues that what distinguishes the two is Virgil's idea of destiny, one in which Aeneas supplicates himself to the gods, embodying what Glover sees as Christian piety.

⁕

Aeneas is not at all a hero of the type of Achilles, and if we come to the *Aeneid* with preconceived opinions of what the hero of an epic should be, we run the risk of disappointment and also of losing Virgil's judgment upon human life. Virgil obviously did not intend to make a copy of Homer's Achilles or of any of Homer's heroes. That was a feat to be left to Quintus of Smyrna. If, as it is, there is an air of anachronism about Virgil's Aeneas, there would have been a far profounder anachronism about him if in the age of Augustus he had been a real Homeric hero. The world, as we have seen, had moved far and fast since Homer's day. Plato's repudiation of Homer meant that a new outlook and new principles were needed in view of new conditions of life and the new thoughts which they waked. In its turn the impulse, with which we connect the literature of Athens, and such names as Euripides, Plato, and Aristotle, was itself spent, though not before it had made an imperishable contribution to the growth of mankind. The world was awaiting another fresh impulse, and, till this should come, it was occupied in analyzing, coordinating, and developing its existing stock of ideas, not without some consciousness that they were already inadequate.

It was at this moment that Virgil wrote, and as he was a poet rather than a mere scholar or antiquarian, he sought to bring his Aeneas into connexion with his own age, while, if possible, still keeping him a Homeric hero. It was hardly to be done. If Aeneas as the ideal hero was to be the "heir of all ages," it would be difficult to keep the simplicity of Homer's outlook and philosophy. Aeneas could not stand in Achilles' relation to men. He must have new virtues which had been discovered since Homer's day, if he was to be a hero near the hearts of Virgil's contemporaries—the new private virtues which Menander and Cleanthes and many more were finding out, and the new political virtues which Alexander and the Ptolemies, Julius and Augustus, were revealing to the world. Aeneas, again, could not stand in Achilles' relation to heaven. The gods no longer came among men in bodily form, they were far away; and yet perhaps they were not so very far away after all—

deum namque ire per omnes. [1]

This is another reason why Aeneas does not appeal to us as Achilles does. The fusion of the Homeric and the modern types is not complete. Virgil's Aeneas is two heroes in one, perhaps more, for beside the Homeric hero and the modern hero one feels sometimes that we have another creature, which is not a hero at all, but an idea[2], an allegory of a virtue, and a political virtue at that, partially incarnated.

To understand the character and the poem of which it is the center, it will be helpful to analyze the various elements in Aeneas. In this process we shall necessarily lose our consciousness of what we have felt to be the great defect of the hero, his want of unity, and we shall probably gain a clearer notion of what the poet intended.

First of all, there is Aeneas conceived as a Homeric hero. Aeneas has of course the heroic manner, in measure, but not quite the manner of Homeric heroes, a more magnificent, a more courtly manner. He has the wealth of the Homeric hero, and his habit of giving splendid presents and receiving them. At times, Virgil would have us think, he feels the same wild delight in battle which we find in Homer's heroes. "Lie there now, terrible one! No mother's love shall lay thee in the sod, or place thy limbs beneath thine heavy ancestral tomb. To birds of prey shalt thou be left, or borne down in the eddying water, where hungry fish shall suck thy wounds."[3] This is what Virgil remembers to have read in the *Iliad;* he blends what Odysseus says to Socus with Achilles' words to Lycaon.[4] But the words are still Homer's; they do not belong to Aeneas. Again, the reservation of eight captured youths to be sacrificed to the Manes of Pallas[5] can be defended by the Homeric parallel of Achilles slaying Trojans over the pyre of Patroclus[6] and by more awful contemporary parallels, but still it is not convincing. Augustus may have ordered or performed a human sacrifice[7], but when Virgil transfers this to Aeneas, the reader feels the justice of Aristotle's paradox: "there is no reason why *some* events that have actually happened should not conform to the law of the probable and possible."[8] This may have been an actual event, but it is not "probable" here.

But perhaps the most incongruous Homeric touch in Virgil's story of Aeneas is the beautifying of the hero by his mother to enable him unconsciously to win Dido. That Aeneas is "like a god in face and shoulders" we can well believe, but the addition of the "purple light of youth"[9] to a man of years, "long tost on land and sea," worn to grandeur by war and travel, is surely a triumph of imitation over imagination.

This perhaps will be best realized if we consider for a moment the passage, or passages, in the *Odyssey* which Virgil had in mind. Twice Athene changes the aspect of Odysseus. First, at his meeting with Nausicaa, the goddess, after his bath, "made him greater and more mighty to behold, and from his head caused deep curling locks to flow, like the hyacinth flower . . . Then to the shore of the sea went Odysseus apart, and sat down, glowing in beauty and grace, and the princess marvelled at him."[10] And very naturally, for she was a young girl, and the goddess knew it, and made her appeal to the imagination in a true and natural way.

Again, when Odysseus makes himself known to his wife, the poet uses the very words, and the simile that follows them, once again. Penelope "sat down over against Odysseus in the light of the fire. Now he was standing by the tall pillar, looking down and waiting to know if perchance his noble wife would speak to him when her eyes beheld him. But she sat long in silence, and amazement came upon her soul, and now she would look upon him steadfastly with her eyes, and now again she knew him not." Odysseus withdraws, and bathes, and comes back, and "Athene shed great beauty from his head downwards, and [made him] greater and more mighty to behold, and from his head caused deep curling locks to flow, like the hyacinth flower."[11] Once more it is an appeal to the imagination. Penelope has still a final test to make before she will be sure, but in her mind she sees her husband as he was twenty years before, young, strong and tall, as she had always pictured him during the long years of his absence. Homer is justified.

But is Virgil justified? People tell us that youth and beauty are not without their appeal to women in middle life or toward it, but the reader can hardly think of Dido as Venus would seem to have done. She was not Nausicaa. Nor can the poet claim Homer's plea in the second case, for Aeneas and Dido had never met before.[12] In fact, it is a piece of imitation, dull and unconvincing, as nearly all the purely Homeric touches are in the character and the story of Aeneas.[13]

Virgil's Aeneas implies a new relation to heaven. While the whole question of Olympus and the gods will have to be reserved for separate treatment at more length, it will be convenient to anticipate a few points of importance. Greek thinkers had moved, and brought mankind with them, beyond the Olympus of Homer. Men no longer might expect to

> Have sight of Proteus rising from the sea,
> Or hear old Triton blow his wreathed horn.

There was a gain, however, in their loss, for it was a deepening consciousness of the real character of the Divine nature that carried men away from Olympus to look for divinity in a higher region. The divine was more remote, but it was more divine. It had less contact with humanity, but it was freer from the weaknesses and the vices of humanity. It was perhaps less interested in the individual, but it might exercise a wider and a firmer power over the universe.

The Homeric gods, in accordance with epic usage, had to watch over Aeneas, but they were gods in whom no one really believed. Hence Virgil handles them with a caution that excludes warmth. Though Aeneas is favoured with one theophany after another, and is for the while re-assured by them, he is not on such easy terms with the gods as was Achilles. He sees them less frequently, and his relations are more formal. In fact, the complete rejection of the Homeric pantheon by educated people in favour of eastern religion or Greek philosophy was too strong for the poet.[14]

Yet Virgil is far from refusing the idea of some divine government of the world. Some of the philosophers had rejected the Homeric theology, just because it did not sufficiently relate the world with the gods. They traced the world's origin back to divine intelligence, they recognized the diviner element in man's nature, his power of remembering and re-discovering the divine "ideas," and they leant to a belief in the moral government of the universe. With the gradual direction of philosophy to individual life, men came to believe in a personal concern of heaven with the individual man. If Fate is hard and unrelenting, it has recognized the individual, and on the whole the

individual may accept it without resentment. Hence Cleanthes bade
Fate lead him in the destined way and he would be fearless, though,
as he reminded himself meanwhile, there was no question about his
following.[15] Man is thus entirely dependent upon the divine, and of
this Aeneas is always conscious. It was, however, a consciousness never
before presented in poetry, and Virgil, in loyalty to the traditions of
the epic, endeavoured to present it by the means of the old, incredible
Homeric gods. This was indeed to pour new wine into old bottles,
with the inevitable result.

This idea of Destiny, perhaps of Providence, is the dominant one
in Virgil, and it is one of the things in which he is furthest from
Homer.

Destiny, as M. Boissier remarks, has its place in Homer. His heroes
often know well that they are doomed to fall, but as a rule they forget
it and act as if they had not the knowledge. The action is only now
and again darkened by the shadow of Fate, but in general we have the
free development of the individual's story, as he carelessly abandons
himself to the fever of life, and forgets the menaces of the future in
the interests of the present.[16] The same idea is well developed by M.
Girard in his chapter on "Man in Homer and Hesiod." In particular
he instances Hector leaving child and wife for a death he foresaw, but
the prevailing tone of the poem he finds, with Arnold, in the words
of Sarpedon to Glaucus—

> But now a thousand fates of death stand over us, which mortal
> man may not flee from nor avoid; then let us on, and give a
> glory, or obtain it ourselves.[17]

The Greek and the Trojan heroes in the *Iliad* recognize Destiny
well enough, but they make up their own minds, and are ready to
accept the consequences. They survey the world for themselves, look
facts well in the face, and then shape their own courses. If the gods
intervene, these calculations may be upset, it is true, but this is accident after all.

Aeneas, on the contrary, is entirely in the hands of heaven, and
for guidance keeps his eyes fixed on superior powers. He resigns
himself to Providence as a willing, if not entirely intelligent, agent.
Wherever his great quest is concerned, he is a man of prayer,

anxiously waiting for a sign from heaven, which never fails him. It is the attitude of the Roman general taking the auspices.

> Haud equidem sine mente, reor, sine numine divom adsumus
> et portus *delati* intramus amicos[18] (*A.* v. 56).

So says Aeneas, when wind and storm drive him out of his course, and land him at his father's grave in Sicily. *Delati* is the whole story of his voyage in one word—an involuntary quest, perpetually over-ruled by a somewhat unintelligible divine will, but with a happy result. The hero, like a medieval saint, has surrendered his own will, though not with the same restfulness of mind.[19]

Aeneas then is the chosen vessel of Destiny from first to last—*fato profugus*;[20] he is guided by fate throughout all his wanderings—

> Nate dea, quo fata trahunt retrahuntque sequamur; quidquid
> erit, superanda omnis fortuna ferendo est (*A.* v. 709),

says one of his captains.[21] He so entirely subordinates himself to Fate, and, in spite of Virgil's showing him to us "this way and that dividing the swift mind," he so frequently flies to prayer rather than to reflection and resolution, that the reader feels that life is after all made clear to him even if it is not easy, and that his pilgrimage is tedious rather than dark or perplexing.

It was a Roman conviction that Rome was under the special care of heaven—a belief which great Roman generals extended to cover their own personal fortunes. "It was not by numbers," says Cicero, "that we overcame the Spaniards, nor by our strength the Gauls, the Carthaginians by our cunning, or the Greeks by our arts, nor lastly was it by that sense, which is the peculiar and natural gift of this race and land, that we overcame the Italians themselves and the Latins; but by piety (*pietas*) and by regard for the divine (*religio*), and by this sole wisdom—our recognition that all things are ruled and directed by the will of the immortal gods—by these things we have overcome all races and peoples."[22]

As this utterance is from a speech, we may take it to represent the belief rather of Cicero's audience than of himself, and this assumption is confirmed by similar language addressed to the Romans by

Horace.[23] Probably Virgil shared this popular feeling more than either
Cicero or Horace could, and consistently with his habit of showing
the future in the past, the spiritual sequence of events from principles,
he endows Aeneas with this thoroughly Roman attitude towards the
gods. Aeneas, the founder of the race, like all his most eminent descendants, holds the belief that his country—for he calls Italy his *patria*—is
beloved and chosen of heaven; like them, he subordinates himself to
heaven's purpose for his country, and, on every occasion, seeks to learn
at once, and in the directest possible way, what is the will of the gods;
and, once more like them, he finds that heaven never fails Rome.

One or two questions naturally rise at this point. We may ask
whether this Roman view, that Rome is the supreme thing for which
Providence should care, is a true one; but there is another inquiry which
bears more closely upon Aeneas. Has he any real conviction that the
gods care for him? They care for Rome—that is evident enough—and
for Aeneas as the destined founder of Rome. But do they care for the
man as apart from the agent?[24] Does he feel that they care for him?

On the whole, the answer is fairly clear. No one could well be
more loyal than Aeneas to the bidding of heaven, but his loyalty gives
him little joy. He is a man who has known affliction, who has seen
the gods in person destroying what he had loved above all things—his
native city;[25] who has been driven, and expects to be driven, over land
and sea by these same gods to a goal foreign to his hopes and affec-
tions. He realizes that in the end some advantage will accrue to his
people, or their descendants, from all that he undergoes, and he is
willing to work for them. Sorrow, it will be seen, has not cramped him,
but rather has broadened and deepened his nature. He lives for others;
and because he is told that the planting of Rome will be a blessing to
his people, he makes Rome "his love and his country"—

hic amor, haec patria est. (*A.* iv. 346)

If his comrades grow weary, and despair, he has words of hope and
cheerfulness for them. But for himself? For himself, he only expects
the repetition of the past. There is little comfort, little hope for
himself. Even his goddess-mother seems to think as much of the ultimate Augustus as of her son. Does any one, god or man, think about
Aeneas and his happiness? His thoughts are ever of wars behind him

and wars before him; and he hates war. He has nothing to which to
look forward, and only too much to which to look back.

> Et nimium meminisse necesse est[26] (*A.* vi. 514)
> Infandum, regina, iubes renovare dolorem[27] (*A.* ii. 3).

And with these thoughts he is perhaps the most solitary figure in
literature.

Virgil is true here to human experience, for with his story of
pain, and with a doubt at his heart, Aeneas could hardly be other
than he is. He can never forget the story he tells to Dido.[28] The poet
has seized the meaning of the fall of Troy, and interpreted it in this
quiet, wounded, self-obliterating man. If Virgil's hand shakes here
and there, his picture, as he saw it in his mind, is true. Underneath the
trappings of the Homeric hero is the warrior-sage, who has sounded
human sorrow, and who, though he cannot solve the riddle, will not
believe that all is vanity and a striving after wind.

NOTES

1. *G.* iv. 221, "for God pervades all."
2. Goethe's word. He told Eckermann (Oct. 29, 1823) "You must do
   some degree of violence to yourself to get out of the idea."
3. *A.* x. 557 (Mackail).
4. *Il.* xi. 452, and xxi. 122.
5. xi. 81 *vinxerat et post terga manus, quos mitteret umbris* | *inferias,
   caeso sparsurus sanguine flammas*; cf x. 517–20.
6. *Il.* xxiii. 22–3. In Il. 175–6 Dr Leaf finds a "moral
   condemnation of the act" by the poet possible, though not
   inevitable, in the Greek . . .
7. Suet. *Aug.* 15.
8. *Poetics*, ix. 9.
9. *A.* i. 588.
10. *Odyssey*, vi. 229f.
11. *Odyssey*, xxiii. 156.
12. It may be objected that Teucer had told Dido of Aeneas long
    before (*A.* i. 619, a point made by Heinze, *Vergils epische Technik*,
    p. 119), and that there was a picture of Aeneas in Dido's temple

(*A.* i. 488). It will hardly be maintained that it can have been a photographic likeness.

13. Sainte-Beuve has some excellent criticism on this episode of the beautification. *Étude sur Virgile*, 274–6.

14. Cf. Sainte-Beuve, *Étude sur Virgile*, p. 276: "Avec lui (Virgil) on est déjà dans la mythologie; avec Homère on était dans la religion."

15. Cleanthes *ap.* Epictetus, *Manual*, 52, end of book.

16. *La Religion romaine*, i. p. 244.

17. Girard, *Le Sentiment religieux en Grèce*, pp. 70–5; Arnold, *On Translating Homer*, p. 18; *Iliad* xii. 310–28. Translated by Purves.

18. "Not in truth, I deem, without the thought or the will of the gods are we here, driven as we are into a friendly haven." Years add beauty to such a couplet.

19. A Christian saying of the second century. It is in the homily known as Second Clement, 6, 7.

20. *A.* i. 2. "an exile of destiny."

21. "Goddess-born whither Fate draws us, onward or backward, let us follow; come what may, every chance must be overcome by bearing it."

22. Cicero, *de Harusp. Resp.* 9. 19. Cf. Warde Fowler, *Religious Experience of the Roman people*, pp. 249 ff., with notes.

23. *Dis te minorem quod geris imperas*, and other utterances of the kind.

24. Cicero's Stoic said they did. Cf. *de natura deorum* ii. 65, 164.

25. *A.* ii. 608 f., 622.

26. "But too good cause is there to remember."

27. "Too cruel to be told, O queen, is the sorrow you bid me revive."

28. Aeneas' words to Dido, *Aen.* iv. 340, give the keynote of his character.

> mi si fata meis paterentur ducere vitam
> auspiciis et sponte mea componere curas,
> urbem Troianam primum dulcisque meorum
> reliquias colerem, Priami tecta alta manerent
> et recidiva manu posuissem Pergama victis.
> sed nunc Italiam, etc.

ALICE'S ADVENTURES IN WONDERLAND (LEWIS CARROLL)

"Alice's Adventures in Wonderland" by Kathleen Blake, in *Play, Games, and Sport:* *The Literary Works of Lewis Carroll* (1974)

INTRODUCTION

In her 1974 book, *Play, Games, and Sport: The Literary Works of Lewis Carroll*, Kathleen Blake analyzes the games Alice plays in Wonderland and the way these games mark crucial stages in her journey. At first, Alice does what the creatures tell her to do, following confusing and arbitrary rules as she goes from game to game. Blake contends, however, that, as Alice becomes aware of the freedom she has, she sees these games as irrational. By becoming a "spoilsport" and rejecting the rules thrust upon her, Alice learns to control her own fate, assert her own will, and escape the game world she has created. Alice gains self-understanding and self-mastery during her heroic journey, despite many frustrations. For Blake, Alice's maturation parallels ours. For life is indeed a strange journey with games governed by many seemingly arbitrary rules we often do not understand. Thus

Blake, Kathleen. "*Alice's Adventures in Wonderland.*" *Play, Games, and Sport: The Literary Works of Lewis Carroll.* Ithaca, N.Y.: Cornell UP, 1974. 108–31.

Alice's journey both mirrors and inscribes the way we come
to understand the world.

∽✥∾

At the outset of *Alice in Wonderland*, Alice, somewhat bored with
the book being read to her, considers amusing herself with a sort of
play—making a daisy chain; she would do this for the fun of it, in
spite of the trouble of getting up to pick the flowers. However, this
type of play is not really what Alice prefers; typically, she likes social
games, games with rules, of a more strictly structured character than
is involved in daisy-chaining. Even when thrown back upon her
solitary self, Alice is fond of pretending to be two people, so that,
besides giving herself good advice, scolding herself to tears, she has
also been known to play a game of croquet against herself (*W*, pp.
25, 32–33).

Given a choice, Alice would prefer to have other people around.
As she falls down the rabbit hole, talking aloud to herself the while,
she feel the absence of listeners, the opportunity of "showing off
her knowledge." This suggests the importance of relative mastery
in Alice's view of social relations, which are games insofar as they
are undertaken out of the pure pleasure of competitive self-asser-
tiveness. Language for Alice is to some extent a way of impressing
others; she likes to say "latitude" and "longitude," without any
notion of their meaning, but only because they are so satisfy-
ingly "grand" to say. On the other hand, she reflects that a lack of
knowledge of a word, for instance, having to ask an inhabitant of
the other side of the globe what the name of his country is, would
put her at a psychological disadvantage. She determines not to be
caught out (*W*, pp. 27–28).

Alice has a game attitude, with which goes a great concern for
the terms and rules of play. She is on the lookout to learn these so
as to fit in and even master the peculiar universe she has entered. In
the first chapter Alice's abiding interest in rules is introduced. For
example, she remarks that she hopes to find a book of rules for shut-
ting up like a telescope, and she recalls disapprovingly stories she has
heard of children who had been burned and eaten up by wild beasts,
"all because they *would* not remember the simple rules their friends

had taught them." She is strict in her views about obeying rules. Once she even boxed her own ears for cheating at the croquet game she was playing with herself (*W*, pp. 30–33).

Alice entertains a self-satisfied, even smug opinion of herself as a rule-abiding little girl. In most cases the narrator's attitude is close to her own.[1] The possibility of great narrative distance or of narrative irony at the expense of the character is diminished by the fact that, as is sometimes suggested, Alice is listening and reacting to the narrator while living the adventures which he is at that moment relating. In one notable instance, just after the narrator remarks her fondness for pretending to be two people, Alice responds as if she had heard this: "'But it's no use now . . . to pretend to be two people! Why, there's hardly enough of me left to make *one* respectable person!'" (*W*, p. 33).
[...]

A lack of stable rule-structure plagues Wonderland (and Looking-Glass land), but this does not ensure that the player will be immune from others' incursions. It gives him less, not more security against being imposed upon, and this is as true in the caucus-race as later in the croquet game. [...] In a sense, the White Knight's song celebrates a generalized concept of play, but it is one contrasted to work, not to games. Although in certain works Carroll seems to lament the turning of games into sport, as I hope to show, it is risky to theorize that he must also lament the turning of free play into games. The Alice narratives do not appear to offer good enough or many enough instances of primitive play to make this a valid point of reference in discussing the novels.

The world Alice enters does not operate according to mental structures of an age younger than herself—an innocent and flamboyant realm of presocialized freedom and unrule-bound self-expression. If this were the case the creatures would not be so insistent on her submission to their games. Rather this world represents an older level of mental organization, characterized by an addiction to games with rules, with which Alice is expected to play along.
[...]

Let us go forward now with *Alice's Adventures*. In the rough interplay of Wonderland, Alice is content, initially, to put up with a hard time. She is acquiescent and accepts a very humble position:

she is mistaken for the housemaid by the White Rabbit and goes on an errand for him. This is as strange as if at home, besides having to submit to the normal authorities, she were to be ordered about by animals, the very cat. Alice imagines being ordered by Dinah to watch a mouse-hole. She supposes though that at home she could count on some protection against such servitude, from the same "them" who are the usual authorities (*W*, p. 56). Alice even wishes she were back home, where besides being sure of one's size one isn't "ordered about by mice and rabbits." "'I almost wish I hadn't gone down that rabbit hole,'" she adds, "'and yet—and yet'" (*W*, p. 58). After all, Alice is willing to stick it out. She still wants to see the lovely garden, and can't resist the very curiousness of this new world. So she chooses to go on in her subordinate role. She trembles at the White Rabbit's voice, though in actual fact she is a thousand times his size and has no need to be afraid (*W*, p. 59). And later, once out of the Rabbit's house and much reduced in size, she fears being eaten by the puppy. Her encounter with him resembles "having a game of play with a cart horse" (*W*, p. 65). In all the games she enters into in Wonderland, Alice labors under a disadvantage of about this proportion.

On several occasions she feels the disadvantage quite strongly, as for example in the Caterpillar encounter. She hates being contradicted and feels she's losing her temper, and yet she swallows it down and maintains her politeness (*W*, p. 72). Consider also this instance of Alice's really heroic considerateness of others in the face of the signal lack of anyone's consideration for herself: though one of her great desires has been to achieve and stabilize her natural size, she actually shrinks herself to a diminutive nine inches before approaching the Duchess's house, because "'it'll never do to come upon them this size: why, I should frighten them out of their wits!'" (*W*, p. 78).

"Pig and Pepper" is a chapter largely about will, or willfulness. Alice notes to herself how dreadfully all the Wonderland creatures argue. The song sung by the Duchess to the baby is in all probability a parody of a poem which teaches

> Speak gently! It is better far
> To rule by love than fear.

The original is all about curbing one's outspoken urgency into gentleness. The Duchess's song, on the other hand, recommends an unleashed battle of wills, which assumes that one's little boy's willfulness is not to be coaxed and tamed but quite simply overpowered:

> Speak roughly to your little boy,
> And beat him when he sneezes
> He only does it to annoy,
> Because he knows it teases. [*W*, p. 85 and n. 3][2]

The Duchess's remedy for insurgency is capital punishment (*W*, p. 84).

Alice, as we have seen, is not very assertive of her own will but rather seeks direction from others. The chapter opens with her "wondering what to do next" (*W*, p. 79). The creatures she encounters refuse to be of much help. The advice received from the Caterpillar, for example, had been excessively cryptic (*W*, p. 73). And now the Frog-Footman remains obdurately unhelpful when Alice begs to know, "'But what am I to do!'" At last she does take the initiative, and dismissing the Frog-Footman as "perfectly idiotic," she opens the door herself and walks into the Duchess's house. Still she has not yet learned much about willfulness as she remains "timid" with the Duchess, afraid of displaying a lack of "good manners" in presuming to begin the conversation herself (*W*, pp. 81–83).

With the Cheshire Cat she is equally timid. She inquires like a dutiful child, "'Would you tell me, please, which way I ought to go from here?'" But the Cheshire Cat is as perverse as the Footman in refusing to give Alice the direction she wants. He throws the question back to her: "'That depends a good deal on where you want to get to!'" Alice doesn't know where she wants to go; she says she doesn't much care. But she adds, "'so long as I get somewhere.'" She wants a goal, and she wants someone else to set it for her. This need is not satisfied by the Cat's response: that she can go any way she likes, that it doesn't matter which way she goes, as no matter whom she goes among will be mad (*W*, pp. 88–89). Alice is very reluctant to go among mad people and even more so to be told she must be mad too, for being in Wonderland. As a polite, well-lessoned little girl, she stakes a lot on her sanity.

At this juncture she is saved from directionlessness, though, for the Cheshire Cat mentions the Queen's croquet game, which Alice would like very much to attend (if asked). The Cat intimates an invitation by remarking, "'You'll see me there'" (*W*, p. 89). Now at midpoint in the book, Alice receives the clearest goal she has had yet. She does not make or even actively choose her own game universe, but she is eager to join in any that offers, once fairly invited.

The Mad Tea-Party shows again Alice's interest in where activities lead, where they get to. She finds these mad creatures with their endless circulating around the tea table very incompatible. Alice asks the embarrassing question, which the Mad Hatter does not choose to answer, what happens when you arrive back at your original place? This concern to know where it will all end is typical of the game-playing mentality, which conceives activity as linear, as going from point X to point Y. But given the infinite extensibility of most processes, or their circular nature, which yields a similar inconclusiveness (as seen in the caucus-race as well as in the Mad Tea Party), a stop rule is absolutely necessary. The stop rule is what Alice wants to know.

Alice likes riddles; she is eager and determined to apply herself, but not to such as the Mad Hatter asks, because she feels that riddles without answers are a waste of her time (*W*, pp. 95, 97). Though the game, the riddle, is quite literally a waste of time in terms of practical use, it is felt as a waste in psychological terms if it does not allow of a solution, a gratifying sense of closure and triumph. Play activity begins arbitrarily; it is simple enough to begin drawing everything that starts with an M, as the three sisters undertake to do in the Dormouse's story. "'Why with an M?' said Alice. 'Why not?' said the March Hare" (*W*, p. 103). One might, with ingenuity, find a way to draw mousetraps, moon, memory, muchness, etc. (It's all in how one defines terms, sets up rules.) But perhaps Alice has another doubt concerning this enterprise—how could one ever leave off drawing things that begin with an M?

In any event, Alice alternates between an attempt to play along civilly with the Tea-Partyers, and dismay at their outrageousness. At one point she promises "humbly" not to interrupt the Dormouse again. And yet this is in apology for speaking "very angrily" to him. She overlooks the Hatter's calling her "stupid," but this after accusing him of rudeness and after snapping at him sharply (*W*, pp. 101, 102, 94). Finally she cannot bear their provocations and walks off in disgust, although, interestingly, she somewhat regrets this bold action, as she keeps looking back "half hoping that they would call after her." Only when they show no signs of wanting her back does she denounce them (to herself) once and for all: "'At any rate I'll never go *there* again,' said Alice. . . . 'It's the stupidest tea-party I ever was at in all my life!'" (*W*, pp. 103–104).

Alice thus demonstrates some capacity to reject past destinations of her own accord, though she cannot as yet propose future ones on the strength of her own will. However, given a purpose, she is persistent in working to achieve it. She does finally get into the garden where the croquet match is being held.

At the start of "The Queen's Croquet-Ground" Alice exhibits increased self-confidence and unwillingness to defer to others. Though she is polite to the Queen, she remarks to herself, "'They're only a pack of cards, after all. I needn't be afraid of them!'" She disclaims responsibility for the situation in which she has merely happened to become involved, the dilemma of the three spade-card gardeners. And when the Queen attempts to enforce her responsibility by punishing her, Alice silences the Queen with a "'Nonsense.'" Apparently she is allowed to get away with this impertinence because she is "only a child," no serious threat to the card world (*W*, pp. 108–109).

Alice is on no one's side now, but only standing up for herself. She is anything but deferential, laughing to hear that the Duchess has boxed the Queen's ears, and without pity at learning of the Duchess's scheduled execution for that act (*W*, p. 111).

The croquet game itself typifies the games of Wonderland. It frustrates Alice because of the maddening absence of fixity in rules or terms: "'I don't think they play at all fairly,' Alice began, in rather a complaining tone, 'and they all quarrel so dreadfully one can't hear oneself speak—and they don't seem to have any rules in particular: at least, if there are, nobody attends to them—and you've no idea how confusing it is all the things being alive: for instance, there's the arch I've got to go through next walking about at the other end of the ground—and I should have croqueted the Queen's hedgehog just now, only it ran away when it saw mine coming!'" (*W*, p. 113). The rules are not only confusing or altogether lacking, but self-contradictory. For example, as far as Alice can see, there is no waiting for turns, and still the Queen decrees execution for missing a turn (*W*, pp. 112, 115). The coherence essential to a game is impossible.

Since the pieces, or terms, in the game are alive and ever-transforming or escaping, they cannot contribute the necessary definition and reliability. The flamingos keep twisting temperamentally about, the hedgehogs run off to fight with each other, and the soldiers walk away from their positions as arches to remove participants condemned by the Queen. Because of the complete devastation of the playing field and the players, the game can never be concluded (*W*, p. 124).

The soldier/arches provide a good example of the definition of terms by attributes and the interrelation of terms and rules in a game. When they are arches they are defined according to a rule of relationship to the rest of the game: fixed positions through which the balls must be struck in a certain sequence in order to win. But when they are soldiers they are defined according to the rule: those who do the Queen's bidding and who arrest those she accuses.

For similar fluctuations in terms according to their attributes, and consequent fluctuations in the rules governing them, we may remember Alice as little girl/serpent, the fish/footman, the baby/pig. It doesn't matter to the Pigeon what Alice is per se, but only what her attributes are. Both a serpent and a little girl "eat eggs"; therefore in the Pigeon's mind they are equivalent terms, both governed by an obnoxious rule of behavior (*W*, pp. 76–77). Judging by his face, Alice would have taken the creature she meets outside the Duchess's door to be a fish (presumably he should act according to fish rules), but since he is in livery, she defines him as a footman, and expects him to act accordingly (*W*, pp. 79–80). As a baby, the creature in Alice's arms should not exhibit the attributes of "grunting," but as a pig it displays this attribute quite properly and according to rule (*W*, p. 87).

Wonderland is a game world which ostensibly values definition and clarity, although it signally fails to achieve these. The Duchess congratulates Alice for her clear way of putting things (in particular, her ability to distinguish between mustard and a bird, something that is beyond the Duchess's power). The Duchess's own precept is "Be what you would seem to be," but she, like other Wonderland characters, has a fatal penchant for confusion, with the result of total incoherence: "'Never imagine yourself not to be otherwise than what it might appear to others that what you were or might have been was not otherwise than what you had been would have appeared to them to be otherwise'" (*W*, pp. 121–122).

Terms and rules must remain constant if one is to know what universe one is dealing with. The croquet game does not meet this criterion. Two of the basic requirements for play as formulated in game theory are lacking: (1) Alice is not cognizant of all the terms and rules, and (2) therefore she cannot play rationally (maximize utility or undertake to play a winning strategy). "Alice soon came to the conclusion that it was a very difficult game indeed" (*W*, p. 112). And though it is impossible to play correctly, the penalty is great for a false move, as the whole spirit of this game is one of capital risk. Alice is getting uneasy. Though she had previously displayed some bravado in saying "Nonsense" to the Queen and recalling that she needn't fear mere cards, she is being ordered about more than ever in her life before, and she fears a dispute with the Queen, for then, "'What would become of me?'" (*W*, pp. 125, 112).

Wonderland is a competitive, have and have-not world, as in the Duchess's moral: "The more there is of mine, the less there is of yours." What makes the world go round?—minding one's own business, which, as far as the Duchess is concerned, amounts to the same thing as love (*W*, pp. 122, 120–121). For her, love means self-love.

Because she is dealing with such a world, Alice feels it politic to flatter the Queen; what she says has a certain sinister accuracy, namely, the Queen is so likely to win, it's hardly worth finishing the game (*W*, p. 114). The Queen may not be able to win at croquet, strictly speaking, through lack of opponents to finish up (unless perhaps they may be considered to forfeit upon disappearing from the game). But she may be playing at something simpler: another version of Fury and the Mouse. (Carroll describes the Red Queen of *Looking-Glass* in "'Alice' on the Stage" as "a sort of embodiment of ungovernable passion—a blind and aimless Fury," and the Queen of Hearts is not far different.) It is no wonder that Alice chooses to escape this game. The threat of losing one's head is literally and according to the common idiom the threat of losing all control.[3]

In spite of herself, Alice is still eager enough to believe that the systems she encounters will be decipherable, rational. Her reasoning goes something as follows: it is true, the creatures assume authority over me in the most galling manner and order me about as if I were at lessons, but if I can figure out by observation (certainly no one bothers to clue me in) the terms and rules by which the system operates, then when I'm in power (I'm only a little girl now, but bound to grow up someday), I'll be able to employ them according to my will, in effect, enjoy the pleasures of mastery.

It is typical of Alice to be very "much pleased at having found out a new kind of rule." "'Maybe it's always pepper that makes people hot-tempered . . . and vinegar that makes them sour—and camomile that makes them bitter—and—and barley sugar and such things that make children sweet-tempered'" (W, pp. 119–120). Alice plans how she will manage things when *she's* a Duchess.

So Alice's faith in rational games persists. Her quickness in figuring out a sequence according to implied rules and her concern for what happens at the end are demonstrated by her questioning of the Mock Turtle, who did ten hours of lessons the first day, nine the second, and so on (which is why they are called lessons). Alice finds this a curious plan and is intrigued enough to figure that "'the eleventh day must have been a holiday?'" "'And how did you manage on the twelfth?'" But the Mock Turtle, like the Mad Hatter, turns the conversation, frustrating Alice of a definite stop rule and clear outcome (W, p. 130).

Of special interest about the Lobster Quadrille is that it is specifically identified as a game (W, pp. 130–131). This emphasizes again the basic circularity, the real pointlessness of play, which like a dance is primitively more of a here-we-go-round-and-round activity than a getting-somewhere activity, though as we have seen, competitive games parade a certain point-X to point-Y linearity, where in practical terms point Y is not anymore somewhere than point X except that one player gets there first. And the only practicality in games is that of the pleasure they produce, the pleasure of final victory in a game nine times out of ten replacing the pleasure of step-by-step in a dance. Alice does not have much sympathy for the latter; it makes her nervous.

The Gryphon and Mock Turtle dance "round and round Alice" while they sing their very symmetrical refrain:

> Will you, won't you, will you, won't you,
>   Will you join the dance?
> Will you, won't you, will you, won't you,
>   Won't you join the dance?

But she has a strongly developed time and direction sense and really dislikes the infinity threatened by such circularity. She feels "very glad that it was over at last" (*W*, pp. 133–135).

Alice had still been allowing herself to be reprimanded for "nonsense" in Chapter X, but in Chapter XI she begins to show a good deal less docility under abuse.

She is pleased with herself for being able to identify all the figures at the trial, for example, the judge because he has a wig (again, a term defined by its attribute with an implied rule of proper function). She is pleased because she knows the word "jurors." The jurors themselves, on the other hand, are so bad at clear definition of terms that they are afraid of forgetting their own names. This makes Alice indignant, and she calls them "stupid things." She cannot bear the jurors' incapacity; a squeaking pencil is the last straw. So she takes away the offending object. Alice is becoming self-assured and bold (*W*, pp. 144–145).

The White Rabbit is a sort of master of ceremonies and tries to insist on the rules to be observed in court, for instance, by giving the King whispered instructions. He is quite ineffectual, but Alice is still curious to see what will come of the proceedings. Apparently, "'though they haven't much evidence yet,'" she thinks they might manage it in the long run (*W*, pp. 146, 151–152).

Alice is growing. Increase in size correlates with increase in boldness. Always before a food or drink had caused her to grow; this time she is in some sense doing it on her own. Whereas in the past, for example in the White Rabbit's house, large size had not mitigated an irrational timidity, now it represents and reinforces a larger courage. True, she is at first still meek: "'I can't help it [if] I'm growing.'" But then more boldly she answers the Dormouse—"'Don't talk nonsense'"—about having no right to grow. Alice is simply assuming more rights. With her increased power she is no longer trapped in any situation where she might not choose to remain. It would no longer be a matter of escape for her to leave, but of simply walking out. Nevertheless, she *decides* to stay (*W*, pp. 147–148).

The last chapter shows Alice in her final transformation from assiduous and obedient aspirant, intent on working her way up from the bottom toward command of the system; now she is rebel and overthrower of that system. Though surprised, she is willing to respond to the call to give evidence, and she is dismayed, apologetic, at accidentally upsetting the jurybox; she is even solicitous for the jurymen's lives. She obeys the King's order to put them back in their places, and yet observes that it wouldn't much matter whether they went in feet or head first. Likewise, she remarks, "It doesn't matter a bit" which way the jury writes down a piece of evidence, as both are equally meaningless (*W*, pp. 153–156).

Alice's increasing rebelliousness climaxes in actual revolt when "Rule Forty-two" is invoked against her: "All persons more than a mile high to leave the court." She refuses to go for three reasons: (1) she is not a mile high, not in the category of those to whom the rule might apply and hence not bound by it; (2) it is not a regular rule, but just invented, hence not binding; (3) "'I shan't go, at any rate.'" The third is perhaps the most significant reason, as it implies: even if your game were coherent and consistent, which it isn't, I shouldn't have to play it unless I chose, which I don't (*W*, p. 156).

This time Alice does not simply remove herself from the game, which would leave the game itself intact. Instead she actively disrupts it. She declares the evidence meaningless (because of the ambiguity and confusion of terms caused by vague pronoun reference in the poem attributed to the Knave of Hearts), and she refuses to hold her tongue (*W*, pp. 158–159). Alice is now so large that she is completely unafraid, and a palpable threat to the court. She challenges it with a loud "'Stuff and Nonsense,'" and declares for the second time, but now out loud rather than harmlessly to herself, "'Who cares for *you.* . . . You're nothing but a pack of cards!'" (*W*, p. 161). The game must destroy or evict her, for it cannot maintain itself in the disruptive presence of a spoilsport.[4] This is what Alice has learned to be, through her lessons in frustration and her increasing awareness of the foundation of play systems upon pure will. Alice is beginning to recognize the rudiments of a Fury-and-the-Mouse model—in the unilateral proclamations of the Dodo, in the outrageous answerless riddles of the Mad Hatter, in the shifting terms and rules of a capital-risk croquet that renders the Queen of Hearts sure to win, and now in a court that invents laws as it goes, and against Alice. If terms, rules, and whole games are founded upon fiat—why not hers as well as theirs? Volition remains to Alice; she is not finally a Mouse.

But the end of *Wonderland* is difficult to interpret. Does Alice succeed in destroying the game? Or does it succeed in evicting her, by ejecting her from her dream? She challenges the cards, but it is they who fly at her (*W*, p. 161). I tend toward the former interpretation. As Piaget points out, play and dream are related, as they are both the ego's strategies of incorporating reality. But more control is maintained in play, for one remains aware of its voluntary status and the fact that one can end it when one chooses. In a dream the nightmare might very well continue indefinitely, for one cannot will to wake up.[5] However, one can will not to play, even in a dream, and thus end the nightmare, if it consists of a game world, by ending the game. This is what Alice does; hers is the initiative. I agree in a certain sense with Empson's statement that "the triumphant close of *Wonderland* is that she [Alice] has outgrown her fancies and can afford to wake and despise them," except that I would add that it is the choosing not to play others' mad games that wakes her.[6]

The end is a triumph insofar as Alice extricates herself from the game world altogether. To a true spoilsport, none of the rules of the game apply, even the rule, a common insurance of the inviolability of parlor games, which says that willful displacement of the pieces forfeits the game.[7] One must be very strong-minded to abolish the nagging compulsion of such a rule. But Alice has developed into a very strong-minded little girl.

NOTES

1. Cf. Harry Levin, "Wonderland Revisited," *Kenyon Review*, XXVII (Autumn 1965), 595: "No novelist has identified more intimately with the point of view of his heroine."
2. See also John Mackay Shaw, *The Parodies of Lewis Carroll and Their Originals*, catalog of an exhibition with notes (Florida State University, 1960).

3. Carroll, "'Alice' on the Stage," from *The Theatre* (April 1887), rprt. in Collingwood, ed., *Diversions and Digressions*, p. 171; see Henkle, "Comedies of Liberation," p. 72, and Greenacre, *Swift and Carroll*, pp. 243–244.

4. See Huizinga, *Homo Ludens*, p. 11: "The spoil-sport shatters the play-world itself. By withdrawing from the game he reveals the relativity and fragility of the play-world in which he had temporarily shut himself with others." This is why he is much less tolerated by other players even than the cheat.

5. Piaget, *Play, Dreams and Imitation*, Chap. 7, especially pp. 179f.

6. Empson, p. 270.

7. See *Hoyle's Games*, rev. by R. F. Foster (New York, 1926), p. 178. The forfeiture rule is sometimes understood, sometimes made explicit, as in this edition.

BEOWULF

"Beowulf"
by W. P. Ker,
in *Epic and Romance:*
Essays on Medieval Literature (1908)

INTRODUCTION

In *Epic and Romance: Essays on Medieval Literature* (1897), Scottish critic W.P. Ker traces the romance tale to the "Teutonic Epic" journey described in the *Beowulf* poem. Arguing for *Beowulf's* aesthetic unity while pointing out what he sees as its shortcomings, Ker cites the *Odyssey* and the *Iliad* as epic journeys that symbolize the human experience. Similarly, Ker finds that Beowulf is indeed an epic hero and the *Beowulf* poem a testimony to the values— both pre- and post-Christian—found in later literary versions of the hero's journey. Thus, Beowulf's journey reflects the moral concerns of a war-waging age and looks forward to the way the romance literature that follows this age builds upon them.

Ker, W. P. *"Beowulf" Epic and Romance: Essays on Medieval Literature*. London: Macmillan, 1908. 158–75.

The poem of *Beowulf* has been sorely tried; critics have long been at work on the body of it, to discover how it is made. It gives many openings for theories of agglutination and adulteration. Many things in it are plainly incongruous. The pedigree of Grendel is not authentic; the Christian sentiments and morals are not in keeping with the heroic or the mythical substance of the poem; the conduct of the narrative is not always clear or easy to follow. These difficulties and contradictions have to be explained; the composition of the poem has to be analysed; what is old has to be separated from what is new and adventitious; and the various senses and degrees of "old" and "new" have to be determined, in the criticism of the poem. With all this, however, the poem continues to possess at least an apparent and external unity. It is an extant book, whatever the history of its composition may have been; the book of the adventures of Beowulf, written out fair by two scribes in the tenth century; an epic poem, with a prologue at the beginning, and a judgment pronounced on the life of the hero at the end; a single book, considered as such by its transcribers, and making a claim to be so considered.

Before any process of disintegration is begun, this claim should be taken into account; the poem deserves to be appreciated as it stands. Whatever may be the secrets of its authorship, it exists as a single continuous narrative poem; and whatever its faults may be, it holds a position by itself, and a place of some honour, as the one extant poem of considerable length in the group to which it belongs. It has a meaning and value apart from the questions of its origin and its mode of production. Its present value as a poem is not affected by proofs or arguments regarding the way in which it may have been patched or edited. The patchwork theory has no power to make new faults in the poem; it can only point out what faults exist, and draw inferences from them. It does not take away from any dignity the book may possess in its present form, that it has been subjected to the same kind of examination as the *Iliad*. The poem may be reviewed as it stands, in order to find out what sort of thing passed for heroic poetry with the English at the time the present copy of the poem was written. However the result was obtained, *Beowulf* is, at any rate, the specimen by which the Teutonic epic poetry must be judged. It is the largest monument extant. There is nothing beyond it, in that kind, in respect of size and completeness. If the old Teutonic epic is judged to have failed, it must be because *Beowulf* is a failure.

Taking the most cursory view of the story of *Beowulf*, it is easy to recognise that the unity of the plot is not like the unity of the *Iliad* or the *Odyssey*. One is inclined at first to reckon *Beowulf* along with those epics of which Aristotle speaks, the *Heracleids* and *Theseids*, the authors of which "imagined that because Heracles was one person the story of his life could not fail to have unity."[1]

It is impossible to reduce the poem of *Beowulf* to the scale of Aristotle's *Odyssey* without revealing the faults of structure in the English poem:—

> A man in want of work goes abroad to the house of a certain king troubled by Harpies, and having accomplished the purification of the house returns home with honour. Long afterwards, having become king in his own country, he kills a dragon, but is at the same time choked by the venom of it. His people lament for him and build his tomb.

Aristotle made a summary of the Homeric poem, because he wished to show how simple its construction really was, apart from the episodes. It is impossible, by any process of reduction and simplification, to get rid of the duality in *Beowulf*. It has many episodes, quite consistent with a general unity of action, but there is something more than episodes, there is a sequel. It is as if to the *Odyssey* there had been added some later books telling in full of the old age of Odysseus, far from the sea, and his death at the hands of his son Telegonus. The adventure with the dragon is separate from the earlier adventures. It is only connected with them because the same person is involved in both.

It is plain from Aristotle's words that the *Iliad* and the *Odyssey* were in this, as in all respects, above and beyond the other Greek epics known to Aristotle. Homer had not to wait for *Beowulf* to serve as a foil to his excellence. That was provided in the other epic poems of Greece, in the cycle of Troy, in the epic stories of Theseus and Heracles. It seems probable that the poem of *Beowulf* may be at least as well knit as the *Little Iliad*, the Greek cyclic poem of which

Aristotle names the principal incidents, contrasting its variety with the simplicity of the *Iliad* and *Odyssey*.

Indeed it is clear that the plan of *Beowulf* might easily have been much worse, that is, more lax and diffuse, than it is. This meagre amount of praise will be allowed by the most grudging critics, if they will only think of the masses of French epic, and imagine the extent to which a French company of poets might have prolonged the narrative of the hero's life—the *Enfances*, the *Chevalerie*—before reaching the *Death of Beowulf*.

At line 2200 in *Beowulf* comes the long interval of time, the fifty years between the adventure at Heorot and the fight between Beowulf and the dragon. Two thousand lines are given to the first story, a thousand to the *Death of Beowulf*. Two thousand lines are occupied with the narrative of Beowulf's expedition, his voyage to Denmark, his fight with Grendel and Grendel's mother, his return to the land of the Gauts and his report of the whole matter to King Hygelac. In this part of the poem, taken by itself, there is no defect of unity. The action is one, with different parts all easily and naturally included between the first voyage and the return. It is amplified and complicated with details, but none of these introduce any new main interests. *Beowulf* is not like the *Heracleids* and *Theseids*. It transgresses the limits of the Homeric unity, by adding a sequel; but for all that it is not a mere string of adventures, like the bad epic in Horace's *Art of Poetry*, or the innocent plays described by Sir Philip Sidney and Cervantes. A third of the whole poem is detached, a separate adventure. The first two-thirds taken by themselves form a complete poem, with a single action; while, in the orthodox epic manner, various allusions and explanations are introduced regarding the past history of the personages involved, and the history of other people famous in tradition. The adventure at Heorot, taken by itself, would pass the scrutiny of Aristotle or Horace, as far as concerns the lines of its composition.

There is variety in it, but the variety is kept in order and not allowed to interfere or compete with the main story. The past history is disclosed, and the subordinate novels are interpolated, as in the *Odyssey*, in the course of an evening's conversation in hall, or in some other interval in the action. In the introduction of accessory matter, standing in different degrees of relevance to the main plot, the practice of *Beowulf* is not essentially different from that of classical epic.

In the *Iliad* we are allowed to catch something of the story of the old time before Agamemnon,—the war of Thebes, Lycurgus, Jason, Heracles,—and even of things less widely notable, less of a concern to the world than the voyage of Argo, such as, for instance, the business of Nestor in his youth. In *Beowulf*, in a similar way, the inexhaustible world outside the story is partly represented by means of allusions and digressions. The tragedy of Finnesburh is sung by the harper, and his song is reported at some length, not merely referred to in passing. The stories of Thrytho, of Heremod, of Sigemund the Waelsing and Fitela his son (Sigmund and Sinfiotli), are introduced like the stories of Lycurgus or of Jason in Homer. They are illustrations of the action, taken from other cycles. The fortunes of the Danish and Gautish kings, the fall of Hygelac, the feuds with Sweden, these matters come into closer relation with the story. They are not so much illustrations taken in from without, as points of attachment between the history of *Beowulf* and the untold history all round it, the history of the persons concerned, along with Beowulf himself, in the vicissitudes of the Danish and Gautish kingdoms.

In the fragments of *Waldere*, also, there are allusions to other stories. In *Waldere* there has been lost a poem much longer and fuller than the *Lay of Hildebrand*, or any of the poems of the "Elder Edda"—a poem more like *Beowulf* than any of those now extant. The references to Weland, to Widia Weland's son, to Hama and Theodoric, are of the same sort as the references in *Beowulf* to the story of Froda and Ingeld, or the references in the *Iliad* to the adventures of Tydeus.

In the episodic passages of *Beowulf* there are, curiously, the same degrees of relevance as in the *Iliad* and *Odyssey*.

Some of them are necessary to the proper fulness of the story, though not essential parts of the plot. Such are the references to *Beowulf*'s swimming-match; and such, in the *Odyssey*, is the tale told to Alcinous.

The allusions to the wars of Hygelac have the same value as the references in the *Iliad* and the *Odyssey* to such portions of the tale of Troy, and of the return of the Greek lords, as are not immediately connected with the anger of Achilles, or the return of Odysseus. The tale of *Finnesburh* in *Beowulf* is purely an interlude, as much as the ballad of *Ares and Aphrodite* in the *Odyssey*.

Many of the references to other legends in the *Iliad* are illustrative and comparative, like the passages about Heremod or Thrytho in *Beowulf.* "Ares suffered when Otus and Ephialtes kept him in a brazen vat, Hera suffered and Hades suffered, and were shot with the arrows of the son of Amphitryon" (*Il.* v. 385). The long parenthetical story of Heracles in a speech of Agamemnon (*Il.* xx. 98) has the same irrelevance of association, and has incurred the same critical suspicions, as the contrast of Hygd and Thrytho, a fairly long passage out of a wholly different story, introduced in *Beowulf* on the very slightest of suggestions.

Thus in *Beowulf* and in the Homeric poems there are episodes that are strictly relevant and consistent, filling up the epic plan, opening out the perspective of the story; also episodes that without being strictly relevant are rightly proportioned and subordinated, like the interlude of Finnesburh, decoration added to the structure, but not overloading it, nor interfering with the design; and, thirdly, episodes that seem to be irrelevant, and may possibly be interpolations. All these kinds have the effect of increasing the mass as well as the variety of the work, and they give to *Beowulf* the character of a poem which, in dealing with one action out of an heroic cycle, is able, by the way, to hint at and partially represent a great number of other stories.

It is not in the episodes alone that *Beowulf* has an advantage over the shorter and more summary poems. The frequent episodes are only part of the general liberality of the narrative.

The narrative is far more cramped than in *Homer*; but when compared with the short method of the Northern poems, not to speak of the ballads, it comes out as itself Homeric by contrast. It succeeds in representing pretty fully and continuously, not by mere allusions and implications, certain portions of heroic life and action. The principal actions in *Beowulf* are curiously trivial, taken by themselves. All around them are the rumours of great heroic and tragic events, and the scene and the personages are heroic and magnificent. But the plot in itself has no very great poetical value; as compared with the tragic themes of the Niblung legend, with the tale of Finnesburh, or even with the historical seriousness of the *Maldon* poem, it lacks weight. The largest of the extant poems of this school has the least important subject-matter; while things essentially and in the abstract more important, like the tragedy of Froda and Ingeld, are thrust away into the corners of the poem.

In the killing of a monster like Grendel, or in the killing of a dragon, there is nothing particularly interesting; no complication to make a fit subject for epic. *Beowulf* is defective from the first in respect of plot.

The story of Grendel and his mother is one that has been told in myriads of ways; there is nothing commoner, except dragons. The killing of dragons and other monsters is the regular occupation of the heroes of old wives' tales; and it is difficult to give individuality or epic dignity to commonplaces of this sort. This, however, is accomplished in the poem of *Beowulf.* Nothing can make the story of Grendel dramatic like the story of Waldere or of Finnesburh. But the poet has, at any rate, in connexion with this simple theme, given a rendering, consistent, adequate, and well-proportioned, of certain aspects of life and certain representative characters in an heroic age.

The characters in *Beowulf* are not much more than types; not much more clearly individual than the persons of a comedy of Terence. In the shorter Northern poems there are the characters of Brynhild and Gudrun; there is nothing in *Beowulf* to compare with them, although in *Beowulf* the personages are consistent with them-selves, and intelligible.

Hrothgar is the generous king whose qualities were in Northern history transferred to his nephew Hrothulf (Hrolf Kraki), the type of peaceful strength, a man of war living quietly in the intervals of war.

Beowulf is like him in magnanimity, but his character is less uniform. He is not one of the more cruel adventurers, like Starkad in the myth, or some of the men of the Icelandic Sagas. But he is an adventurer with something strange and not altogether safe in his disposition. His youth was like that of the lubberly younger sons in the fairy stories. "They said that he was slack." Though he does not swagger like a Berserk, nor "gab" like the Paladins of Charlemagne, he is ready on provocation to boast of what he has done. The pathetic sentiment of his farewell to Hrothgar is possibly to be ascribed, in the details of its rhetoric, to the common affection of Anglo-Saxon poetry for the elegiac mood; but the softer passages are not out of keeping with the wilder moments of *Beowulf,* and they add greatly to the interest of his character. He is more variable, more dramatic, than the king and queen of the Danes, or any of the secondary personages.

Wealhtheo, the queen, represents the poetical idea of a noble lady. There is nothing complex or strongly dramatic in her character.

Hunferth, the envious man, brought in as a foil to Beowulf, is not caricatured or exaggerated. His sourness is that of a critic and a politician, disinclined to accept newcomers on their own valuation. He is not a figure of envy in a moral allegory.

In the latter part of the poem it is impossible to find in the character of Wiglaf more than the general and abstract qualities of the "loyal servitor."

Yet all those abstract and typical characters are introduced in such a way as to complete and fill up the picture. The general impression is one of variety and complexity, though the elements of it are simple enough.

With a plot like that of *Beowulf* it might seem that there was danger of a lapse from the more serious kind of heroic composition into a more trivial kind. Certainly there is nothing in the plain story to give much help to the author; nothing in Grendel to fascinate or tempt a poet with a story made to his hand.

The plot of *Beowulf* is not more serious than that of a thousand easy-going romances of chivalry, and of fairy tales beyond all number.

The strength of what may be called an epic tradition is shown in the superiority of *Beowulf* to the temptations of cheap romantic commonplace. Beowulf, the hero, is, after all, something different from the giant-killer of popular stories, the dragonslayer of the romantic schools. It is the virtue and the triumph of the poet of *Beowulf* that when all is done the characters of the poem remain distinct in the memory, that the thoughts and sentiments of the poem are remembered as significant, in a way that is not the way of the common romance. Although the incidents that take up the principal part of the scene of *Beowulf* are among the commonest in popular stories, it is impossible to mistake the poem for one of the ordinary tales of terror and wonder. The essential part of the poem is the drama of characters; though the plot happens to be such that the characters are never made to undergo a tragic ordeal like that of so many of the other Teutonic stories. It is not incorrect to say of the poem of *Beowulf* that the main story is really less important to the imagination than the accessories by which the characters are defined and distinguished. It is the defect of the poem this should be so. There is a constitutional weakness in it.

Although the two stories of *Beowulf* are both commonplace, there is a difference between the story of Grendel and the story of the dragon.

The story of the dragon is more of a commonplace than the other. Almost every one of any distinction, and many quite ordinary people in certain periods of history have killed dragons; from Hercules and Bellerophon to Gawain, who, on different occasions, narrowly escaped the fate of Beowulf; from Harald Hardrada (who killed two at least) to More of More Hall who killed the dragon of Wantley.

The latter part of *Beowulf* is a tissue of commonplaces of every kind: the dragon and its treasure; the devastation of the land; the hero against the dragon; the defection of his companions; the loyalty of one of them; the fight with the dragon; the dragon killed, and the hero dying from the flame and the venom of it; these are common-places of the story, and in addition to these there are commonplaces of sentiment, the old theme of this transitory life that "fareth as a fantasy," the lament for the glory passed away; and the equally common theme of loyalty and treason in contrast. Everything is commonplace, while everything is also magnificent in its way, and set forth in the right epic style, with elegiac passages here and there. Everything is commonplace except the allusions to matters of historical tradition, such as the death of Ongentheow, the death of Hygelac. With these exceptions, there is nothing in the latter part of *Beowulf* that might not have been taken at almost any time from the common stock of fables and appropriate sentiments, familiar to every maker or hearer of poetry from the days of the English conquest of Britain, and long before that. It is not to be denied that the common-places here are handled with some discretion; though commonplace, they are not mean or dull.[2]

The story of Grendel and his mother is also common, but not as common as the dragon. The function of this story is considerably different from the other, and the class to which it belongs is differently distributed in literature. Both are stories of the killing of monsters, both belong naturally to legends of heroes like Theseus or Hercules.

But for literature there is this difference between them, that dragons belong more appropriately to the more fantastic kinds of narrative, while stories of the deliverance of a house from a pestilent goblin are much more capable of sober treatment and verisimilitude. Dragons are more easily distinguished and set aside as fabulous monsters than is the family of Grendel. Thus the story of Grendel is much better fitted than the dragon story for a composition like *Beowulf*, which includes a considerable amount of the detail of common experience and ordinary life. Dragons are easily scared from the neighbourhood of sober experience; they have to be looked for in the mountains and caverns of romance or fable. Whereas Grendel remains a possibility in the middle of common life, long after the last dragon has been disposed of.

The people who tell fairy stories like the *Well of the World's End*, the *Knight of the Red Shield*, the *Castle East o' the Sun and West o' the Moon*, have no belief, have neither belief nor disbelief, in the adventures of them. But the same people have other stories of which they take a different view, stories of wonderful things more near to their own experience. Many a man to whom the *Well of the World's End* is an idea, a fancy, has in his mind a story like that of Grendel which he believes, which makes him afraid. The bogle that comes to a house at night and throttles the goodman is a creature more hardy than the dragon, and more persevering. Stories like that of Beowulf and Grendel are to be found along with other popular stories in collections; but they are to be distinguished from them. There are popular heroes of tradition to this day who are called to do for lonely houses the service done by Beowulf for the house of Hrothgar.

Peer Gynt (not Ibsen's Peer Gynt, who is sophisticated, but the original Peter) is a lonely deer-stalker on the fells, who is asked by his neighbour to come and keep his house for him, which is infested with trolls. Peer Gynt clears them out,[3] and goes back to his deer-stalking. The story is plainly one that touches the facts of life more nearly than stories of *Shortshanks* or the *Blue Belt*. The trolls are a possibility.

The story of Uistean Mor mac Ghille Phadrig is another of the same sort.[4] It is not, like the *Battle of the Birds* or *Conal Gulban*, a thing of pure fantasy. It is a story that may pass for true when the others have lost everything but their pure imaginative value as stories. Here, again, in the West Highlands, the champion is called upon like Beowulf and Peer Gynt to save his neighbours from a warlock. And it is matter of history that Bishop Gudmund Arason of Holar in Iceland had to suppress a creature with a seal's head, Selkolla, that played the game of Grendel.[5]

There are people, no doubt, for whom Peer Gynt and the trolls, Uistean Mor and the warlock, even Selkolla that Bishop Gudmund killed, are as impossible as the dragon in the end of the poem of *Beowulf*. But it is certain that stories like those of Grendel are commonly believed in many places where dragons are extinct. The story of Beowulf and Grendel is not wildly fantastic or improbable; it agrees with the conditions of real life, as they have been commonly understood at all times except those of peculiar enlightenment and rationalism. It is not to be compared with the Phaeacian stories of the adventures of Odysseus. Those stories in the *Odyssey* are plainly and intentionally in a different order of imagination from the story of the killing of the suitors. They are pure romance, and if any hearer of the *Odyssey* in ancient times was led to go in search of the island of Calypso, he might come back with the same confession as the seeker for the wonders of Broceliande,—*fol i alai*. But there are other wonderful things in the *Iliad* and the *Odyssey* which are equally improbable to the modern rationalist and sceptic; yet by no means of the same kind of wonder as Calypso or the Sirens. Probably few of the earliest hearers of the *Odyssey* thought of the Sirens or of Calypso as anywhere near them, while many of them must have had their grandmothers' testimony for things like the portents before the death of the suitors. Grendel in the poem of *Beowulf* is in the same order of existence as these portents. If they are superstitions, they are among the most persistent; and they are superstitions, rather than creatures of romance. The fight with Grendel is not of the same kind of adventure as Sigurd at the hedge of flame, or Svipdag at the enchanted castle. And the episode of Grendel's mother is further from matter of fact than the story of Grendel himself. The description of the desolate water is justly recognised as one of the masterpieces of the old English poetry; it deserves all that has been said of it as a passage of romance in the middle of epic. Beowulf's descent under the water, his fight with the warlock's mother, the darkness of that "sea dingle," the light of the mysterious sword, all this, if less admirably worked out than the first description of the dolorous mere, is quite as far from Heorot and the report of the table-talk of Hrothgar, Beowulf, and Hunferth. It is also a different sort of thing from the fight with Grendel. There is more of supernatural incident, more romantic ornament, less of that concentration in the struggle which makes the fight with Grendel almost as good in its way as its Icelandic counterpart, the wrestling of Grettir and Glam.

The story of *Beowulf*, which in the fight with Grendel has analogies with the plainer kind of goblin story, rather alters its tone in the fight with Grendel's mother. There are parallels in *Grettis Saga*, and elsewhere, to encounters like this, with a hag or ogress under water; stories of this sort have been found no less credible than stories of haunting warlocks like Grendel. But this second story is not told in the same way as the first. It has more of the fashion and temper of mythical fable or romance, and less of matter of fact. More particularly, the old sword, the sword of light, in the possession of Grendel's dam in her house under the water, makes one think of other legends of mysterious swords, like that of Helgi, and the "glaives of light" that are in the keeping of divers "gyre carlines" in the *West Highland Tales*. Further, the whole scheme is a common one in popular stories, especially in Celtic stories of giants; after the giant is killed his mother comes to avenge him.

Nevertheless, the controlling power in the story of *Beowulf* is not that of any kind of romance or fantastic invention; neither the original fantasy of popular stories nor the literary embellishments of romantic schools of poetry. There are things in *Beowulf* that may be compared to things in the fairy tales; and, again, there are passages of high value for their use of the motive of pure awe and mystery. But the poem is made what it is by the power with which the characters are kept in right relation to their circumstances. The hero is not lost or carried away in his adventures. The introduction, the arrival in Heorot, and the conclusion, the return of Beowulf to his own country, are quite unlike the manner of pure romance; and these are the parts of the work by which it is most accurately to be judged.

The adventure of Grendel is put in its right proportion when it is related by Beowulf to Hygelac. The repetition of the story, in a shorter form, and in the mouth of the hero himself, gives strength and body to a theme that was in danger of appearing trivial and fantastic. The popular story-teller has done his work when he has told the adventures of the giant-killer; the epic poet has failed, if he has done no more than this.

The character and personage of Beowulf must be brought out and impressed on the audience; it is the poet's hero that they are bound to admire. He appeals to them, not directly, but with unmistakable force and emphasis, to say that they have beheld ("as may unworthiness define") the nature of the hero, and to give him their praises.

The beauty and the strength of the poem of *Beowulf*, as of all true epic, depend mainly upon its comprehensive power, its inclusion of various aspects, its faculty of changing the mood of the story. The fight with Grendel is an adventure of one sort, grim, unrelieved, touching close upon the springs of mortal terror, the recollection or the apprehension of real adversaries possibly to be met with in the darkness. The fight with Grendel's mother touches on other motives; the terror is further away from human habitations, and it is accompanied with a charm and a beauty, the beauty of the Gorgon, such as is absent from the first adventure. It would have loosened the tension and broken the unity of the scene, if any such irrelevances had been admitted into the story of the fight with Grendel. The fight with Grendel's mother is fought under other conditions; the stress is not the same; the hero goes out to conquer, he is beset by no such apprehension as in the case of the night attack. The poet is at this point free to make use of a new set of motives, and here it is rather the scene than the action that is made vivid to the mind. But after this excursion the story comes back to its heroic beginning; and the conversation of Beowulf with his hosts in Denmark, and the report that he gives to his kin in Gautland, are enough to reduce to its right episodic dimensions the fantasy of the adventure under the sea. In the latter part of the poem there is still another distribution of interest. The conversation of the personages is still to be found occasionally carried on in the steady tones of people who have lives of their own, and belong to a world where the tunes are not all in one key. At the same time, it cannot be denied that the story of the *Death of Beowulf* is inclined to monotony. The epic variety and independence are obliterated by the too obviously pathetic intention. The character of this part of the poem is that of a late school of heroic poetry attempting, and with some success, to extract the spirit of an older kind of poetry, and to represent in one scene an heroic ideal or example, with emphasis and with concentration of all the available matter. But while the end of the poem may lose in some things by comparison with the stronger earlier parts, it is not so wholly lost in the charms of pathetic meditation as to forget the martial tone and the more resolute air altogether. There was a danger that Beowulf should be transformed into a sort of Amadis, a mirror of the earlier chivalry; with a loyal servitor attending upon his death, and uttering the rhetorical panegyric of an abstract ideal. But this danger is avoided, at least in part. Beowulf is still, in his death, a sharer in the fortunes of the Northern houses; he keeps his history. The fight with the dragon is shot through with reminiscences of the Gautish wars: Wiglaf speaks his sorrow for the champion of the Gauts; the virtues of Beowulf are not those of a fictitious paragon king, but of a man who would be missed in the day when the enemies of the Gauts should come upon them.

The epic keeps its hold upon what went before, and on what is to come. Its construction is solid, not flat. It is exposed to the attractions of all kinds of subordinate and partial literature,—the fairy story, the conventional romance, the pathetic legend,—and it escapes them all by taking them all up as moments, as episodes and points of view, governed by the conception, or the comprehension, of some of the possibilities of human character in a certain form of society. It does not impose any one view on the reader; it gives what it is the proper task of the higher kind of fiction to give—the play of life in different moods and under different aspects.

NOTES

1. *Poet.* 1451 a.
2. It has been shown recently by Dr. Edward Sievers that Beowulf's dragon corresponds in many points to the dragon killed by Frotho, father of Haldanus, in Saxo, Book II. The dragon is not wholly commonplace, but has some particular distinctive traits. See *Berichte der Königl. Sächs. Gesellschaft der Wissenschaften*, 6 Juli 1895.
3. Asbjörnsen, *Norske Huldre-Eventyr og Folkesagn. At renske Huset* is the phrase—"to cleanse the house." Cf. *Heorot is gefaelsod*, "Heorot is cleansed," in *Beowulf*.
4. J. F. Campbell, *Tales of the West Highlands*, ii. p. 99. The reference to this story in *Catriona* (p. 174) will be remembered.
5. *Biskupa Sögur*, i. p. 604.

DAVID COPPERFIELD
(CHARLES DICKENS)

"David Copperfield and the Emergence of the Homeless Hero"
by Beth F. Herst,
in *The Dickens Hero: Selfhood and Alienation in the Dickens World* (1990)

INTRODUCTION

Beth Herst notes how David Copperfield marks a turn in the Dickens hero, this time combining two previously used hero types: the parentless orphan protagonist of such early novels as *Oliver Twist* and *Nicholas Nickleby* and the natural hero–imperfect and fallible–of *Martin Chuzzlewit.* Displaced in the world, homeless and parentless, David, amid a pain-filled journey, attains a "full, and integrated, selfhood." While Copperfield's journey is not complete, neither are ours; his herculean efforts and his perseverance raise this everyman's journey to heroic stature.

Herst, Beth F. "David Copperfield and the Emergence of the Homeless Hero." *The Dickens Hero: Selfhood and Alienation in the Dickens World.* New York: St. Martin's Press, 1990. 43–66.

With the publication in May 1849 of the first installment of his 'autobiography', David Copperfield joins ranks with Jane Eyre and Arthur Pendennis, two no less determinedly unheroic literary figures whose personal histories had likewise recently been given to the public. Parallels between the trio's stories, not least the coincidence of their meditative, retrospective tone, have often been noted, and so too has the popularity of this confessional mode at mid-century (with 'In Memoriam' and 'The Prelude' appearing the following year). All three novels are tales of initiation and development. All locate their interest in the private world of individual experience, not the public arena of the 'social problem'. And all deliberately call into question conventional notions of literary 'heroism': *Copperfield* with David's celebrated opening, 'Whether I shall turn out to be the hero of my own life' (*David Copperfield* 1), masking a host of other questions; *Pendennis* with the figure of Pen himself, good-hearted and erring, 'who does not claim to be a hero, but only a man and a brother'; and *Jane Eyre* with its author's determination to prove, 'in defiance of the accepted canon', that the heroine of a novel could be poor, obscure, plain and little, and still retain the interest of its readers. Thackeray, in fact, in a letter to Lady Blessington of 6 May 1849, detected the influence of *Pendennis* in *Copperfield*'s opening number. And Q. D. Leavis has made a similar claim for influence on Charlotte Brontë's behalf. Yet David Copperfield is neither a passionate rebel, like Jane, nor a reclaimed worldling, like Pen. Nor does he owe much, if anything, to the literary models who feature so prominently in his own childhood reading and populate his early imaginative world, 'heroes' like Roderick Random, Peregrine Pickle, Humphry Clinker, Tom Jones and Gil Blas (48). David is, rather, a figure new to the world of Dickens's fiction. In him appears, essentially for the first time, a fusion of strains familiar, individually, from the earlier works, strains now brought together in distinctive form. It is a combination which will, in the novels to come, increasingly characterize the male protagonists who stand at their heart. Defining the type—a sad, time-haunted and increasingly alienated figure—it establishes the dimensions of the 'Dickens hero'.

For David Copperfield is the first of Dickens's waifs to grow up, the first adult counterpart to the abandoned child whose image haunts the earlier novels, and of whom young David is clearly another version. In perpetual children like Oliver Twist and Nell, the condition of orphanhood draws largely on the religious, folk and fairy-tale associations that cluster about the figures of foundlings and holy innocents. In both the inherent pathos of the young orphan is underscored by the mythic potential of a single image: an unprotected child wandering amid a hostile adult world. David too, in his early experiences in London and on the Dover road, plainly draws on similar traditions. But in him orphanhood goes on to assume an additional, spiritual dimension, becoming a potent symbol of a larger loss. Want of parents, and its corollary the want of a home, mean want of a fixed identity for David, 'home' now functioning as both the source, and the refuge, of selfhood. For Nicholas Nickleby the death of a father had chiefly meant economic vulnerability. For David Copperfield the loss goes infinitely deeper, his resulting homelessness an emblem of the alienation it is the task of his life to overcome.

In effect, Dickens brings together in *David Copperfield* two major, but previously separate, preoccupations of the early novels. David unites the parentless child—victimized and suppressed—represented by Oliver, Smike, Nell and the Marchioness, with the 'natural' hero—imperfect, unliterary and developing—anticipated in Nicholas Nickleby, attempted in Martin Chuzzlewit and abandoned in Walter Gay. What he does not obviously further, however, is a third, equally important strain which emerges at the end of this early period. For *Copperfield* suspends the exploration tentatively begun in *Martin Chuzzlewit*, and temporarily abandoned in *Dombey and Son*, of the possibilities inherent in linking the experience of the recreated 'hero' with the overtly 'social' preoccupations that are now coming to shape Dickens's artistic concerns. And this would appear to have been a deliberate decision. According to Forster, Dickens's completion of the second chapter of the novel ('I Observe') defined to himself 'more clearly than before, the character of the book; and the propriety of rejecting everything not strictly personal from the name given to it'. The introductory words 'The Copperfield Survey of the World as it Rolled' were, in consequence, dropped from the work's title, which then became 'The Personal History, Adventures, Experience, and Observation of David Copperfield the Younger, of Blunderstone Rookery, which he never meant to be published on any account'. There is some doubt as to the accuracy of Forster's dating of this change. Yet the implication is still clear: the character of the book itself was, for Dickens, 'strictly personal', having less to do with the world as it rolls than one individual's 'personal history' in it. And Barry Westburg has noted a further, significant change in the shortened working title Dickens used for the novel's number plans. While the first number is titled 'The Personal History and Adventures of David Copperfield', in the second number and thereafter 'Adventures' is replaced by 'Experiences'. Choosing deliberately to emphasize the internal rather than the external, Dickens moves David still further from the picaresque mode of his childhood reading. It is a change which anticipates the formulation of the 1856 letter and its 'experiences, trials, perplexities, and confusions inseparable from the making or unmaking of all men'. Nicholas Nickleby and Martin Chuzzlewit, it might be recalled, had adventures. David will have experiences.

[. . .]

The adult David's experience is, in essence, a dramatization of the difficulty of overcoming this childhood inheritance in order to achieve a full, and integrated, selfhood. And it is a dramatization in which Steerforth and Uriah Heep play important roles. In addition to serving as symbolic surrogates for David in his relations with Emily and Agnes—and living testaments to David's continued blindness—the two act as thematic counterparts, subtly refracted images of the novel's central figure and situation. All three play out the same basic configuration: fatherless son, inadequate mother, and a formative childhood experience. But Steerforth and Uriah represent a fundamental failure of self, defining through negative example the meaning of David's own, ultimately successful, struggle. It is precisely the sort of thematic reflection/refraction Dickens tries for, but does not achieve, in *Martin Chuzzlewit* with the juxtaposition of young Martin, Tom Pinch, Mark Tapley and John Westlock.

The absence of a 'steadfast and judicious father' (275), an absence that defines Steerforth's life no less than David's, ultimately proves fatal in the former's case. He is himself aware of what this want has meant: "'I wish with all my soul I had been better guided! . . . I wish with all my soul I could guide myself better!'" (274). His present inability to guide himself plainly stems from the earlier lack. Gifted with abilities which might have made him a 'hero' in eyes less partial than David's—the fascination of his manner is well conveyed—Steerforth is incapable of directing his talents, and of directing, or controlling himself. Indulged since childhood—his mother, David learns at Salem House, 'was a widow, and rich, and would do almost anything, it was said, that he asked her' (86)—he has never lost the child's instinctive tendency to treat other personalities as mere adjuncts to his own. Self, running rampant, prevents truly mutual, and truly human, interaction, as Steerforth's 'love' affairs with Rosa Dartle and Little Emily prove. Each time the woman becomes, in Rosa's words, "'a doll, a trifle for the occupation of an idle hour, to be dropped, and taken up, and trifled with'" (686). Diminishing others to the status of objects, Steerforth equally diminishes himself. He is right to be, as he tells David he is, "'afraid of myself'" (274), for, in the end, the selfishness which is the essence of his nature can lead him to nothing more than a 'heroic' death on the deck of a sinking ship. It has no more positive potential.

And Uriah Heep presents the companion piece to this, the psychological obverse of Steerforth's fatal egotism. Uriah's venomous account of his charity education clearly reveals that society has for years systematically denied him all outward expression of his natural ambitions and needs, insisting instead on a degrading and self-denying humbleness: "'We was to be umble to this person, and umble to that; and to pull off our caps here, and to make bows there; and always to know our place, and abase ourselves before our betters. And we had such a lot of betters!'" (490). The self, so long suppressed in this way, now naturally seeks revenge in the very thing habitually withheld from it, power—as 'naturally' as David seeks confirmation of his genteel status through friendship with Steerforth. Deprived of legitimate psychic fulfilment, Uriah seeks satisfaction in a secret ascendancy, and in doing so twists his already distorted self still further awry.

Both characters function as exaggerated reflections of David's own competing self-images: the status-less charity boy on the one hand, the invulnerable gentleman on the other. The peculiar fascination of repulsion he feels towards Uriah seems rooted in his embodiment of everything David himself feared he would become in the dark days of Murdstone and Grinby, the degradation against which he fought so desperately. That Uriah feels the negative bond in his turn is made evident by his vicious outburst late in the novel, when he is being 'exploded' by Micawber: "'You think it justifiable, do you, Copperfield, you who pride yourself so much on your honor and all the rest of it, to sneak about my place, eavesdropping with my clerk? If it had been *me*, I shouldn't have wondered; for I don't make myself out a gentleman (though I never was in the streets either, as you were, according to Micawber), but being *you*!'" (641). Similarly, something of the fascination Steerforth holds for David obviously resides in his assured possession of the status Uriah, and his example, call into question. Even at Salem House, David is attracted by Steerforth's social image—'his nice voice, and his fine face, and his easy manner, and his curling hair' (75)—which contrasts so markedly with Uriah's creeping lowness. And when they meet again as adults his admiration for Steerforth's style and manner—his ease with servants, his social grace, his 'gentlemanly' accomplishments—is just as compulsively undiscriminating.

Emblems of a radical failure of self, these distorted reflections embody a fate that clearly threatens David too. But he is not surrounded by negative exemplars alone. If Steerforth and Uriah illustrate the consequences of a fatal self-estrangement, Tommy Traddles, yet another of *David Copperfield*'s fatherless sons, demonstrates the potential of a properly disciplined self to secure a refuge. Where Steerforth and Uriah destroy homes, Traddles creates one. This, surely, is the significance of the house for which he and Sophy work and plan: "'Then, when we stroll into the squares, and great streets, and see a house to let, sometimes we look up at it, and say, how would *that* do, if I was made a judge?'" (725). Traddles functions in many ways as a more convincingly realized version of Tom Pinch in *Martin Chuzzlewit*, minus the explicit moralizing and the rhetoric of insistent pathos. With his genial peculiarities—the comic head of hair and the skeletons—his simple nature and quiet virtues, Tommy offers an alternative to the spurious 'heroic' glamour of Steerforth. Early detecting the selfishness lurking beneath Steerforth's surface charm, Traddles's patience, determination and good sense define the sort of domesticated, moral heroism David himself must embrace, his ability to estimate such heroism at its true worth serving as an index of his own growing maturity. Tommy embodies too the positive answer to Murdstone 'firmness': determination, energy and self-reliance, motivated and softened by love for his 'dearest girl' (347). These are the qualities—'perseverance', 'patient and continuous energy'—which David's experience will slowly teach him, and to which his older self will look back as 'the strong part of my character' (517). It is, in fact, only by learning the sort of self-denial Traddles represents that David prepares himself to achieve the ultimate self-realization Agnes holds out.

The respective places of Agnes, and Dora too, within the pattern of David's life should by now be evident: one is the true angel in his house, the other the embodiment of David's false domestic ideal. Given the thematic importance of 'home' in the novel, Dora's comic inadequacies as housekeeper assume a particular significance, linking her still more closely to the long-dead mother of David's boyhood. They are the symbol of her inability to provide for David's deepest needs, of her failure to furnish a spiritual no less than a material home. David characterizes their housekeeping by saying 'nothing had a place of its own' (548) and that includes Dora's husband. It is a failure, or rather a lack, David himself soon recognizes: 'I did feel, sometimes, for a little while, that I could have wished my wife had been my counsellor; had had more character and purpose, to sustain me and improve me by; had been endowed with power to fill up the void which somewhere seemed to be about me' (552). This sense of a particular lack is soon assimilated by David to the conviction that it is a universal fate. Acknowledging in his disappointment evidence of his own weakness, of the undisciplined state of his own heart, he sees in it too a natural regret for things lost, or never found, that attends the progress from child to man. Even before her death Dora, like Steerforth, serves David as an emblem of lost youth and promise unfulfilled, as well as of a more personal blindness and unwitting self-betrayal:

> When I thought of the airy dreams of youth that are incapable
> of realisation, I thought of the better state preceding manhood
> that I had outgrown; and then the contented days with Agnes,
> in the dear old house, arose before me, like spectres of the dead
> that might have some renewal in another world, but never
> more could be reanimated here. (595)

That 'old unhappy loss or want of something' (551) which haunts David is, in fact, a compound of the general loss time brings in its

wake, the specific early deprivation of the home he has ever since been
seeking, and the want of selfhood attendant upon the quest. And Dora,
the inadequate home-maker, can neither compensate for, nor supply,
any of these. It is entirely appropriate, perhaps inevitable, that David
should forever find himself reading Annie Strong's resonant words—
'the first mistaken impulse of an undisciplined heart'—'inscribed
upon the walls of houses' (595) in dreams. For his own inability to find
a home in Dora's 'baby-house' (553) is a clear indication of just how
mistaken his own heart has been in choosing a wife who can offer him
no more than a 'make-believe of housekeeping' (553).

It is Agnes, the 'little housekeeper' (190) in earnest, who is
David's true mate. Long before he learns to recognize his particular
love for her, David has cherished the 'general fancy as if Agnes were
one of the elements of my natural home' (419). And he himself
acknowledges the larger meaning of the role. Agnes is the source
of his best self: 'She so filled my heart with such good resolutions,
strengthened my weakness so, by her example, so directed ... the
wandering ardor and unsettled purpose within me, that all the little
good I have done, and all the harm I have forborne, I solemnly
believe I may refer to her' (443). Although Dora holds the pens,
it is Agnes and her inspiration which are associated with David's
'growing reputation' (595) as a novelist and his discovery of his true
vocation. In this too she consistently serves as his good angel, urging
him to work and to a full acceptance of the responsibilities his fame
brings with it (698, 721). Agnes is not only the treasury of David's
'earliest and brightest hopes' (699), his muse and his moral guide.
In his bereavement she explicitly becomes too 'a sacred presence in
my lonely house' (695). In her he finds the 'peace and happiness'
(484), the perfect domestic joy he has so long, and so fruitlessly,
been seeking and something more: a rock to found his love, and
self, upon. David's absence from England not only teaches him the
undisciplined nature of his heart, but brings him too to acknowledge his own responsibility for its errors. In his wanderings abroad
he learns to give a name to the 'old unhappy loss' and to accept the
unalterable fact of its irrevocability:

Home, in its best sense, was for me no more. She in whom I
might have inspired a dearer love, I had taught to be my sister.

> She would marry and have new claimants on her tenderness, and in doing it, would never know the love for her that had grown up in my heart. It was right that I should have to pay the forfeit of my headlong passion. What I had reaped, I had sown. (710–711)

Having made for so long a 'mystery' (699) of his own heart, it is right that that heart should now be a secret to the woman who possesses it. There is a symmetry, a poetic justice to his fate that David the author clearly appreciates: 'I had bestowed my passionate tenderness upon another object; and what I might have done, I had not done: and what Agnes was to me, I and her own noble heart had made her' (700). In acknowledging his own error, David measures too his distance from the conventional 'happily ever after' of the conventional novel 'hero'. He has married his fairy-tale princess and the marriage proved not the end of his story but the beginning of a larger loss, a loss forever present to him in the figure of the 'sister' who could, and should, have been his wife.

Yet, in the end, David is allowed not only to love his 'sister' but to marry her too. In effect, he both acknowledges the lesson time has taught him, the impossibility of retracing the road not taken—'Home was very dear to me, and Agnes too—but she was not mine—she was never to be mine. She might have been, but that was past!' (701)—and proves it wrong. For Agnes herself embodies a seeming defiance of time and change which coexists uneasily with the insistence on mutability that pervades David's written memory. Where Dora becomes 'the blossom withered in its bloom upon the tree' (598), an emblem of the inevitable law 'of change in everything' (635) David hears sounding in the bells of Canterbury cathedral, Agnes remains frozen in time, forever associated with the 'tranquil brightness' (191) of the stained-glass window in whose frame David first placed her as a child. That is the glory of her final confession to the time-haunted David: she has loved him all her life, and never changed (739). Agnes's intended symbolic function within David's life history seems clear. She fills the void in his heart and mind precisely because she represents 'home in its best sense' (710). Embracing her as his wife, David holds within his arms 'the centre of myself' (740), a centre he has lacked for so long. The homeless hero has overcome his spiritual

orphanhood and found in Agnes a home at last. She is the end of
a journey begun many years ago, the completion, as David himself
indicates, of the circle of his life:

> Long miles of road then opened out before my mind: and,
> toiling on, I saw a ragged way-worn boy, forsaken and
> neglected, who should come to call even the heart now beating
> against mine, his own. (739)

As a 'happy ending' it is doubly problematic, in the fact of its presence as well as its form. Is David after all to achieve nothing more or
less than the familiar 'heros" reward? Yet it is important to distinguish
here between intentional limitation and imaginative failure. Agnes's
apparent immunity to the novel's own laws of change must be the
source of some dissatisfaction, for that defies the narrative's very
organizing principle. Additionally, to a twentieth-century sensibility,
the figure from the stained-glass window, eternally pointing upwards,
must be still more unsettling in her capacity as an emblem of mature
emotional fulfilment. As Alexander Welsh has demonstrated, the
symbolic associations of the angel in the house have a disturbing
tendency to become conflated with those of the angel of death. And
the stillness and tranquillity so consistently associated with Agnes
do carry with them intimations of this ultimate stasis. She represents
a denial of energy, her union with David constituting a limitation,
a diminution, a loss. But it is a loss that forms part of an essential
pattern. Robin Gilmour, in his excellent essay 'Memory in *David
Copperfield*', identifies David's movement from child-wife to angel-
bride, so inseparable from his own self-discovery—and so unsettling
for modern readers—as designedly forming a state of emotional
contraction. It marks, in his estimation, a loss of passionate intensity
which balances David's increasing material success, and explains his
narrative's tone of quiet melancholy. Viewed in this light, Agnes and
the depleted domesticity she represents become a part of David's
general chastening, a deliberate embodiment of the limits he must
learn to accept. Through the medium of his retrospective narration,
David does, in fact, resign himself to the inevitable losses time brings
in its wake. But that they should be inevitable is itself a source of
continuing regret. There is a price to be paid in the substitution of

'domestic joy' (741) for a more spontaneous, freer emotion, a price registered in the voice of David's recollection itself. And there are other shadows qualifying, if not subverting, the 'happy ending' of his history. The very fact of David's narrative suggests a continuity of past into present—the way-worn boy forever toiling on in memory—that resists the closure he attempts to invoke. Why, after all, is David writing his personal history that is never meant to be published on any account? He himself never resolves the issue, but David's last retrospect, his final deliberate act as author, in which the crocodile book and that 'old acquaintance Brooks of Sheffield' (748) turn up yet again, speaks unmistakably of a past that is never truly over, a history never finally ended. Even the Murdstones reappear, by report, at the novel's close, reenacting beyond its confines another *David Copperfield*. Dickens may allow his hero, this once at least, to come home, to achieve a compromised closure, but he pays an emotional price for the privilege. And for his successors the cost will mount steadily higher.

DON QUIXOTE
(MIGUEL DE CERVANTES)

"Don Quixote"
by Sir Walter Alexander Raleigh,
in *Some Authors: A Collection of Literary Essays,*
1896–1916 (1923)

INTRODUCTION

English critic Sir Walter Alexander Raleigh focuses on the
chivalric code that determines the path Don Quixote follows
on his journey. As one who dedicates his life to this code,
Don Quixote resembles a kind of religious saint. His spiritual
journey highlights the many rewards of following abstract
ideals and the many illusions that such ideals suffer upon us.
Contrasting the Don's idealism with Sancho's pragmatism,
Raleigh finds they are both aspects of the human journey,
one bounded by imagination and grounded in reality.

A Spanish knight, about fifty years of age, who lived in great poverty
in a village of La Mancha, gave himself up so entirely to reading the

---

Raleigh, Sir Walter Alexander. "Don Quixote." *Some Authors: A Collection of
Literary Essays, 1896–1916*. Freeport, NY: Books for Libraries Press, 1968 (first
printed 1923). 27–40.

romances of chivalry, of which he had a large collection, that in the
end they turned his brain, and nothing would satisfy him but that he
must ride abroad on his old horse, armed with spear and helmet, a
knight-errant, to encounter all adventures, and to redress the innu-
merable wrongs of the world. He induced a neighbour of his, a poor
and ignorant peasant called Sancho Panza, mounted on a very good
ass, to accompany him as squire. The knight saw the world only in the
mirror of his beloved romances; he mistook inns for enchanted castles,
windmills for giants, and country wenches for exiled princesses. His
high spirit and his courage never failed him, but his illusions led him
into endless trouble. In the name of justice and chivalry he intruded
himself on all whom he met, and assaulted all whom he took to be
making an oppressive or discourteous use of power. He and his poor
squire were beaten, trounced, cheated, and ridiculed on all hands, until
in the end, by the kindliness of his old friends in the village, and with
the help of some new friends who had been touched by the amiable
and generous character of his illusions, the knight was cured of his
whimsies and was led back to his home in the village, there to die.[1]

That is the story of Don Quixote: it seems a slight framework for
what, without much extravagance, may be called the wisest and most
splendid book in the world. It is an old man's book; there is in it all
the wisdom of a fiery heart that has learned patience. Shakespeare and
Cervantes died on the same day, but if Cervantes had died at the same
age as Shakespeare we should have had no *Don Quixote*. Shakespeare
himself has written nothing so full of the diverse stuff of experience,
so quietly and steadily illuminated by gentle wisdom, so open-eyed
in discerning the strength of the world; and Shakespeare himself is
not more courageous in championing the rights of the gallant heart.
Suppose the Governor of Barataria had been called on to decide the
cause between these two great authors. His judgments were often
wonderfully simple and obvious. Perhaps he would have ruled that
whereas Shakespeare died at the age of fifty-two and Cervantes lived
seventeen years longer, a man shall give his days and nights to the
study of Shakespeare until he is older than ever Shakespeare was, and
then, for the solace of his later years, shall pass on to the graver school
of Cervantes. Not every man lives longer than Shakespeare; and, of
those who do, not every man masters the art and craft of growing
older with the passage of years, so that, by this rule, the Spanish

gentleman would have a much smaller circle of intimates than the High Bailiff's son of Stratford. And so he has; yet his world-wide popularity is none the less assured. He has always attracted, and will always attract, a great company of readers who take a simple and legitimate delight in the comic distresses of the deluded Don, in the tricks put upon him, in the woful absurdity of his appearance, in the many love-stories and love-songs that he hears, in the variety of the characters that he meets, in the wealth of the incidents and events that spring up, a joyous crop, wherever he sets his foot, and not least, perhaps, in the beatings, poundings, scratchings, and tumblings in the mire that are his daily portion. That is to say, those who care little or nothing for Don Quixote may yet take pleasure in the life that is in his book; and his book is full of life.

We have no very ample record of the life experiences of Cervantes, which are distilled in this, his greatest book.[2] We know that he was a soldier, and fought against the Turks at Lepanto, where his left hand was maimed for life; that he was made prisoner some years later by the Moors, and suffered five years' captivity at Algiers; that he attempted with others to escape, and when discovered and cross-examined took the whole responsibility on himself; that at last he was ransomed by the efforts of his family and friends, and returned to Spain, there to live as best he could the life of a poor man of letters, with intermittent Government employ, for thirty-six more years. He wrote sonnets and plays, pawned his family's goods, and was well acquainted with the inside of prisons. He published the First Part of *Don Quixote* in 1605—that is to say, in his fifty-eighth year—and thenceforward enjoyed a high reputation, though his poverty continued. In 1615 the Second Part of *Don Quixote* appeared, wherein the author makes delightful play with the First Part by treating it as a book well known to all the characters of the story. In the following year he died, clothed in the Franciscan habit, and was buried in the convent of the Barefooted Trinitarian Nuns in Madrid. No stone marks his grave, but his spirit still wanders the world in the person of the finest gentleman of all the realms of fact and fable, who still maintains in discourse with all whom he meets that the thing of which the world has most need is knights-errant, to do honour to women, to fight for the cause of the oppressed, and to right the wrong. 'This, then, gentlemen,' he may still be heard saying, 'it is to be a knight-errant, and what I have spoken of is the order of chivalry, in the which, as I have already said, I, though a sinner, have made profession; the same which these famous knights profess do I profess; and that is why I am travelling through these deserts and solitary places, in quest of adventures, with deliberate resolve to offer my arm and my person to the most dangerous adventure which fortune may present, in aid of the weak and needy.' And the world is still incredulous and dazed. 'By these words which he uttered', says the author in brief comment on the foregoing speech, 'the travellers were quite convinced that Don Quixote was out of his wits.'

It has often been said, and is still sometimes repeated by good students of Cervantes, that his main object in writing *Don Quixote* was to put an end to the influence of the romances of chivalry. It is true that these romances were the fashionable reading of his age, that many of them were trash, and that some of them were pernicious trash. It is true also that the very scheme of his book lends itself to a scathing exposure of their weaknesses, and that the moral is pointed in the scene of the Inquisition of the Books, where the priest, the barber, the housekeeper, and the niece destroy the greater part of his library by fire. But how came it that Cervantes knew the romances so well, and dwelt on some of their incidents in such loving detail? Moreover, it is worth noting that not a few of them are excluded by name from the general condemnation. *Amadis of Gaul* is spared, because it is 'the best of all books of the kind'. Equal praise is given to *Palmerin of England*; while of *Tirante the White* the priest himself declares that it is a treasure of delight and a mine of pastime.

> 'Truly, I declare to you, gossip, that in its style this is the best book in the world. Here the knights eat and sleep, and die in their beds, and make their wills before they die, with other things in which the rest of the books of this kind are wanting.'

But even stronger evidence of the esteem that Cervantes felt for the best of the romances is to be found in his habit of linking their names with the poems of Homer and Virgil. So, in the course of instruction given by Don Quixote to Sancho Panza, while they dwelt in the wilds of the Sierra Morena, Ulysses is cited as the model of prudence and patience, Aeneas as the greatest of pious sons and expert captains, and Amadis as the 'pole star, the morning star, the sun of valiant and enamoured knights, whom all we have to copy, who do battle under the banner of love and chivalry'. It would indeed be a strange thing if a book which is so brave an exercise of the creative imagination, were mainly destructive in its aim, and deserved no higher honour than a scavenger. The truth is that the book is so many-sided that all kinds of tastes and beliefs can find their warrant in it. The soul of it is an irony so profound that but few of its readers have explored it to the depths. It is like a mine, deep below deep; and much good treasure is to be found at the more easily accessible levels. All irony criticizes the imperfect ideas and theories of mankind, not by substituting for them other ideas and other theories, less imperfect, but by placing the facts of life, in mute comment, alongside of the theories. The Ruler of the World is the great master of irony; and man has been permitted to share some part of his enjoyment in the purifying power of fact. The weaker and more querulous members of the race commonly try to enlist the facts in the service of their pet ideas. A grave and deep spirit like Cervantes knows that the facts will endure no such servitude. They will not take orders from those who call for their verdict, nor will they be content to speak only when they are asked to speak. They intrude suddenly, in the most amazing and irrelevant fashion, on the carefully ordered plans of humanity. They cannot be explained away, and many a man who thought to have guarded himself against surprise has been surprised by love and death.

Everyone sees the irony of *Don Quixote* in its first degree, and enjoys it in its more obvious forms. This absurd old gentleman, who tries to put his antiquated ideas into action in a busy, selfish, prosy world, is a figure of fun even to the meanest intelligence. But, with more thought, there comes a check to our frivolity. Is not all virtue and all goodness in the same case as Don Quixote? Does the author, after all, mean to say that the world is right, and that those who try to better it are wrong? If that is what he means, how is it that at every step of our journey we come to like the Don better, until in the end we can hardly put a limit to our love and reverence for him? Is it possible that the criticism is double-edged, and that what we are celebrating with our laughter is the failure of the world?

A wonderful thing in Cervantes's handling of his story is his absolute honesty and candour. He does not mince matters. His world behaves as the world may be expected to behave when its daily interests are violently disordered by a lunatic. Failure upon failure dogs the steps of poor Don Quixote, and he has no popularity to redeem his material disasters. 'He who writes of me', says the Don pensively, in his discussion with the bachelor Sampson, 'will please very few'; and the only comfort the bachelor can find for him is that the number of fools is infinite, and that the First Part of his adventures has delighted them all. As an example of Cervantes's treatment take one of the earliest of these adventures, the rescue of the boy Andres from the hands of his oppressor. As he rode away from the inn, on the first day of his knighthood, while yet he was unfurnished with a squire, Don Quixote heard cries of complaint from a thicket near by. He thanked Heaven for giving him so early an opportunity of service, and turned his horse aside to where he found a farmer beating a boy. Don Quixote, with all knightly formality, called the farmer a coward, and challenged him to single combat. The farmer, terrified by the strange apparition, explained that the boy was his servant and by gross carelessness had lost sheep for him at the rate of one a day. The matter was at last settled by the farmer liberating the boy and promising to pay him in full his arrears of wages; whereupon the knight rode away, well pleased. Then the farmer tied up the boy again, and beat him more severely than ever, till at the last he loosed him, and told him to go and seek redress from his champion. 'So the boy departed sobbing, and his master stayed behind laughing, and after this manner did the valorous Don Quixote right that wrong.' Later on, when the knight and his squire are in the wilds, with the company whom chance has gathered around them, the boy appears again, and Don Quixote narrates the story of his deliverance as an illustration of the benefits conferred on the world by knight-errantry.

> 'All that your worship says is true,' replies the lad, 'but the end of the business was very much the contrary of what your worship imagines.' 'How contrary?' said Don Quixote. 'Did he not pay thee, then?' 'He not only did not pay me,' said the boy, 'but as soon as your worship had got outside the wood, and

we were alone, he tied me again to the same tree, and gave me so many lashes that he left me flayed like St. Bartholomew; and at every lash he gave me, he uttered some jest or scoff, to make a mock of your worship; and if I had not felt so much pain, I would have laughed at what he said.... For all this your worship is to blame, because if you had held on your way, and had not meddled with other people's business, my master would have been content to give me a dozen or two lashes, and afterwards he would have released me and paid me what he owed. But as your worship insulted him and called him bad names, his anger was kindled, and as he could not avenge himself on you, he let fly the tempest on me.'

Don Quixote sadly admits his error, and confesses that he ought to have remembered that 'no churl keeps the word he gives if he finds that it does not suit him to keep it'. But he promises Andres that he will yet see him righted; and with that the boy's terror awakes. 'For the love of God, sir knight-errant,' he says, 'if you meet me again, and see me being cut to pieces, do not rescue me, nor help me, but leave me to my pain; for, however great it be, it cannot be greater than will come to me from the help of your worship—whom, with all the knights-errant ever born into the world, may God confound!' With that he ran away, and Don Quixote stood very much abashed by his story, so that the rest of the company had to take great care that they did not laugh outright and put him to confusion.

At no point in the story does Cervantes permit the reader to forget that the righter of wrongs must not look in this world for either success or praise. The indignities heaped upon that gentle and heroic soul almost revolt the reader, as Charles Lamb remarked. He is beaten and kicked; he has his teeth knocked out, and consoles himself with the thought that these hardships are incident to his profession; his face is all bedaubed with mud, and he answers with grave politeness to the mocks of those who deride him. When he stands sentry on the back of his horse at the inn, to guard the sleepers, the stable wench, Maritornes, gets him to reach up his hand to an upper window, or rather a round hole in the wall of the hayloft, whereupon she slips a running noose over his wrist and ties the rope firmly to a bar within the loft. In this posture, and in continual danger of being hung by the arm if his horse should move away, he stands till dawn, when four travellers knock at the gate of the inn. He at once challenges them for their discourtesy in disturbing the slumbers of those whom he is guarding. Even the Duke and the Duchess, who feel kindly to Don Quixote and take him under their care, are quite ready to play rough practical jokes on him. It is while he is their guest that his face is all scratched and clawed by frightened cats turned loose in his bedroom at night. His friends in the village were kinder than this, but they, to get him home, carried him through the country in a latticed cage on poles, like a wild beast, for the admiration of the populace; and he bethought himself, 'As I am a new knight in the world, and the first that hath revived the forgotten exercise of chivalry, these are newly invented forms of enchantment.' His spirit rises superior to all his misfortunes, and his mind remains as serene as a cloudless sky.

But Don Quixote, it may be objected, is mad. Here the irony of Cervantes finds a deeper level. Don Quixote is a high-minded idealist, who sees all things by the light of his own lofty preconceptions. To him every woman is beautiful and adorable; everything that is said to him is worthy to be heard with attention and respect; every community of men, even the casual assemblage of lodgers at an inn, is a society founded on strict rules of mutual consideration and esteem. He shapes his behaviour in accordance with these ideas, and is laughed at for his pains. But he has a squire, Sancho Panza, who is a realist and loves food and sleep, who sees the world as it is, by the light of common day. Sancho, it might be supposed, is sane, and supplies a sure standard whereby to measure his master's deviations from the normal. Not at all; Sancho, in his own way, is as mad as his master. If the one is betrayed by fantasy, the other is betrayed, with as ludicrous a result, by common sense. The thing is well seen in the question of the island, the government of which is to be intrusted to Sancho when Don Quixote comes into his kingdom. Sancho, though he would have seen through the pretences of any merely corrupt bargainer, recognizes at once that his master is disinterested and truthful, and he believes all he hears about the island. He spends much thought on the scheme, and passes many criticisms on it. Sometimes he protests that he is quite unfit for the position of a governor, and that his wife would cut a poor figure as a governor's lady. At other times he

vehemently asserts that many men of much less ability than himself
are governors, and eat every day off silver plate. Then he hears that, if
an island should not come to hand, he is to be rewarded with a slice
of a continent, and at once he stipulates that his domain shall be situ-
ated on the coast, so that he may put his subjects to a profitable use
by selling them into slavery. It is not a gloss upon Cervantes to say
that Sancho is mad; the suggestion is made, with significant repetition, in the book itself. 'As the Lord liveth,' says the barber, addressing
the squire, 'I begin to think that thou oughtest to keep him company
in the cage, and that thou art as much enchanted as he. In an evil day
wast thou impregnated with his promises, and it was a sorrowful hour
when the island of thy longings entered thy skull.'

So these two, in the opinion of the neighbours, are both mad, yet
most of the wisdom of the book is theirs, and when neither of them
is talking, the book falls into mere commonplace. And this also is
many times recognized and commented on in the book itself. Sometimes it is the knight, and sometimes the squire, whose conversation
makes the hearers marvel that one who talks with so much wisdom,
justice, and discernment should act so foolishly. Certainly the book
is a paradise of delightful discourse wherein all topics are handled
and are presented in a new guise. The dramatic setting, which is the
meaning of the book, is never forgotten; yet the things said are so
good that when they are taken out of their setting they shine still,
though with diminished splendour. What could be better than Don
Quixote's treatment of the question of lineage, when he is considering his future claim to marry the beautiful daughter of a Christian
or paynim King? 'There are two kinds of lineage,' he remarks. 'The
difference is this—that some were what they are not, and others are
what they were not; and when the thing is looked into I might prove
to be one of those who had a great and famous origin, with which the
King, my father-in-law who is to be, must be content.' Or what could
be wiser than Sancho's account of his resignation of the governor-
ship? 'Yesterday morning I left the island as I found it, with the same
streets, houses, and tiles which they had when I went there. I have
borrowed nothing of nobody, nor mixed myself up with the making
of profits, and though I thought to make some profitable laws, I
did not make any of them, for I was afraid they would not be kept,
which would be just the same as if they had never been made.' Many

of those who come across the pair in the course of their wanderings fall under the fascination of their talk. Not only so, but the world of imagination in which the two wanderers live proves so attractive, the infection of their ideas is so strong, that, long before the end of the story is reached, a motley company of people, from the Duke and Duchess down to the villagers, have set their own business aside in order to take part in the make-believe, and to be the persons of Don Quixote's dream. There was never any Kingdom of Barataria; but the hearts of all who knew him were set on seeing how Sancho would comport himself in the office of Governor, so the Duke lent a village for the purpose, and it was put in order and furnished with officers of State for the part that it had to play. In this way some of the fancies of the talkers almost struggle into existence, and the dream of Don Quixote makes the happiness it does not find.

Nothing in the story is more touching than the steadily growing attachment and mutual admiration of the knight and the squire. Each deeply respects the wisdom of the other, though Don Quixote, whose taste in speech is courtly, many times complains of Sancho's swarm of proverbs. Each is influenced by the other; the knight insists on treating the squire with the courtesies due to an equal, and poor Sancho, in the end, declares that not all the governments of the world shall tempt him away from the service of his beloved master. What, then, are we to think, and what does their creator think, of those two madmen, whose lips drop wisdom? 'Mark you, Sancho,' said Don Quixote, 'there are two kinds of beauty—one of the soul, and another of the body. That of the soul excelleth in knowledge, in modesty, in fine conduct, in liberality and good breeding; and all these virtues are found in, and may belong to, an ugly man. . . . I see full well, Sancho, that I am not beautiful, but I know also that I am not deformed, and it is enough for a man of honour to be no monster; he may be well loved, if he possesses those gifts of soul which I have mentioned.' Sometimes, at the height of his frenzy, the knight seems almost inspired. So, when the shepherds have entertained him, he offers, by way of thanks, to maintain against all comers the fame and beauty of the shepherdesses, and utters his wonderful little speech on gratitude:

'For the most part, he who receives is inferior to him who gives; and hence God is above all, because he is, above all, the great giver; and the gifts of man cannot be equal to those of God, for there is an infinite distance between them; and the narrowness and insufficiency of the gifts of man is eked out by gratitude.'

There cannot be too much of this kind of madness. Well may Don Antonio cry out on the bachelor Sampson, who dresses himself as the Knight of the Silver Moon and overthrows Don Quixote in fight:

'O sir, may God forgive you the wrong you have done to all the world in desiring to make a sane man of the most gracious madman that the world contains! Do you not perceive that the profit which shall come from the healing of Don Quixote can never be equal to the pleasure which is caused by his ecstasies?'

What if the world itself is mad, not with the ecstasy of Don Quixote, nor with the thrifty madness of Sancho, but with a flat kind of madness, a makeshift compromise between faith and doubt? All men have a vein of Quixotry somewhere in their nature. They can be counted on, in most things, to follow the beaten path of interest and custom, till suddenly there comes along some question on which they refuse to appeal to interest; they take their stand on principle, and are adamant. All men know in themselves the mood of Sancho, when he says:

'I have heard the preachers preach that we should love our Lord for himself alone, without being moved to it by the hope of glory or the fear of pain; but, for my own part, I would love him for what he is able to do for me.'

These two moods, the mood of Quixote and the mood of Sancho, seem to divide between them most of the splendours and most of the comforts of human life. It is rare to find either mood in its perfection. A man who should consistently indulge in himself the mood of the unregenerate Sancho would be a rogue, though, if he preserved good temper in his doings, he would be a pleasant rogue. The man who should maintain in himself the mood of Quixote would be something very like a saint. The saints of the Church Militant would find no puzzle and no obscurity in the character of the Knight of La Mancha.

Some of them, perhaps, would understand, better than Don Quixote understood, that the full record of his doings, compiled by Cervantes, is both a tribute to the saintly character, and a criticism of it. They certainly could not fail to discover the religious kernel of the book, as the world, in the easy confidence of its own superiority, has failed to discover it. They would know that whoso loseth his life shall save it; they would not find it difficult to understand how Don Quixote, and, in his own degree, Sancho, was willing to be a fool, that he, and the world with him, might be made wise. Above all, they would appreciate the more squalid misadventures of Don Quixote, for, unlike the public, which recognizes the saint by his aureole, they would know, none better, that the way they have chosen is the way of contempt, and that Christianity was nursed in a manger.

NOTES

1. Miguel de Cervantes Saavedra, born at Alcalá de Henares, 1547; died at Madrid, 23 April 1616.

2. The authentic facts concerning the life of Cervantes have been collected and stated with admirable scholarly precision by Professor Fitzmaurice-Kelly, in his recent *Miguel de Cervantes Saavedra, a Memoir* (Clarendon Press, 1913). In this biography is embodied all that can be learned from the large array of documents discovered and published within the last twenty years by the late Cristobal Pérez Pastor. The resulting addition to our knowledge will disappoint those who are not accustomed to the perspective of the law. A man's small debts and worries are recorded on parchment; the crucial events of his life find no historian but himself. To compile a life of Cervantes from this wilderness of documents is as difficult as it must always be to write the life of a soldier and poet from the evidence supplied by his washing-bills and tax-papers. Mr. Fitzmaurice-Kelly has performed his task modestly and judiciously.

THE EPIC OF GILGAMESH

"*The Epic of Gilgamesh* and the Hero's Journey,"
by Merritt Moseley,
University of North Carolina at Asheville

One definition of a hero is a person who, through genius or courage or might, can accomplish what a normal person cannot. By this standard, the journey of Gilgamesh, the ancient Mesopotamian figure at the heart of *The Epic of Gilgamesh*, is splendidly heroic. He actually undertakes two daunting journeys; in the first, accompanied by his friend Enkidu, he walks from his kingdom Uruk, in what is now southern Iraq, to northern Lebanon in six days. The poem specifies that the two heroes cover 50 leagues a day, "a walk of a month and a half" (Kovacs 31), an accomplishment that (even before they kill a watchful divinity) can only be called heroic. And later, bereaved by the death of his beloved Enkidu, Gilgamesh does something even more astonishing: He travels to the ends of the earth, braving all sorts of threats, in an effort to discover the secret of life.

The hero, as a literary figure, is associated with the genre of epic. Despite the modern titling of *The Epic of Gilgamesh*, the term is anachronistic, originating with the Greek epics written long after Gilgamesh. Nevertheless, the usual understanding of an epic poem is something like "a long narrative poem describing heroic events that happen over a period of time," and under these terms it *is* indeed the epic of Gilgamesh (George 3). There are two kinds of epic: the traditional epic told over a long period by anonymous tellers before being written down, like *The Iliad* or *Beowulf;* and the literary epic, written as a self-consciously artistic composition by a single author. *The Epic of Gilgamesh* is of the former definition; it may have been under construction for over a thousand years before reaching the state in which it was rediscovered. But epics of both kinds share several conventions with *Gilgamesh*: the large spatial scope of the action; the inclusion of mighty battles, perhaps against superhuman or semi-divine opponents; an arduous journey; the participation of the divine realm in the action, as the epic hero's undertakings are important enough to engage the attention of gods; and a hero who is the greatest of men and sometimes even more than human. Homer's hero Achilles is the son of a goddess. Gilgamesh is even more divine: He is two-thirds god, only one-third man. Importantly, though, he like Achilles is still mortal. As a tavern-keeper reminds Gilgamesh in the Old Babylonian version, "When the gods created mankind, / they fixed Death for mankind, / and held back Life in their own hands" (Kovacs 85).

The Epic of Gilgamesh is the world's oldest known story, though it became available to the world at large only in 1872, when George Smith published the part of the story related to the flood, of interest to him because of its linkages with the Hebrew Bible. He had translated it from clay tablets found in the library of Ashurbanipal, an Assyrian king (668–627 BCE), whose capital was Nineveh. Since that time many other fragments have been found in many parts of southwestern Asia, translated, and published. Ancient Mesopotamian texts were inscribed in cuneiform, normally on clay tablets (or as is the case with Gilgamesh, in cylinder seals). It is remarkable that so much textual evidence of Gilgamesh has survived. The story of Gilgamesh goes back thousands of years before the Common Era (BCE). Gilgamesh himself may have been a real person. One document, the *Sumerian King List*, says that he was "the fifth king in the first dynasty of Uruk, which historians place in the Second Early Dynastic Period of Sumer (ca. 2700–2500)" (Tigay 13). If Gilgamesh was indeed a real figure, little is known of him other than that he ruled over Uruk, built the city wall, and rebuilt a shrine to a god, all deeds which are attributed to him in the poem itself.

Scholars do know the name of one of the authors of one version of the epic, an exorcist-priest named Sîn-leqi-unninni, who may have lived in Uruk sometime after 1600 BCE (12). The three main versions of the epic are the one attributed to Sîn-leqi-unninni, (known as the Old Babylonian version) and two later ones called the eleven-tablet and the twelve-tablet forms of the Standard Babylonian version. The twelfth tablet is a piece of narrative only loosely connected to the earlier part, relating a descent into the underworld, and some editors omit it. But other parts of even the eleven-tablet version are probably later additions, episodes co-opted from other tales (Abusch 615). After all, a great deal of change takes place during a thousand years or more of epic fermentation. The story of Utnapishtim and the flood—the part of *Gilgamesh* that originally excited Western scholars most—seems to have been carried over from another Babylonian story, the *Myth of Atrahasis*. It is not included in the Old Babylonian version (617).

There are a number of modern translations. Some are very scholarly and include references to the history and language of the Sumerian culture. Others offer a continuous poetic narrative, more readable but less reliable as a representation of the original ancient texts. Still others omit absent lines (due to the breakage of the tablets) and offer cautious hypotheses about missing or unexplained information. Some modern readers find this last approach confusing or troubling. One reason for their dissatisfaction is the imperfect state of the text. Important explanations seem to be missing; chunks of the plot are gone and must be inferred. But this should not deter a serious reader for long.

More troubling for some readers is the question of motivation: *Why do the characters do the things they do?* For instance, when Gilgamesh and Enkidu decide to go to the Cedar Forest and kill Humbaba, its divine protector, the text (which is also imperfect at this point) gives only a sketchy idea of their aims. It is true that Gilgamesh says to his mother, Ninsun,

> I must travel a long way to where Humbaba is,
> I must face fighting such as I have not known,
> and I must travel on a road that I do not know!
> Until the time that I go and return,
> until I reach the Cedar Forest,

until I kill Humbaba the Terrible,
and eradicate from the land something baneful that Shamash
hates,
intercede with Shamash on my behalf! (Kovacs 25–26; Tablet III,
lines 24–31)

Humbaba lives a long way off and has done nothing to threaten
the people of Uruk, whatever his standing in the eyes of Shamash
(the Sun God). In the following lines—"If I kill Humbaba and cut
his Cedar [?] / let there be rejoicing all over the land [?]"—another
explanation is implied, and after killing Humbaba, Gilgamesh takes
the cedar to make a gigantic door for the city wall. But the most
important motivation is a desire for heroic fame. Gilgamesh reminds
his friend Enkidu that no man lives forever: "As for human beings,
their days are numbered, and whatever they keep trying to achieve
is but wind!" (20, II, 230–1). Therefore, fame is their only chance at
eternal life: "Should I fall, I will have established my fame" (line 236).
In lines from the Old Babylonian version, he makes this aim more
explicit:

I will make the land hear how mighty is the Scion of Uruk!
I will set my hand to it and will chop down the Cedar,
I will establish for myself a Name for eternity! (Kovacs 21)

Is this a good reason? For modern readers, killing another living
being, pulling out his tongue, and stealing his cedar just to make a
name for oneself is ethically suspect. But an ancient Sumerian had
no hope for an afterlife with rewards and punishments (instead he
would have expected a shadowy underworld of the dead, resembling
neither heaven nor hell). In some sense, one's ability to remain alive
after death depended upon leaving a famous name. And the way to
win fame in this world was by daring deeds of violence.
      This is not the only difference between Gilgamesh and the
modern model of the hero. If we think a hero ought to be brave but
self-sacrificing, noble, modest, and good, then Gilgamesh falls short
in all but bravery. He is, by our standards, vainglorious and boastful.
He does speak of the things he has done for the people of Uruk,
but his accomplishments as king, like his assault on Humbaba, seem

designed to burnish his own fame, and for the most part he is utterly self-centered. He gives little thought to the ordinary men and women among whom he lives or does so only as means to satisfy his own desires. Though missing lines prevent us from knowing exactly how he does it, we do know that Gilgamesh frightens the people of Uruk. His people complain to Anu, the Sky God, and their complaints hint at violence and sexual rapaciousness:

> There is no rival who can raise a weapon against him.
> His fellows stand [at the alert], attentive to his [orders?],
> Gilgamesh does not leave a son to his father,
> day and night he arrogantly . . .
> Is he the shepherd of Uruk-Haven,
> is he their shepherd . . . bold, eminent, knowing, and *wise*?
> Gilgamesh does not leave a girl to *her mother* [?]! (5, I, 67–74)

In fact these excesses, and the divine creation of Gilgamesh's rival, Enkidu, launch the events that make up *The Epic of Gilgamesh*.

The nature of the gods also bewilders some modern readers. There are many of them, of course, Mesopotamia being a polytheistic culture. As in other polytheistic systems, pleasing one god may displease another (as we also see with Odysseus or Aeneas). The gods also act from obscure motives. For instance, the imposition of the flood, by contrast with the account in the book of Genesis, is capricious. Utnapishtim tells Gilgamesh, "The hearts of the Great Gods moved them to inflict the Flood" (97, XI, 14). The Atrahasis fragment, the source of this part of *The Epic of Gilgamesh*, specifies that people had become so numerous on the earth that their noise was keeping Enlil from sleep (Heidel 226).

The gods are also anything but remote from men. A god whispers the secret of the flood to Utnapishtim, apparently because he likes him (though unlike Noah, Utnapishtim is not said to be more virtuous than all the other human beings, who were later killed in the flood). Ishtar, the goddess of love, proposes to Gilgamesh. When he rejects her advances—contemptuously, reminding her of the poor life expectancy of her previous lovers—she arranges for the Bull of Heaven to attack Uruk. Enkidu and Gilgamesh kill the Bull of Heaven, another successful heroic venture against the divine, paralleling their murder of

Humbaba. Remarkably, Enkidu, a mere man, wrenches off the bull's hindquarter and flings it into the face of the goddess (this proves to be going a step too far).

There are, to be sure, reasons to feel distanced from Gilgamesh. He is partly divine, in complete command of a city and its people, the love object of the Goddess of Love, stronger than anybody else on earth and handsomer, too. And yet the power of *The Epic of Gilgamesh* comes from its universal human qualities. The fact that a book is old is not enough to give it power over readers. Everyone can understand *The Epic of Gilgamesh* because everyone must grow up, everyone must love, and everyone must die.

Enkidu, Gilgamesh's heroic but entirely human counterpart, enacts the process of growing up; in fact, he enacts the maturation of the entire human species. To be sure, his birth is unusual. In answer to the complaint of the men of Uruk about Gilgamesh's intolerable behavior, the gods instruct Aruru (the mother goddess) to create someone to counter him. From a piece of clay, she sculpts Enkidu, who is a creature entirely of nature:

> His whole body was shaggy with hair,
> he had a full head of hair like a woman,
> his locks billowed in profusion like Ashnan.
> He knew neither people nor settled living,
> but wore a garment like Sumukan.
> He ate grasses with the gazelles,
> and jostled at the watering hole with the animals;
> as with animals, his thirst was slaked with [mere] water. (Kovacs 6, I, 86–93)

Allied with wild animals, Enkidu protects them from a trapper. When the trapper seeks assistance from Gilgamesh, he sends a harlot, who seduces Enkidu and, in effect, makes him human:

> But when he turned his attention to his animals,
> the gazelles saw Enkidu and darted off . . .
> Enkidu was diminished, his running was not as before.
> But then he drew himself up, for his understanding had broadened. (9, I, 178–79, 183–84).

Like Adam and Eve, Enkidu has fallen into adulthood, become fully human, through sex. Estranged from the animals, he then recapitulates the human movement from nature to culture: He moves to the city. Under the harlot's tutelage he becomes "civilized." In the Old Babylonian account,

> Enkidu ate the food until he was sated,
> He drank the beer—seven jugs!—and became expansive and sang with joy!
> He was elated and his face glowed.
> He splashed his shaggy body with water,
> and rubbed himself with oil, and turned into a human.
> He put on some clothing and became like a warrior [?].
> He took up his weapon and chased lions so that the shepherds could rest at night. (16)

Now drinking beer—an artificial human product—instead of the natural water, wearing textile clothing instead of his earlier skins, and siding with his fellow human beings against the animals, Enkidu has turned into a human. Like anyone's maturation from child into adult, Enkidu's is fraught with both gains and losses. His understanding is broadened, yet his running is slowed. He has a human relationship (with the harlot Shamhat), yet he has lost his friends among the animals. Later, as he faces death, Enkidu curses both Shamhat and the trapper, but Gilgamesh reminds him that his "fall," via the harlot's wiles introduced him to bread and wine, grand garments, and the friendship of "beautiful Gilgamesh" (63, VII, 128).

It is the loving companionship between Gilgamesh and Enkidu that most humanizes them both. As the epic opens, Gilgamesh is glorified and worshipped, as well as feared, by his subjects. He has his choice of all the women. He is the handsomest of men, proud of his unmatched achievements. But he is also solitary, because he is different in degree from all the other men in his world. When the gods create Enkidu, they explain,

> Let him be equal to his [Gilgamesh's] stormy heart,
> let them be a match for each other so that Uruk may find peace! (5–6, I, 80–81).

"Match" can mean several things, and initially it suggests a violent struggle between equally matched heroes, which is what happens. Enkidu strides into Uruk-Haven, welcomed by the population, and takes up a position blocking "the entry to the marital chamber"— evidently where Gilgamesh is headed to enjoy another man's bride (18, II, 98). A battle ensues, their mighty conflict shaking the wall. Unfortunately, the text is imperfect here, but they seem to fight to a standstill and soon are kissing and becoming friends.

This is the more important way that Enkidu is a match for Gilgamesh. Enkidu cannot defeat him and force him to stop mistreating his people. But by becoming his friend (a role for which only he is qualified, because he is the only man equal to Gilgamesh), he can give Gilgamesh a companion and assist and accompany him on his journey. From this point no more is heard of Gilgamesh molesting the people. From here begin the heroic adventures. Enkidu's friendship has called Gilgamesh to rise above taking petty advantage of his superiority to ordinary human beings and under-take deeds commensurate with his greatness.

That Gilgamesh and Enkidu love each other is clear. Perhaps it makes sense to think of this as a homosexual relationship; certainly Enkidu is powerfully agitated by Ishtar's attempt to seduce his friend. Perhaps it is no more than a lifelong, life-changing companionship of beloved equals. Their love for each other is both the reason for Enkidu's fate and the condition that makes it so poignant. As we have seen, Gilgamesh and Enkidu together undertake exploits that neither could, or would, attempt alone. They kill Humbaba; they reject and humiliate Ishtar; they kill the Bull of Heaven. Although, as we might expect, there is disagreement among the gods about how blameworthy this deed is, one thing they agree upon is that Enkidu must die. Tablet VII begins with the gods in conference (in Gilgamesh's dream), and Anu, father of the gods, declares:

Because they killed the Bull of Heaven and have also slain Humbaba,
the one of them who pulled up the Cedar of the Mountain must die!
Enlil said: "Let Enkidu die, but Gilgamesh must not die!" (59, VII, 4–6)

Enkidu's death, described at great length in the poem, is dreadful for Gilgamesh, who watches with him for twelve days and is inconsolable after his death.

> He covered his friend's face like a bride,
> swooping down over him like an eagle,
> and like a lioness deprived of her cubs
> he keeps pacing to and fro.
> He shears off his curls and heaps them onto the ground,
> ripping off his finery and casting it away as an abomination.
> (70–71; VIII, 47–52)

His grief is understandable and his mourning is extreme: sacrificing to the gods, disregarding his own person, and commissioning a rich and elaborate statue of his friend.

But the strongest result of Endiku's death is Gilgamesh's realization that he, too, can die. As his expedition against Humbaba marked his exterior journey, Gilgamesh's awareness of death marks a stage in Gilgamesh's inner, or psychological, journey. This is a man who has seen people die (during the Bull of Heaven episode, for instance) and who even declared in Tablet II, "As for human beings, their days are numbered" (20, II, 230). But apparently he never realized *he* shared their fate. Perhaps Gilgamesh in his pride was heedless; perhaps he reasoned from his undoubted superiority to all the other people he had ever met that he was exempt from their mortality. The death of Enkidu sobers him:

> I am going to die!—am I not like Enkidu?!
> Deep sadness penetrates my core,
> I fear death, and now roam the wilderness—
> I will set out to the region of Utanapishtim, son of Ubartutu,
> and will go with utmost dispatch! (75; ix, 2–5)

Here begins the most important part of the hero's journey in *The Epic of Gilgamesh*. Utanapishtim is an ancient king who alone survived the flood (a sort of analogue to the biblical Noah), living at the Mouth of the Rivers, the most remote place there is. Newly anxious about death, Gilgamesh proposes to find Utanapishtim and discover the secret of his immortality. After a difficulty journey he reaches the sea, where he has a conversation with a tavern keeper, Siduri. Then he finds Utanapishtim and is surprised to find that he looks like a normal man. Utanapishtim relates the story of the flood and of his escape in something like an ark because the god Ea (breaking ranks with the other gods, who had agreed to kill all mankind without warning) had given him notice of the flood. When it subsided, Enlil declared: "Previously Utanapishtim was a human being. / But now let Utanapishtim and his wife become like us, the gods! / Let Utanapishtim reside far away, at the mouth of the Rivers" (103, XI, 200–202).

Utanapishtim does have the knowledge Gilgamesh seeks—the secret of eternal life. In order to gain it Gilgamesh has to stay awake for six days and seven nights. When he fails at this task, he has a consolatory chance to get renewed youth by means of a magic plant, but he is careless with it and a snake takes it. All that is left is to return to Uruk, and the last lines of the poem mirror the first, praising the city's wall and splendid design.

It doesn't matter if one is great, handsome, strong, ruthless, or of divine origin, all of which Gilgamesh was; one cannot escape death. Gilgamesh does not die in *The Epic of Gilgamesh*, but he does accept his own mortality. The Standard Version, at least in its eleven-tablet form, leads up to the meeting with Utanapishtim, Gilgamesh's failure to achieve immortality or even rejuvenation, and his return to Uruk. He must die, but he can be a great king until then (Utanapishtim was also a king).

The Old Babylonian version lacks the Utanapishtim episode and ends with Gilgamesh learning wisdom from Siduri, the tavern keeper (wise women bookend the poem, with Shamhat teaching Enkidu, and Siduri teaching Gilgamesh, what it means to be human). Siduri's advice is that one cannot avoid death, but one can make the most of life:

> Gilgamesh, where are you wandering?
> The life that you are seeking all around you will not find.
> When the gods created mankind
> they fixed Death for mankind,
> and held back Life in their own hands.
> Now you, Gilgamesh, let your belly be full!
> Be happy day and night,

of each day make a party,
dance in circles day and night!
Let your clothes be sparkling clean,
Let your head be clean, wash yourself with water!
Attend to the little one who holds onto your hand,
let a wife delight in your embrace.
This is the [true] task of *mankind*[?] (85)

Abusch writes that this advice calls on the hero to accept "the value of life and its affirmation in the face of the heroic and the absolute, which can only lead to death" (617). These are two different responses to the question that the *Epic of Gilgamesh* asks of its readers, and of Gilgamesh himself: We all must die. What then?

Whether we dance and rejoice in clean clothes, the love of food and drink, or our spouse and children; whether we set to work to build the city wall and restore the god's sanctuary; whether we enjoy the profound sharing and love of an equal companionship—the lesson of Gilgamesh is that death gives meaning to life. It may be a tragic meaning but, in some measure, it is a meaning denied to the deathless gods themselves. It is a powerful message and one that is no less true for today's readers than for those who, four thousand years ago, told each other tales of the great Gilgamesh, the incomparable king.

WORKS CITED

Abusch, Tzvi, "The Development and Meaning of the Epic of Gilgamesh: An Interpretive Essay," *Journal of the American Oriental Society*, 121 (October–December 2001): 614–622.

Gardner, John and John Maier. *Gilgamesh: Translated from the Sin-leqi-unninni Version*. New York: Alfred A. Knopf, 1984.

George, A. R. *The Babylonian Gilgamesh Epic: Introduction, Critical Edition and Cuneiform Texts*, Vol. I (Oxford: Oxford University Press, 2003).

Heidel, Alexander. *The Gilgamesh Epic and Old Testament Parallels*. Chicago: University of Chicago Press, 1946.

Kovacs, Maureen Gallery. *The Epic of Gilgamesh*. Stanford, Calif.: Stanford University Press, 1985.

Mason, Herbert. *Gilgamesh: A Verse Narrative*. New York New American
    Library, 1972.
Mitchell, Stephen. *Gilgamesh: A New English Version*. New York: Free Press,
    2004.
Tigay, Jeffrey H. *The Evolution of the Gilgamesh Epic*. Philadelphia: University
    of Pennsylvania Press, 1982.

GO TELL IT ON THE MOUNTAIN
(JAMES BALDWIN)

"James Baldwin"
by Robert Bone,
in *The Negro Novel in America* (1965)

INTRODUCTION

In *The Negro Novel in America*, Robert Bone explores
blues as an important subject in James Baldwin's *Go Tell
It on the Mountain*. A musical form derived in part from
the African-American spiritual, blues, according to Bone, is
representative of the "New Negro" or "Harlem Renaissance"
movement as it is now most often referred to. During John
Grimes's internal quest, we hear "the sound of all Negro art
and all Negro religion, for it flows from the cracked-open
heart." Bone contends that John's journey toward sexual and
racial freedom also mirrors Baldwin's life. Ultimately, John's
journey deals with identity, the sense of self he forges amid
two ritualized ways of experiencing suffering: Christianity
and the blues.

Bone, Robert. "James Baldwin." *The Negro Novel in America*. Revised edition.
New Haven, Conn.: Yale UP, 1965. 215–39.

The best of Baldwin's novels is *Go Tell It on the Mountain* (1953), and his best is very good indeed. It ranks with Jean Toomer's *Cane*, Richard Wright's *Native Son*, and Ralph Ellison's *Invisible Man* as a major contribution to American fiction. For this novel cuts through the walls of the store-front church to the essence of Negro experience in America. This is Baldwin's earliest world, his bright and morning star, and it glows with metaphorical intensity. Its emotions are his emotions; its language, his native tongue. The result is a prose of unusual power and authority. One senses in Baldwin's first novel a confidence, control, and mastery of style that he has not attained again in the novel form.

The central event of *Go Tell It on the Mountain* is the religious conversion of an adolescent boy. In a long autobiographical essay, which forms a part of *The Fire Next Time*,[1] Baldwin leaves no doubt that he was writing of his own experience. During the summer of his fourteenth year, he tells us, he succumbed to the spiritual seduction of a woman evangelist. On the night of his conversion, he suddenly found himself lying on the floor before the altar. He describes his trancelike state, the singing and clapping of the saints, and the all-night prayer vigil which helped to bring him "through." He then recalls the circumstances of his life that prompted so pagan and desperate a journey to the throne of Grace.

The overwhelming fact of Baldwin's childhood was his victimization by the white power structure. At first he experienced white power only indirectly, as refracted through the brutality and degradation of the Harlem ghetto. The world beyond the ghetto seemed remote, and scarcely could be linked in a child's imagination to the harrowing conditions of his daily life. And yet a vague terror, transmitted through his parents to the ghetto child, attested to the power of the white world. Meanwhile, in the forefront of his consciousness was a set of fears by no means vague.

To a young boy growing up in the Harlem ghetto, damnation was a clear and present danger: "For the wages of sin were visible everywhere, in every wine-stained and urine-splashed hallway, in every clanging ambulance bell, in every scar on the faces of the pimps and their whores, in every helpless, newborn baby being brought into this danger, in every knife and pistol fight on the Avenue."[2] To such a boy, the store-front church offered a refuge and a sanctuary from the terrors of the street. God and safety became synonymous, and the church, a part of his survival strategy.

Fear, then, was the principal motive of Baldwin's conversion: "I became, during my fourteenth year, for the first time in my life afraid—afraid of the evil within me and afraid of the evil without."[3] As the twin pressures of sex and race began to mount, the adolescent boy struck a desperate bargain with God. In exchange for sanctuary, he surrendered his sexuality, and abandoned any aspirations that might bring him into conflict with white power. He was safe, but walled off from the world; saved, but isolated from experience. This, to Baldwin, is the historical betrayal of the Negro Church. In exchange for the power of the Word, the Negro trades away the personal power of his sex and the social power of his people.

Life on these terms was unacceptable to Baldwin; he did not care to settle for less than his potential as a man. If his deepest longings were thwarted in the church, he would pursue them through his art. Sexual and racial freedom thus became his constant theme. And yet, even in breaking with the church, he pays tribute to its power: "In spite of everything, there was in the life I fled a zest and a joy and a capacity for facing and surviving disaster that are very moving and very rare."[4] We shall confront, then, in *Go Tell It on the Mountain*, a certain complexity of tone. Baldwin maintains an ironic distance from his material, even as he portrays the spiritual force and emotional appeal of storefront Christianity.

So much for the biographical foundations of the novel. The present action commences on the morning of John Grimes' fourteenth birthday, and before the night is out, he is born again in Christ. Part I, "The Seventh Day," introduces us to the boy and his family, his fears and aspirations, and the Temple of the Fire Baptized that is the center of his life. Part II, "The Prayers of the Saints," contains a series of flashbacks in which we share the inmost thoughts and private histories of his Aunt Florence, his mother Elizabeth, and his putative father, Gabriel. Part III, "The Threshing-Floor," returns us to the present and completes the story of the boy's conversion.

Parts I and III are set in Harlem in the spring of 1935. The action of Part II, however, takes place for the most part down home. Florence, Elizabeth, and Gabriel belong to a transitional generation, born roughly between 1875 and 1900. *Go Tell It on the Mountain* is thus a novel of the Great Migration. It traces the process of secularization that occurred when the Negro left the land for the Northern ghettos. This theme, to be sure, is handled ironically. Baldwin's protagonist "gets religion," but he is too young, too frightened, and too innocent to grasp the implications of his choice.

It is through the lives of the adults that we achieve perspective on the boy's conversion. His Aunt Florence has been brought to the evening prayer meeting by her fear of death. She is dying of cancer, and in her extremity humbles herself before God, asking forgiveness of her sins. These have consisted of a driving ambition and a ruthless hardening of heart. Early in her adult life, she left her dying mother to come North, in hopes of bettering her lot. Later, she drove from her side a husband whom she loved: "It had not been her fault that Frank was the way he was, determined to live and die a common nigger" (p. 92).[5] All her deeper feelings have been sacrificed to a futile striving for "whiteness" and respectability. Now she contemplates the wages of her virtue: an agonizing death in a lonely furnished room.

Elizabeth, as she conceives her life, has experienced both the fall and the redemption. Through Richard, she has brought an illegitimate child into the world, but through Gabriel, her error is retrieved. She fell in love with Richard during the last summer of her childhood, and followed him North to Harlem. There they took jobs as chambermaid and elevator boy, hoping to be married soon. Richard is sensitive, intelligent, and determined to educate himself. Late one evening, however, he is arrested and accused of armed robbery. When he protests his innocence, he is beaten savagely by the police. Ultimately he is released, but half hysterical with rage and shame, he commits suicide. Under the impact of this blow, Elizabeth retreats from life. Her subsequent marriage to Gabriel represents safety, timidity, and atonement for her sin.

As Gabriel prays on the night of John's conversion his thoughts revert to the events of his twenty-first year: his own conversion and beginning ministry, his joyless marriage to Deborah, and his brief affair with Esther. Deborah had been raped by white men at the age of sixteen. Thin, ugly, sexless, she is treated by the Negroes as a kind of holy fool. Gabriel, who had been a wild and reckless youth, marries her precisely to mortify the flesh. But he cannot master his desire. He commits adultery with Esther, and, informed that she is pregnant, refuses all emotional support. Esther dies in childbirth, and her son, Royal, who grows to manhood unacknowledged by his father, is killed in a Chicago dive.

Soon after the death of Royal, Deborah dies childless, and Gabriel is left without an heir. When he moves North, however, the Lord sends him a sign in the form of an unwed mother and her father-less child. He marries Elizabeth and promises to raise Johnny as his own son. In the course of time the second Royal is born, and Gabriel rejoices in the fulfillment of God's promise. But John's half brother, the fruit of the prophet's seed, has turned his back on God. Tonight he lies at home with a knife wound, inflicted in a street fight with some whites. To Gabriel, therefore, John's conversion is a bitter irony: "Only the son of the bondwoman stood where the rightful heir should stand" (p. 128).

Through this allusion, Baldwin alerts us to the metaphorical possibilities of his plot. Gabriel's phrase is from Genesis 21:9–10, "And Sarah saw the son of Hagar the Egyptian, which she had born unto Abraham, mocking. Wherefore she said unto Abraham, Cast out this bondwoman and her son: for the son of the bondwoman shall not be heir with my son, even with Isaac." Hagar's bastard son is of course Ishmael, the archetypal outcast. Apparently Baldwin wants us to view Gabriel and Johnny in metaphorical relation to Abraham and Ishmael. This tableau of guilty father and rejected son will serve him as an emblem of race relations in America.

Baldwin sees the Negro quite literally as the bastard child of American civilization. In Gabriel's double involvement with bastardy we have a re-enactment of the white man's historic crime. In Johnny, the innocent victim of Gabriel's hatred, we have an archetypal image of the Negro child. Obliquely, by means of an extended metaphor, Baldwin approaches the very essence of Negro experience. That essence is rejection, and its most destruc-tive consequence is shame. But God, the Heavenly Father, does not reject the Negro utterly. He casts down only to raise up. This is the psychic drama that occurs beneath the surface of John's conversion.

The Negro child, rejected by the whites for reasons that he cannot understand, is afflicted by an overwhelming sense of shame. Something mysterious, he feels, must be wrong with him, that he should be so cruelly ostracized. In time he comes to associate these feelings with the color of his skin—the basis, after all, of his rejection. He feels, and is made to feel, perpetually dirty and unclean:

> John hated sweeping this carpet, for dust arose, clogging his nose and sticking to his sweaty skin, and he felt that should he sweep it forever, the clouds of dust would not diminish, the rug would not be clean. It became in his imagination his impossible, lifelong task, his hard trial, like that of a man he had read about somewhere, whose curse it was to push a boulder up a steep hill. [p. 27]

This quality of Negro life, unending struggle with one's own blackness, is symbolized by Baldwin in the family name, Grimes. One can readily understand how such a sense of personal shame might have been inflamed by contact with the Christian tradition and transformed into an obsession with original sin. Gabriel's sermons take off from such texts as "I am a man of unclean lips," or "He which is filthy, let him be filthy still." The Negro's religious ritual, as Baldwin points out in an early essay, is permeated with color symbolism: "Wash me, cried the slave to his Maker, and I shall be whiter, whiter than snow! For black is the color of evil; only the robes of the saved are white."[6]

Given this attack on the core of the self, how can the Negro respond? If he accepts the white man's equation of blackness with evil, he is lost. Hating his true self, he will undertake the construction of a counter-self along the line that everything "black" he now disowns. To such a man, Christ is a kind of spiritual bleaching cream. Only if the Negro challenges the white man's moral categories can he hope to survive on honorable terms. This involves the sentiment that everything "black" he now embraces, however painfully, as his. There is, in short, the path of self-hatred and the path of self-acceptance. Both are available to Johnny within the framework of the Church, but he is deterred from one by the negative example of his father.

Consider Gabriel. The substance of his life is moral evasion. A preacher of the gospel and secretly the father of an illegitimate child,

he cannot face the evil in himself. In order to preserve his image as
the Lord's anointed, he has sacrificed the lives of those around him. His
principal victim is Johnny, who is not his natural child. In disowning the
bastard, he disowns the "blackness" in himself. Gabriel's psychological
mechanisms are, so to say, white. Throughout his work Baldwin has
described the scapegoat mechanism that is fundamental to the white
man's sense of self. To the question, Who am I?, the white man answers:
I am *white*, that is immaculate, without stain. I am the purified, the
saved, the saintly, the elect. It is the *black* who is the embodiment of evil.
Let him, the son of the bondwoman, pay the price of my sins.

From self-hatred flows not only self-righteousness but self-
glorification as well. From the time of his conversion Gabriel has
been living in a world of compensatory fantasy. He sees the Negro
race as a chosen people and himself as prophet and founder of a royal
line. But if Old Testament materials can be appropriated to buttress
such a fantasy world, they also offer a powerful means of grappling
with reality. When the Negro preacher compares the lot of his people
to that of the children of Israel, he provides his flock with a series of
metaphors corresponding to their deepest experience. The Church
thus offers to the Negro masses a ritual enactment of their daily pain.
It is with this poetry of suffering, which Baldwin calls the power of
the Word, that the final section of the novel is concerned.

The first fifteen pages of Part III contain some of Baldwin's
most effective writing. As John Grimes lies before the altar, a
series of visionary states passes through his soul. Dream fragments
and Freudian sequences, lively fantasies and Aesopian allegories,
combine to produce a generally surrealistic effect. Images of darkness and chaos, silence and emptiness, mist and cold—cumulative
patterns developed early in the novel—function now at maximum
intensity. These images of damnation express the state of the soul
when thrust into outer darkness by a rejecting, punishing, castrating
father figure who is the surrogate of a hostile society. The dominant
emotions are shame, despair, guilt, and fear.

At the depth of John's despair, a sound emerges to assuage his
pain:

> He had heard it all his life, but it was only now that his ears
> were opened to this sound that came from the darkness, that

could only come from darkness, that yet bore such sure witness
to the glory of the light. And now in his moaning, and so
far from any help, he heard it in himself—it rose from his
bleeding, his cracked-open heart. It was a sound of rage and
weeping which filled the grave, rage and weeping from time
set free, but bound now in eternity; rage that had no language,
weeping with no voice—which yet spoke now, to John's startled
soul, of boundless melancholy, of the bitterest patience, and the
longest night; of the deepest water, the strongest chains, the
most cruel lash; of humility most wretched, the dungeon most
absolute, of love's bed defiled, and birth dishonored, and most
bloody, unspeakable, sudden death. Yes, the darkness hummed
with murder: the body in the water, the body in the fire, the
body on the tree. John looked down the line of these armies
of darkness, army upon army, and his soul whispered, *Who are
these?* [p. 228]

This is the sound, though John Grimes doesn't know it, of the
blues. It is the sound of Bessie Smith, to which James Baldwin
listened as he wrote *Go Tell It on the Mountain*. It is the sound of
all Negro art and all Negro religion, for it flows from the cracked-
open heart.

On these harsh terms, Baldwin's protagonist discovers his identity. He belongs to those armies of darkness and must forever share
their pain. To the question, Who am I? he can now reply: I am he
who suffers, and yet whose suffering on occasion is "from time set
free." And thereby he discovers his humanity, for only man can ritu-
alize his pain. We are now very close to that plane of human experience where art and religion intersect. What Baldwin wants us to feel
is the emotional pressure exerted on the Negro's cultural forms by
his exposure to white oppression. And finally to comprehend that
these forms alone, through their power of transforming suffering,
have enabled him to survive his terrible ordeal.

NOTES

1. *The Fire Next Time* (New York, Dial Press, 1963), p. 29–61.
2. *Ibid.*, p. 34.

3. *Ibid.*, p. 30.
4. *Ibid.*, p. 55.
5. All page references are to the Dial Press editions of the novels.
6. *Notes of a Native Son*, p. 21.

JANE EYRE
(CHARLOTTE BRONTË)

"*Jane Eyre* and the Hero's Journey"
by Merritt Moseley,
University of North Carolina at Asheville

When Charlotte Brontë was writing *Jane Eyre*, she gave careful thought to what sort of heroine she wished to present. Her sisters Anne and Emily were also at work on their own first novels. Charlotte, according to an obituary account:

> told her sisters that they were wrong—even morally wrong—in making their heroines beautiful as a matter of course. They replied that it was impossible to make a heroine interesting on any other terms. Her answer was, "I will prove to you that you are wrong; I will show you a heroine as plain and as small as myself, who shall be as interesting as any of yours." (Gaskell II, 9)

We know that "heroine" may mean no more than female protagonist, but with Jane Eyre, Charlotte Brontë created a character to whom the term applies with nearly its full range of heroic associations.

As a heroine Jane has distinct disadvantages. Jane Austen in *Northanger Abbey* wrote ironically of its heroine Catherine Morland, "No one who had ever seen Catherine Morland in her infancy, would have supposed her born to be an heroine. Her situation in life, the character of her father and mother, her own person and disposition, were all equally against her" (Austen 1005). Catherine Morland's "problem" is that she is the contented and comfortable child of a happy home. Jane's is almost the opposite. Like Catherine, she is an orphan of a clergyman—one who caused an estrangement between his wife and her family when he married her, because he was poor, followed almost immediately by the death of both from typhus—now being barely tolerated by her maternal relatives, the wealthy and pompous Reeds. She is little. Her personality is an odd mixture of the self-effacing and the touchily aggressive. She hates more passionately and more openly than most Victorian women, or at least the ones portrayed in novels (Doreen Roberts identifies her capacity for hate as "an oblique way of measuring her capacity to love" [145]). And she is not beautiful—this trait is one of the most emphasized in the book. In Chapter III one of the Reed servants, Abbot, declares, "if she were a nice, pretty child, one might compassionate her forlornness; but one really cannot care for such a little toad as that" (21). She sums up her own disadvantages later when she thinks Mr. Rochester is banishing her from his love:

> "Do you think, because I am poor, obscure, plain, and little, I am soulless and heartless?—You think wrong!—I have as much soul as you,—and full as much heart! And if God had gifted me with some beauty and much wealth, I should have made it as hard for you to leave me, as it is now for me to leave you." (216)

Jane's lack of beauty—though sometimes it seems just the lack of the preferred kind of beauty—is represented as a defect, but through the course of the novel the customary polarities (of the sort taken for granted by Charlotte Brontë's sisters) come to be reversed. Beautiful women, particularly if they are large, with copious ringlets of dark hair and a noble bust—presumably the preferred kind of beauty for more conventional men—are shown to be false. Jane's looks are honest and the index of an honest, brave, and independent character. Likewise she is indifferent to conventional standards of male beauty, and she and Rochester speak candidly to each other about their "ugliness."

Jane Eyre is a *Bildungsroman,* a common Victorian fictional type, sometimes called an apprenticeship novel or a novel of development (other well-known examples are Charles Dickens's *David Copperfield* and *Great Expectations,* George Eliot's *The Mill on the Floss,* and William Makepeace Thackeray's *Pendennis.* Twentieth-century examples include David Herbert Lawrence's *Sons and Lovers* and James Joyce's *A Portrait of the Artist as a Young Man*). Jerome Buckley sums up the features of the Bildungsroman as: "childhood, the conflict of generations, provinciality, the larger society, self-education, alienation, ordeal by love, the search for a vocation and a working philosophy"(18)—a useful list that can mislead unless adjusted for gender. Middle-class Victorian women did not usually seek, or find, careers, so "vocation" needs to mean some kind of calling other than paid employment. Similarly, girls and women were much less able to move around freely. Unlike David Copperfield, Jane Eyre cannot move to London and live in a flat while seeking a living. Jane actually moves around much more than most Victorian female protagonists.

Others of Buckley's characteristics apply very strongly to *Jane Eyre:* For instance, "two love affairs or sexual encounters, one debasing, one exalting" can describe Jane's experience with Mr. Rochester and St. John Rivers, and her "first schooling, even if not totally inadequate, may be frustrating insofar as it may suggest options not available to [her] in [her] current setting" (17). Jane also embodies in a strong way the *Bildungsroman* protagonist's search for a model or preceptor (someone to whom she or he may be "apprenticed"), the clearest example of which is Miss Temple at Lowood School. Jane does not find a vocation in the modern sense of a career; her journey ends in marriage and a family. But she does pursue important goals in the course of *Jane Eyre,* and reaching these constitutes the decisive and, in the world of the text, happy ending of her quest.

Let Jane identify her two drives: Very early in her narration of her story, she explains her pitiful consolations for the miserable way her relatives treat her: "To this crib I always took my doll; human beings must love something, and in the dearth of worthier objects of affection, I contrived to find a pleasure in loving and cherishing a faded graven image, shabby as a miniature scarecrow" (23). To her guardian aunt, she insists, "You think I have no feelings, and that I can do without one bit of love or kindness; but I cannot live so: and you have no pity" (30). When Aunt Reed sends her off to school—partly to get her out of the way, partly shaken by Jane's fierce self-assertion—Jane makes a friend of a sweet, self-effacing Christian girl, Helen Burns, to whom she announces:

> "if others don't love me I would rather die than live—I cannot bear to be solitary and hated, Helen. Look here; to gain some real affection from you, or Miss Temple, or any other whom I truly love, I would willingly submit to have the bone of my arm broken, or to let a bull toss me, or to stand behind a kicking horse, and let it dash its hoof at my chest,—"
>
> "Hush, Jane," says Helen, "you think too much of the love of human beings . . ." (58-59)

Helen has a point, perhaps, though the novel suggests that she thinks too *little* of human love, in part because she is doomed to die and the human world (which has treated her as badly as it has treated Jane) is no longer her main concern. But a powerful need to love and be loved is one of the drives that propels Jane's story.

The other is a need for liberty. Just after her denunciation of Aunt Reed, Jane says, "It seemed as if an invisible bond had burst, and that I had struggled out into unhoped-for liberty" (30). At first it is a freedom purchased by scaring her aunt a little; soon she is liberated from her early home at Gateshead and allowed to go to school. Years later, Jane makes her major (and deservedly famous) statement on freedom while new to her position as governess at Thornfield:

> Millions are condemned to a stiller doom than mine, and millions are in silent revolt against their lot. Nobody knows how many rebellions besides political rebellions ferment in the masses of life which people earth. Women are supposed to be very calm generally: but women feel just as men feel: they need exercise for their faculties, and a field for their efforts as much as their brothers do; they suffer from too rigid a restraint, too absolute a stagnation, precisely as men would suffer; and it is

narrow-minded in their more privileged fellow-creatures to say
that they ought to confine themselves to making puddings and
knitting stockings, to playing on the piano and embroidering
bags. (93)

This language of restraint and confinement, of revolt and rebellion, explains why some contemporary readers took Currer Bell
(the pseudonym under which Brontë published her novel) to be a
dangerous radical.

Neither of Jane's two needs—for liberty and for love—are easy
to achieve or reconcile (and this is part of the message of *Jane Eyre*:
Liberty and love are in some ways at war in the lives of all of us). They
drive the novel, which is structured very much like a pilgrim's progress, as a movement through symbolic scenes. There are five stages
in Jane's progress, identified by the five places she lives in the course
of the book. These are Gateshead, Chapters 1–3; Lowood, Chapters
4–10; Thornfield, Chapters 11–27; Moor House, Chapters 28–35;
and finally Ferndean, Chapters 36–37. Clearly the major part of the
novel is the long central section in which Jane moves to Thornfield,
falls in love with Mr. Rochester and receives his love in return, but
flees him after learning he is married. This stage also presents other
important developments, including an interlude when she visits the
dying Aunt Reed, finds out something about her own family, and has
the satisfaction of seeing the ruination of the Gateshead family by a
providential system of justice. But each of them, save the last, short
section set at Ferndean, enacts the same basic pattern: Jane is imprisoned, then liberated, usually by something that is or at least seems to
be supernatural.

At Gateshead, for instance, she is literally imprisoned. As
punishment for an entirely justified retaliation against her spoiled
and obnoxious cousin John, her aunt orders her locked in the "red
room." Terrified because it was the room in which her uncle died, she
has some kind of fit after she sees an apparently supernatural light
gleaming on the wall. Her fit brings Mr. Lloyd, a kindly apothecary,
the first person to show her any kindness. It is Mr. Lloyd who first
suggests she might go to school, and he volunteers to speak to Aunt
Reed about this plan. It is after arrangements have been made, but
before she can leave, that she finds unhoped-for liberty: "my soul

began to expand, to exult, with the strangest sense of freedom, of triumph, I ever felt" (30).

The scene of the next act of Jane's drama, Lowood School, falls short of her dreams of freedom, despite being a change from Gateshead. She is mistreated there as well, particularly by the odious, hypocritical director, the clergyman Mr. Brocklehurst. Life for the girls of Lowood is hard and heavily restricted. After a wave of typhus kills many of the pupils and Brocklehurst is disgraced, life there becomes more pleasant, though Jane never claims to rejoice in the teacher's role. She does, indeed, find loving companionship, first from Helen Burns, then from Miss Temple. Her life at Gateshead had been without affection. With Helen things are different. As Jane says, "I never tired of Helen Burns; nor ever ceased to cherish for her a sentiment of attachment, as strong, tender, and respectful as any that ever animated my heart" (66). But this declaration accompanies the news that Helen was ill at this time—fatally ill, as it turns out. She dies in Jane's arms. Miss Temple, unlike Helen, is never Jane's equal but the much-admired head teacher of the school. She shows Jane kindness and protects her from injustice. Jane mentions her "delight in pleasing her teachers, especially such as I loved" (71), but Miss Temple is the teacher she loves. Her marriage and departure from Lowood spur Jane's own departure. The day Miss Temple leaves, Jane relates:

> I tired of the routine of eight years in one afternoon. I desired liberty; for liberty I gasped; for liberty I uttered a prayer; it seemed scattered on the wind then faintly blowing. I abandoned it and framed a humbler supplication; for change, stimulus; that petition, too seemed swept off into vague space; "Then," I cried, half desperate, "grant me at least a new servitude!" (72)

Again Jane's progress receives supernatural assistance; as she wonders how to get a job, a "kind fairy, in my absence, had surely dropped the required suggestion on my pillow"—that she should advertise (73).

Neither the "kind fairy," nor the visionary gleam at Gateshead, perhaps, is meant entirely seriously. But they are part of an impor-

tant pattern that will become stronger, that shows "the divine intention is distinctly perceptible as it works in the world" (Vargish 63).
Is this God? Not exactly; but Jane moves through a world that is
Providentially ordered, and when she needs supernatural assistance,
it arrives.

The Thornfield Act finally gives Jane a full-bodied erotic love
and, after vicissitudes, some of them rather cruelly imposed by Mr.
Rochester, she is engaged to be married. Some of Mr. Rochester's
behavior, a kind of smothering love enacted through planning Jane's
life and even her wardrobe for her, worries Jane and threatens her
autonomy, and she is determined to preserve her independence after
marriage rather than become his plaything. Worse, of course, is the
discovery on what was to be her wedding day that he is not legally
eligible to marry her, having a living wife. What follows is her greatest
threat. Mr. Rochester implores Jane to live with him as his mistress.
We must understand that part of her (her heart, her feelings) really
wants to do this. Her love draws her very strongly to Rochester. But
this love would be satisfied at too high a price. She once again faces
imprisonment. The Thornfield section, too, ends with an act of liberation, and once again she receives a supernatural monition: As she lies
in her bed, thinking back on the red room at Gateshead, she sees a
white human form that tells her, "My daughter, flee temptation," to
which she answers, "Mother, I will" (272). The next day she steals
away and travels aimlessly to another part of England where, nearly
starving, she winds up on the doorstep of a family that turns out to
be her only living relatives. Providential protection can go no further
than this.

At Moor House Jane achieves the greatest independence possible
for a woman. She has a job, as schoolteacher, and a cottage of her
own. She earns her own living and is answerable to no one. Calling
herself Jane Elliott, she is even anonymous. But love again compli-
cates her situation. For one thing, she still loves Mr. Rochester; for
another, her cousin, the frigid clergyman St. John Rivers, attempts to
claim her. Having rejected love without marriage with Mr. Rochester,
she is now offered (or threatened with) marriage without love from
Rivers. The first time he saw her, he flatly says that "The grace and
harmony of beauty are quite wanting in those features" (289). And
he never quite says that he loves her, only that he wants her to marry

him and accompany him to India as a Christian missionary. Though
not lovable, Rivers has a powerful effect on Jane. She admits that she
venerates him. When he orders her to stop the study of German and
learn Hindustani, she frets but complies, explaining that "I fell under
a freezing spell. When he said 'go,' I went; 'come,' I came; 'do this,' I
did it. But I did not love my servitude. I wished, many a time, he had
continued to neglect me" (339). The contrast with Mr. Rochester is
emphasized in many ways. We remember that Jane's quest for "a new
servitude" led her to Thornfield and Rochester and that, though he
actually was her employer, he was very hesitant to give her instructions or assume authority over her.

The climax of the Moor House section comes when Rivers presses
Jane to marry him. His proposals (repeated several times) are remarkably loveless: "It is not personal, but mental endowments they"—God
and nature—"have given you; you are formed for labour, not for love. A
missionary's wife you must—shall be. You shall be mine" (343). Rivers
insists she accompany him and, in order to do so properly, become his
wife. Jane suspects he will expect her to "endure all the forms of love"
(345), though his chill repels her. "I scorn your idea of love," she tells
him, "I scorn the counterfeit sentiment you offer: yes, St. John, and I
scorn you when you offer it" (348). As John Maynard writes, "In St.
John, Jane finds a far more serious threat to her independence than
any Rochester ever posed. St. John will turn her sexual feelings in a
totalitarian way to his own ends" (134). Yet his peculiar power operates on her, particularly when he has the good sense to speak gently to
her, and she is under some danger of complying with him when once
again the natural order of events is ruptured. It begins with a feeling:
"My heart beat fast and thick; I heard its throb. Suddenly it stood still
to an inexpressible feeling that thrilled it through, and passed at once
to my head and extremities," and then a voice somewhere cries, "Jane!
Jane! Jane!" (357). It is the voice of Rochester, miraculously calling her
(and liberating her from Rivers). It is a voice Jane considers nothing
less than "the work of nature" (358).

The last act is a short one. Jane returns and finds Thornfield a ruin
and Rochester not much better. He has been blinded and maimed in
the fire that burned down his house and killed his wife. He now lives, a
reduced and miserable man, at his other house, Ferndean. She quickly
reconciles with him, and they marry and have a family. As the novel

ends, they have been married ten years and he has partly recovered his wounded faculties. At Ferndean he is now free to marry her, as he was not at Thornfield. But the other changes are more important. Rochester is now in need of Jane's help, as he was once before when they first met and he was lamed by falling from his horse. He has become poorer. Moreover, Jane has become richer, though not really wealthy. She has gained an inheritance and thus some financial independence; she has been independently employed; she has had another suitor (as Rochester had previous erotic experience). Though Jane has earlier insisted to Rochester that they are equal, she had stipulated that this is *before God*. Now they are closer to being equal in a worldly sense, in part because Rochester, previously a magnetic, physically powerful man in the prime of life, is now weakened and helpless (his blinding may also symbolize being able to see Jane more clearly [Carpenter 53]). Brontë does not suggest that they are wholly equal, or either fully independent, though Jane, referring to her inheritance, announces, "I am an independent woman now" (370). Conventional inequality remains, and the "violence attached to Rochester's regeneration/reformation speaks to the difficulty of achieving the necessary changes in society as a whole" (Ward 23).

Yet there is not much about society as a whole in *Jane Eyre*—it is the story of an individual's growth and development—and particularly at the end, where Jane and her husband retreat to a Ferndean "deep buried in a wood" (366). What makes the conclusion of *Jane Eyre* a "happy ending" is not just that it ends with marriage—that is the conventional happy ending of the conventional marriage plot—but that it allows the heroine's journey to proceed, through a series of important personal growth stages, to a satisfying working philosophy and personal integrity. Thomas Vargish comments that "The straightforward agreement between poetic justice, the meting out of merited punishments and rewards, and providential intention, the completion of God's design in the novel, allows Jane at the end to combine love for Rochester with Christian rectitude" (64). It is true that Jane's refusal to live with the married Rochester was traced to "the law given by God; sanctioned by man" (Brontë 270), and that Mrs. Rochester's death squares their marriage with that law. But the more important reconciliation is between Jane's lifelong and powerful desire to love and be loved and her equally strong and lifelong need to be free. Marriage, as she describes it rhapsodically in the novel's closing paragraphs, calls for no infringement on her independence:

> I know no weariness of my Edward's society; he knows none of mine, any more than we each do of the pulsation of the heart that beats in our separate bosoms; consequently, we are ever together. To be together is for us to be at once as free as in solitude, as gay as in company. (384)

Solitude is wonderful for freedom, not so well-adapted to love; but Jane testifies that she has found a way, driven by a strong, passionate, determined selfhood and aided by a providential system, to bring the two into harmony.

WORKS CITED

Austen, Jane. *Northanger Abbey. The Complete Novels of Jane Austen*. New York; Penguin, 1980.

Brontë, Charlotte. *Jane Eyre*. 1847; New York: Norton, 2001.

Buckley, Jerome Hamilton. *Season of Youth: The Bildungsroman from Dickens to Golding*. Cambridge: Harvard UP, 1974.

Carpenter, Mary Wilson, "Blinding the Hero," *Differences: A Journal of Feminist Cultural Studies* 17 (Fall 2006): 52–68.

Gaskell, E. C. *The Life of Charlotte Brontë*, 2 vols. New York: D. Appleton & Co., 1857.

Maynard, John. *Charlotte Brontë and Sexuality*. Cambridge: Cambridge University Press, 1984.

Qualls, Barry. *The Secular Pilgrims of Victorian Fiction: The Novel as a Book of Life*. Cambridge: Cambridge UP, 1982.

Roberts, Doreen, "*Jane Eyre* and 'The Warped System of Things.'" *Reading the Victorian Novel: Detail into Form*, ed. Ian Gregor. Totowa, N.J.: Barnes & Noble, 1980: 131–49.

Vargish, Thomas. *The Providential Aesthetic in Victorian Fiction*. Charlottesville: University Press of Virginia, 1985.

Ward, Maryanne. "Romancing the Ending: Adaptations in Nineteenth-Century Closure," *The Journal of the Midwest Modern Language Association* 29 (Spring 1996): 15–31.

JULIUS CAESAR
(WILLIAM SHAKESPEARE)

"The Political Odyssey: Shakespeare's
Exploration of Ethics in *Julius Caesar*"
by Matthew Sims,
Lee University

The complex political and ethical issues of *Julius Caesar* (1599) make interpretation of the play difficult. Ernest Schanzer, for example, has rightly labeled *Julius Caesar* as one of Shakespeare's most controversial plays. He points out that commentators still disagree on such basic items as the identity of the principal character, whether or not the play is a tragedy, and perhaps, most importantly, whether or not Shakespeare intended Caesar's murder to be considered damnable or praiseworthy. Along with *Measure for Measure* and *Antony and Cleopatra*, Schanzer views *Julius Caesar* as a problematic text in which no particular moral response seems to be unequivocally appropriate. As he states:

> The reader of Shakespeare's play is consequently faced with a difficult choice. Is he to throw in his lot with Dover Wilson and Cassius, and regard Shakespeare's Caesar as a boastful tyrant, strutting blindly to his well-merited doom, and the assassination as a glorious act of liberation? Or is he to follow Mark Hunter and Mark Antony, and look at him as "the noblest man that ever lived in the tide of times," and at the assassination as a hideous crime? (Schanzer 6)

Shakespeare was of course not the first great writer to wrestle with the nature of Caesar's murder. The medieval Italian poet Dante famously expressed his disgust with Brutus by placing him (along with Judas Iscariot) in *The Divine Comedy* in the ninth circle of hell as an eternal punishment for his political sins. According to D.S. Brewer, Caesar's death was generally regarded as a crime, and Brutus was perceived as a criminal up until 1590, an attitude reflected in the *Mirror for Magistrates* (Brewer 53). Yet as Mildred Hartsock observes, in Plutarch's biography of Caesar, Shakespeare's original source for the play, Caesar was mortally hated because he wanted to be king. As Hartsock states, "The fact is that the Caesar of Plutarch provides clear motivation for tyrannicide" (58). In writing *Julius Caesar*, therefore, Shakespeare had finally found a historical subject fit for a play focusing on moral decision-making and political power. *Julius Caesar* is a kind of odyssey in which Brutus attempts to navigate his ship of state through the murky depths of Roman politics and all its sordid ironies and ethical dilemmas. There are three main stages to the political odyssey of *Julius Caesar*. First, Brutus's quest to preserve the Roman Republic from the possible tyranny of Caesar; second, the rhetoric of Mark Antony at Caesar's funeral and its impact on the political situation in Rome; and third, the defeat of Brutus and the conspirators by Mark Antony and Octavius. By focusing on both the causes and the consequences of Brutus's decision to partake in the conspiracy against Caesar, Shakespeare forces his audience to grapple with the problematic nature of ethics when applied to the political realm. As we shall see, the vast discrepancy between Brutus's intent to save the Republic and the catastrophic effects of his decision to murder Caesar is an irony that contributes to the moral ambiguity of the play.

The political journey for Brutus begins with his sincere desire to preserve the republican liberty of Rome against the threat of possible tyranny. When Cassius first attempts to persuade Brutus to join the conspiracy against Caesar, Brutus informs him that he remains loyal to the Roman Republic, not to Caesar. As he tells Cassius: "If it be aught toward the general good, set honor in one eye and death i' the other and I will look on both indifferently" (1.1. 85-87). This statement reveals Brutus to be a man of high principles, a loyal Roman who dearly prizes the political liberty of the republic threatened by Caesar's rising popularity. In this passage, we clearly see Brutus's concern for the general populace of Rome. His emphasis on the general good as opposed to the safety of his own life suggests a utilitarian conviction that one ought to work for the sake of the common good, not primarily for one's own happiness. Two scenes later we find Brutus trying to unravel the conclusion that he has already committed himself to, namely the fact that Caesar's tyranny must be prevented through his death. In this soliloquy Brutus argues that Caesar must be killed like a "serpent in the shell" if justice is to be served (2.1. 10–36). In syllogistic fashion, Brutus calculates how Caesar will probably abuse his power once he attains it and therefore, since power naturally corrupts, Caesar must be stopped. As Joseph Houppert observes, "He kills Caesar not because he is a tyrant in fact, but because he may become one" (Houppert 4). Although many critics have interpreted Brutus's decision to murder Caesar as a moral flaw, Joseph Houppert argues that in fact it is a failure of logic, not a failure of virtue, that traps Brutus in this scene. Such an interpretation gains support in the scene where Cassius pleads with Brutus that Mark Antony should not outlive the death of Caesar. Brutus, however, responds that only Caesar's death is necessary for the triumph of justice:

> Our course will seem too bloody, Caius Cassius,
> To cut the head off and then hack the limbs,
> Like wrath in death and envy afterwards;
> For Antony is but a limb of Caesar.
> Let's be sacrificers but not butchers, Caius.
> We all stand up against the spirit of Caesar,
> And in the spirit of men there is no blood.
> O, that we then could come by Caesar's spirit
> And not dismember Caesar! But, alas,
> Caesar must bleed for it. And, gentle friends,
> Let's kill him boldly, but not wrathfully.
> Let's carve him as a dish fit for the gods,
> Not hew him as a carcass fit for hounds.
> And let our hearts, as subtle masters do,
> Stir up their servants to an act of rage

And after seem to chide 'em. This shall make
Our purpose necessary and not envious;
Which so appearing to the common eyes,
We shall be called purgers, not murderers. (2.1. 175–193)

This speech cleverly depicts how Brutus's personal benevolence
and his rigid standard of public justice collide with disastrous consequences. Compelled to murder Caesar for the sake of the general
good, Brutus nevertheless fails to understand that Mark Antony's
death is required as well. Yet, despite the hints of compassion and
idealism in Brutus, this speech ends on a much more pragmatic note
as Brutus expresses his desire to be known as a "purger" instead of
a "murderer." There is more than a hint of Machiavellian ethos here
as the noble Brutus attempts to disguise his murder as a sacrifice
instead of what it really is, a violent act of butchery. In the eyes of
Brutus, Caesar's assassination has become a hallowed event, not
merely a mercenary act of bloodshed but rather a sacramental means
to achieve, in Brutus's own words, "a piece of work that will make
sick men whole." Of course, as Brutus is reminded by Ligarius, those
who are *whole* (i.e. Caesar) must also be made *sick*. The tragic price
for republican freedom, Brutus sadly acknowledges, is that Caesar
"must bleed for it."

This rhetorical attempt by Brutus to define their murder as
a sacrifice and to make their conspiracy appear necessary to all
Romans implies a deepening contradiction in Brutus's motive for
murder. Whereas before this speech Brutus had used honor as his
justification for the conspiracy against Caesar, now he appears
to cloak his motives in deceptive fashion. Apparently, even the
noble Brutus has been somewhat seduced by the Machiavellian
climate of the conspiracy, a truth foreshadowed by Cassius's earlier
remark: "For who so firm that cannot be seduced?" (1.2. 308).
After the conspirators stab Caesar, Brutus even claims that he
has actually done Caesar a favor, a feeble justification brought on
by Casca's remark that "he that cuts off twenty years of life cuts
off so many years of fearing death." Here, as in his earlier speech,
Brutus refuses to acknowledge Caesar's death as an actual murder
by instead associating Caesar's blood with the imagery of a foun-
tain. Having slain the demagogue who threatened Roman liberty,

Brutus now orders his fellow conspirators to bathe their hands in Caesar's blood. In his speech to Mark Antony, Brutus justifies the bloody deed as a necessary sacrifice and one executed out of compassion for the Roman people: "Our hearts you see not, they are pitiful and pity to the general wrong of Rome hath done this deed on Caesar" (3.1. 164–176). Yet Mark Antony views the corpse of Caesar not as the sacrificial price paid for Roman liberty but rather as an envious act of butchery that has destroyed "the noblest man that ever lived in the tide of times." Brutus, on the other hand, clearly sees this assassination as the debt which has been paid for all of Caesar's hero worship and political ambition, a fact which he makes very clear to Antony: "Our reasons are so full of good regard that were you, Antony, the son of Caesar, you should be satisfied." Here we have the bitter fruit of Ligarius's comment about the *whole being made sick* for the common good. Brutus's willingness to slay Caesar, wash in his blood, and then justify his butchery, all in good conscience, reveals a fundamental truth about the ethical dimensions of politics, that even the noblest of men can be seduced by power when the quest for justice becomes dominated by ideological principles. Perhaps no writer has better expressed the dangers of political ideology than the 20th century Russian novelist Alexander Solzhenitsyn. In his *Gulag Archipelago* he writes:

> To do evil a human being must first of all believe that what he's doing is good or else that it's a well-considered act in conformity with natural law. Fortunately, it is in the nature of the human being to seek a justification for his actions. Macbeth's self-justifications were feeble—and his conscience devoured him. Yes, even Iago was a little lamb too. The imagination and the spiritual strength of Shakespeare's evil doers stopped short at a dozen corpses. Because they had no ideology. Ideology—that is what gives evildoing its long-sought justification and gives the evildoer the necessary steadfastness and determination. That is the social theory which helps to make his acts seem good instead of bad in his own and other's eyes, so that he won't hear reproaches and curses but will receive praise and honors. (Solzhenitsyn 98–99)

As Solzhenitsyn's statement brilliantly articulates, political power is fraught with self-justifications that endorse a kind of "end justifies the means" principle. For example, in his attempt to vindicate his role in the conspiracy at Caesar's funeral, Brutus tells the Roman plebeians that he stabbed Caesar because Caesar's ambition was growing too dangerous for the security of Roman liberty. As Brutus so eloquently says to his audience: "Not that I lov'd Caesar less, but that I lov'd Rome more" (3.2. 21–22). For Brutus, the specific political agenda that allows him to stab his good friend without pangs of conscience is the ideology of the Roman Republic, a senatorial form of government opposed to the concept of tyranny (or, in the case of Caesar, demagogues who might turn into tyrants). Although an avid supporter of republicanism, Brutus refuses to get his hands dirty when faced with the unethical considerations that political survival require. In his personal crusade for justice, Brutus neglects Cassius's shrewd advice that Mark Antony must be killed with Caesar, just as he mistakenly allows Antony to speak after him at Caesar's funeral, a costly mistake that triggers a civil war in Rome, one that ultimately destroys the very form of government that Brutus sought so hard to preserve. The fact that Brutus's political career will be cut short by his moral refusal to execute Mark Antony when he has the chance is an irony that Shakespeare explores in the last half of the play.

The second stage of *Julius Caesar* begins with Mark Antony's funeral oration of Caesar. Shakespeare shifts the attention of the play from Brutus and the conspirators to the explosive power of the Roman mob. It is in Mark Antony's famous "Friends, Romans, countrymen" speech (3.2. 82–266) that Shakespeare most fully explores the tragic dimensions of political power, a world where rhetoric, not sincerity, proves to be the galvanizing force that motivates (and activates) the Roman people. Antony deceives his audience, for example, into believing that Caesar has left every Roman citizen seventy-five drachmas. Furthermore Antony lies about his own skills as an orator, claiming that he has not the "power of speech to stir men's blood," whereas in reality he is the supreme sophist of Rome. Antony's rhetorical power to incite a mass insurrection at Caesar's funeral represents what Allan Bloom has referred to as the theme of Shakespeare's Roman plays, that "the corruption of the people is the key to the mastery of Rome" (83). Commenting on the relationship between the public speaker and the Roman people, Bloom observes:

> The more corrupt the audience, the more brilliant the rhetoric. A good citizen speaks the truth and respects his audience enough to believe that they are competent enough to recognize the common good and virtuous enough to act in accordance with it. The flatterer assumes the baseness of his audience and appeals to its vices, cloaking his enticements in the beauty of his words. Brutus is austere, Antony charming. (83)

So, to be politically successful in Rome one must match a corrupt audience with a corrupt message. According to another critic, Jacqueline Pearson, Antony's funeral speech masks an inner dishonesty, a statement supported by Antony's statement to the crowd, "Look, in this place ran Cassius' dagger through." Commenting on this line, Pearson states that "there is no way he can know, for instance, which dagger made which hole in Caesar's mantle" (163). While Antony repeatedly insists that he does not want to stir the Roman mob to riot against Brutus and the other "honorable" conspirators, the emotional force of his swaying rhetoric has exactly the opposite effect:

> But were I Brutus
> And Brutus Antony, there were an Antony
> Would ruffle up your spirits and put a tongue
> In every wound of Caesar that should move
> The stones of Rome to rise and mutiny. (3.2. 239–243)

Yet Mark Antony does not seem to mind the damaging effects of his speech when these same Romans who previously cheered for Brutus later begin pillaging Rome. This dangerous ability of rhetoric to move the people was foreshadowed by Antony's remark after witnessing Octavio's servant weep at the sight of the dead Caesar: "Passion, I see is catching." Indeed, passion is contagious, and apparently no Roman can more effectively infect others with passion than Mark Antony. More a man of instinct than reason, Antony mirrors the Dionysian quality of the Roman mob as he embraces a truth that Brutus is unable, or unwilling, to accept: that most human beings primarily respond to emotional rhetoric, not rational appeals of justice or vows of sincerity. Thus, after Antony's funeral oration we are told that Brutus and Cassius are both "rid like madmen through the gates of Rome" to which Antony responds: "Belike they had some notice of the people, how I had mov'd them" (3.2. 270–71). Antony's ability to manipulate the passions of the Roman mob through deception and rhetoric supports Machiavelli's political axiom in *The Prince* that "men are so simple and so ready to follow the needs of the moment that the deceiver will always find some one to deceive" (Machiavelli 51). In the following scene, we see the terrifying consequences of Antony's political rhetoric as the poet Cinna encounters the powerful Roman mob that Antony has unleashed on the city. Guilty of sharing the same name as one of the conspirators, Cinna becomes a victim to the senseless mass violence of the plebeians as he is murdered for his "bad verses" (3.3. 27–36). The tragic irony of Rome's political situation, Shakespeare seems to suggest, is that an even greater potential threat to Rome now exists than the "ambitious" Caesar ever was—the Roman people themselves. As Barbara Parker perceptively states, "It may not be an overstatement to assert that the mob is the play's real protagonist, for they control not only Caesar and the other aristocratic characters but virtually the entire course of events" (38).

The last stage of the political journey in *Julius Caesar* focuses on the consequences of the political instability in Rome left by Caesar's death, consequences characterized by civil war, mass bloodshed, and ultimately the demise of the republic itself. The "domestic fury" and "civil strife" earlier prophesied by Mark Antony (3.1. 289–290) come to fulfillment as the armies of Brutus and Cassius gather to fight against the legions of Mark Antony and Octavius at the Battle of Philippi. Perhaps the highest political wisdom that Brutus ever attains in this play is his realization of the human inability to foresee the consequences and effects of particular decisions. As he tells Cassius at his final farewell at Philippi:

> O that a man might know
> The end of this day's business ere it come!
> But it sufficeth that the day will end
> And then the end is known. (5.1. 123–126)

Like Sophocles's Oedipus, another man whose ignorance and intellectual miscalculations cost him dearly, the tragedy of Brutus is the tragedy of man's limited knowledge in a world where political decisions made from the noblest of motives can often backfire and prove catastrophic. From what we know of Brutus, he does try to do the right thing as he sees it, a point emphasized in his statement to Cassius before Philippi: "Did not great Julius bleed for justice sake? What villain touched his body that did stab, and not for Justice?" (4.3. 19–21). Even as he prepares for suicide after his defeat has become inevitable, Brutus claims to have more glory by this "losing day" than either Octavius or Mark Antony will achieve by their "vile conquest." It is interesting to compare the triumphant tone of Brutus's final speech with the actual winner of the civil war, Octavius, a man whose victorious rhetoric ends the play and who will soon become Rome's first emperor—Augustus. In his final moments of life, the political loser Brutus seeks solace in the intrinsic worthiness of his cause and the fact that no man ever was untrue to him. The final impression Shakespeare leaves us of Brutus, found ironically enough in Mark Antony's eulogy, perhaps suggests the problematic nature of condemning a man whose political miscalculations have overshadowed his good intentions for the Roman people:

> This was the noblest Roman of them all.
> All the conspirators save only he
> Did that they did in envy of great Caesar.
> He only in a general honest thought
> And common good to all made one of them. (5.5. 68–72)

Thus ends the last stage of the political odyssey of *Julius Caesar*, a journey that ultimately brought Brutus's quest for Roman liberty to a dead end. Throughout this journey, Shakespeare explores the fragile relationship between personal virtue and the public sphere of politics, a theme that he expresses through one man's feeble attempt to extract justice out of a highly unjust political system. Paradox, not didacticism, marks the tone of this play. The playwright depicts for us in no uncertain terms the problematic role of ethics in a political system that often requires unethical behavior to achieve success. As many critics have pointed out, Shakespeare's complex characterization of Brutus and Caesar lends the play a moral ambiguity so that the reader, like the audience at Caesar's funeral, does not know fully whether to bury Caesar or to praise him. In this same vein, Mildred Hartsock has written that *Julius Caesar* is not just a problem play but rather "a play about a problem: the difficulty—perhaps the impossibility—of knowing the truth of men and of history" (61). One pivotal question that arises from such a reading of *Julius Caesar* is this: Did Shakespeare intend for us to sympathize with Brutus and view him as a noble failure whose loyalty to the republic and concern for the welfare of Rome transcend the disastrous consequences of his actions? Or are we to judge Brutus in more practical terms and therefore condemn him as a walking political disaster whose intellectual hubris and miscalculations paved the way for the end of the Roman Republic? Commenting on this highly problematic question, William and Barbara Rosen have argued that *Julius Caesar* is a play in which "we judge a man not only for what he is but for what he does" and that "consequences are no less important than intentions" (111). In a similar vein, Norman Rabkin interprets the political message of this play as a warning that moral passion and high principles are irrelevant when confronted by the merciless opportunism of a Mark Antony (116). Yet, for all these criticisms made against Brutus, there is no clear evidence from the text that Shakespeare ever attempts to glorify the political success of Mark Antony and Octavius at the expense of Brutus's idealism. While we may think of Brutus's pursuit of justice as being naïve and politically unfeasible, there is no reason to necessarily support the amoral pragmatism of Mark Antony, a Machiavellian demagogue who is defined by sheer political expediency and rhetoric, not high principles and good intentions.

In the end there are no easy solutions to the ethical dilemmas that must be faced by those who thrust themselves into the highest offices of the political arena. Unlike Shakespeare's earlier history play *Henry V*, there is no hero worship in *Julius Caesar*, only real men tainted by their own political enterprises, regardless of whether their motives are guided by envy, ruthless ambition, or the quest for justice. Even Brutus, for all his good intentions, is no saint, a fact made clear by his willingness to dehumanize Caesar by conceiving of his assassination in purely aesthetic terms. Shakespeare suggests that in the brutal game of politics, everyone must get his or her hands a little dirty, and often the dirtier one's hands, the better the chance of success. Such is certainly the case in *Julius Caesar*, a drama that painfully depicts the harsh truth that decisions motivated by concern for the "general good" are no guarantee of success (or survival) in the political realm and the equally tragic realization that often the noblest of intentions can prove to be disastrous in their political consequences. Perhaps such an epiphany is the only definitive conclusion to be formed in a tragedy as highly complex as *Julius Caesar*.

WORKS CITED

Bloom, Allan. *Shakespeare's Politics*. New York: Basic Books, 1964.

Brewer, D.S. "Brutus' Crime: A Footnote to *Julius Caesar*." *The Review of English Studies* Vol. 3, No. 9 (January 1952): 51–54.

Hartsock, Mildred. "The Complexity of *Julius Caesar*." *PMLA* Vol. 81, No. 1 (March 1966): 56–62.

Houppert, Joseph. "Fatal Logic in *Julius Caesar*." *South Atlantic Bulletin* Vol. 39, No. 4 (November 1974): 3–9.

Machiavelli. *The Prince*. (Translated by Thomas Bergin) Arlington Heights, Illinois: Harlan Davidson, 1947.

Parker, Barbara. "'A Thing Unfirm': Plato's *Republic* and Shakespeare's *Julius Caesar*." *Shakespeare Quarterly* Vol. 44, No. 1 (Spring 1993): 30–43.

Pearson, Jacqueline. "Romans and Barbarians: The Structure of Irony in Shakespeare's Roman Tragedies." *Stratford-Upon-Avon Studies* Vol. 20 (1984): 159–182.

Rabkin, Norman. *Shakespeare and the Common Understanding*. New York: Free Press, 1967.

Rosen, William and Barbara. "*Julius Caesar:* 'The Specialty of Rule.'" *Twentieth Century Interpretations of Julius Caesar*. Edited by Leonard Dean. Englewood Cliffs, New Jersey: Prentice-Hall, 1968. 109–115.

Schanzer, Ernest. *The Problem Plays of Shakespeare*. New York: Schocken Books, 1963.

Solzhenitsyn, Alexander. *The Gulag Archipelago* in *Classics of Western Thought: The Twentieth Century*. Edited by Donald Gochberg. New York: Harcourt Brace, 1980.

THE LORD OF THE RINGS
(J.R.R. TOLKIEN)

"Hobbits and Heroism"
by Richard L. Purtill,
in *J.R.R. Tolkien:*
Myth, Morality, and Religion (1984)

INTRODUCTION

In "Hobbits and Heroism," Richard L. Purtill identifies Bilbo
and Frodo's journey as a mythic one and myth itself as a tool
for providing moral instruction. For Purtill, Bilbo and Frodo
are everyday characters who rise to fulfill heroic roles, motivated only by loyalty and love of friends. Thus, hobbits rather
than human beings in *Lord of the Rings* serve as models for
what our lives can become; their journey is ours. For Purtill,
the hobbits embody the "self-sacrificing love" that the human
journey necessitates. Throughout their heroic journey, the
hobbits must provide answers to timeless questions: What
is the nature of good? What is the nature of evil? How do
good and evil operate in human beings? These questions
confront the journeyer at every fork in the path.

Purtill, Richard L. "Hobbits and Heroism." *J.R.R. Tolkien: Myth, Morality, and
Religion*. New York: Harper and Row, 1984. 45–58.

One function of myth is to convey moral values, and as we have seen, Tolkien himself gives as one purpose of his writing "the encouragement of good morals in this real world by the ancient device of exemplifying them in unfamiliar embodiments, that may tend to 'bring them home.'" But how does Tolkien do this? To answer this question it is important to look at Tolkien's whole strategy in his major work, *The Lord of the Rings*. The first thing to realize is that the focus of the book, the "human interest," is not in the human characters, the Men, but in the Hobbits. The traditional kinds of heroes, Aragorn, for example, exist in the story partly to validate by their respect and approval the simple, dogged heroism of the Hobbits.

In many ways Tolkien "facets" character: each individual, and to some extent each race, represents one aspect of a complete human being. He has said specifically that the Elves represent certain human characteristics in isolation: "in fact exterior to my story Elves and Men are just different aspects of the Humane. . . . The Elves represent, as it were, the artistic, aesthetic and purely scientific aspects of human nature raised to a higher level than is actually seen in Men."

Another kind of contrast is made between Men and Hobbits, with Men representing the traditional noble and knightly style of heroism and Hobbits the kind of courage exhibited by the ordinary person who rises to heroism in the face of challenge. Tolkien saw these two kinds of heroic style as interdependent and complementary.

> This last great Tale, coming down from myth and legend to the earth is seen mainly through the eyes of Hobbits: it thus becomes in fact anthropocentric. But through Hobbits, not Men so-called because the last Tale is to exemplify most clearly a recurrent theme: the place in "world politics" of the unforeseen and unforeseeable acts of will and deeds of virtue of the apparently small, ungreat, forgotten in the places of the Wise and Great (good as well as evil). A moral of the whole . . . is the obvious one that without the high and noble the simple and vulgar is utterly mean; and without the simple and ordinary the noble and heroic is meaningless.

To see how Tolkien develops this theme, consider his first book, *The Hobbit*. At the beginning Bilbo Baggins is a somewhat self-important little fellow, set in his ways and suspicious of anything outside his own limited sphere. He is bullied into going on an adventure with a band of Dwarves by Gandalf the wizard, but even in this first encounter he shows the beginnings of courage. After being terrified by talk of death and dragons, he has a fainting fit, but stung by the contempt shown by the Dwarves who have come to enlist his help on their quest, he offers to go along with them, even though he thinks that they have made a mistake in coming to him.

> "I am quite sure you have come to the wrong house. As soon as I saw your funny faces on the door-step, I had my doubts. But treat it as the right one. Tell me what you want done, and I will try it, if I have to walk from here to the East of East and fight the wild were-worms in the Last Desert."

In his next trial of courage, he is sent by the Dwarves to scout out a mysterious campfire that promises some hope of warmth on a miserable rainy night. He is easily captured by the Trolls who are sitting around the fire and has to be rescued by Gandalf, but at least he has had the courage to go when the Dwarves send him. His increased status is symbolized by a sword (only a dagger by human standards) that he receives as his share when the treasure of the Trolls is shared out.

Bilbo's next adventure begins when he and the Dwarves are captured by Goblins when they shelter for the night in a cave. It is Bilbo's yell that awakes Gandalf in the nick of time and enables the wizard to escape and later come to the rescue. But in the rescue Bilbo is separated from the others and wanders into the depths of the Goblin caverns, where he encounters a predatory creature, Gollum. Bilbo keeps him from attacking by the threat of his new-won sword. The ring of invisibility that Bilbo "accidentally" finds on his adventure is again a mark of his increased power, evidenced by his ability to trade riddles with Gollum and make the creature guide him out of the caverns.

When Bilbo does get free of the caverns, he looks for the Dwarves and does not at first find them. At the beginning of his adventure he might simply have abandoned his dangerous adventure and tried to get home. But already he has grown enough in moral stature so that a very uncomfortable thought was growing within him. He wondered whether he ought not, now that he had the magic ring, to go back into the horrible, horrible, tunnels and look for his friends. He had just made up his mind that it was his duty, that he must turn back—and very miserable he felt about it—when he heard voices.

The voices are those of the Dwarves, who have won free with Gandalf's help, and he does not have to carry out his decision. But the reader feels that he would have if he had not found the Dwarves. We are shown, however, that the Dwarves might not have done the same for him.

> The dwarves were grumbling and Gandalf was saying that they could not possibly go on with their journey leaving Mr. Baggins in the hands of the goblins, without trying to find out if he was alive or dead and without trying to rescue him. . . . The dwarves wanted to know why he had ever been brought at all. . . . "He has been more trouble than use so far," said one. "If we have to go back now into those abominable tunnels to look for him, then drat him, I say."

We are not told Bilbo's reaction to this, but the Dwarves are impressed by his escape and the fact that he appears to have crept quietly up on them without their lookout spotting him (he does not tell them about the magic ring). They begin to depend on him, and even though they are rescued from their next scrape by eagles summoned by Gandalf, the Dwarves rely on Bilbo, especially after Gandalf leaves them at the entrance to the great and grim forest of Mirkwood.

In Mirkwood the Dwarves leave the safe path, against Gandalf's advice, and are captured by giant spiders. With his sword, Bilbo manages to kill the spider who attacks him, and

> somehow the killing of the giant spider, all alone by himself in the dark without the help of the wizard or the dwarves or of anyone else, made a great difference to Mr. Baggins. He felt a different person, and much fiercer and bolder in spite

of an empty stomach. . . . The forest was grim and silent, but obviously he had first of all to look for his friends.

Tolkien makes Bilbo's increasing courage plausible to us in two ways—first, by showing us its cause and, second, by reminding us of Bilbo's limitations—his empty stomach and a little later his loneliness without his companions. The idealized heroes of some fantasies never seem to worry about such ordinary things as hunger and loneliness. But because of Bilbo's very ordinariness, we are often reminded of the uncomfortable and even comic side of adventure—and at the same time reminded that ordinary people can act heroically.

Bilbo does rescue the Dwarves with the use of his sword and his magic ring, as well as his wits and a skill at throwing stones he learned as a young Hobbit. The rescue is not a matter of a single hero attacking a group of monsters and hewing them limb from limb: it involves the use of the magic ring to confuse the spiders and lead them away from their prey; Bilbo then creeps back and frees the Dwarves.

The Dwarves are next captured by the Elves who live in the woods, basically good creatures but hostile to Dwarves and protective of their domain. Bilbo frees them by the use of his ring and his wits, and they arrive at the threshold of their goal—the town nearest to the mountain where the dragon broods on his heap of treasure. It is this treasure, stolen from the Dwarves, that they have journeyed to recover. The Dwarves are welcomed by the town and, with ponies supplied by the townspeople, journey to the mountain itself and find the side entrance to the dwarf-caverns inside the mountain where the dragon guards the treasure.

They have not come to fight the dragon but to steal back some of their own treasure. Bilbo is sent down into the dragon's stronghold to begin taking some treasure.

> Then the hobbit slipped on his ring and, warned by the echoes to take more than a hobbit's care to make no sound, he crept noiselessly down, down into the dark. He was trembling with fear, but his little face was set and grim. Already he was a very different hobbit from the one that had run out without a pocket-handkerchief from Bag End long ago. He had not had a pocket-handkerchief for ages. He loosened his dagger in

its sheath, tightened his belt and went on. . . . Going on from
there was the bravest thing he ever did. The tremendous things
that happened afterwards were as nothing compared to it. He
fought the real battle in the tunnel alone, before he even saw
the vast danger that lay in wait.

Bilbo does manage to steal a cup from the treasure, which enrages
the dragon, who flies out of his cave and nearly catches the Dwarves
waiting outside. They scurry into the tunnel, realizing that they have
little chance of escaping with any treasure while Smaug, the dragon,
lives. Bilbo volunteers to go on another scouting mission.

> "Getting rid of dragons is not at all in my line [Bilbo says],
> but I will do my best to think about it. Personally I have no
> hopes at all, and wish I was safe back home. . . . I have got my
> ring and will creep down . . . and see what he is up to. Perhaps
> something will turn up." . . . Naturally the dwarves accepted
> the offer eagerly. Already they had come to respect little Bilbo.
> Now he had become the real leader in their adventure.

This reconnaissance is a partial disaster, because it sends Smaug
off to attack the townspeople who had befriended the Dwarves.
However, Bilbo has seen a weak spot in the dragon's armor, and word
of it gets back to one of the town's defenders, who kills the dragon
with an arrow when the monster attacks the town. Thus Bilbo is
the indirect cause of the dragon's removal, though he never gets any
thanks for it. But now the struggle moves from the traditional heroic
to the political. With the dragon dead, five armies converge on the
dragon's lair to claim the treasure: the Men from the town, Elves
from the wood, Dwarves from the North, and the Goblins and their
wolflike allies.

Men and Elves arrive first, but the Dwarves with Bilbo refuse
to share the treasure, hoping for help from their Dwarvish allies to
the North. Now Bilbo shows a moral courage to match the physical
courage he has shown earlier. To end the impasse, he takes possession of one piece of the treasure particularly beloved by the leader of
the Dwarves and delivers it to the Elves and Men who are besieging
the Dwarves, to use as a bargaining point. Then he goes back to the

Dwarves to face the consequences of his action. Thorin, leader of the Dwarves, is enraged by what he sees as treachery, and Bilbo escapes execution by the Dwarves only with the aid of Gandalf.

The kind of courage exhibited by Bilbo in this incident is not the usual heroism of the folktales. He has to make a lonely moral decision as to rights and wrongs in a complex situation, devise a plan with no help or support from those who should be his friends, and carry it out alone. His return to face the rage of the Dwarves shows another kind of courage, exhibiting a sense of honor and obligation that is chivalrous, almost quixotic. But Bilbo does not speak of honor, he speaks of what he owes to his friends, the "friends" who have done so much less for him than he for them. For all his pretense sometimes to be "business-like" and "sensible," friendship is not a business matter for Bilbo: for him friendship involves giving even if you do not receive. The true word for what he calls friendship is love, the sort of love spoken of by Paul in his First Letter to the Corinthians that "endures long and is kind . . . it is not self-seeking . . . nor does it take account of a wrong that is suffered. It takes no pleasure in injustice, but sides happily with truth."

The coming of the Goblins and their allies returns us from the political to the heroic; the armies of Dwarves, Elves, and Men fight together against the forces of evil and win, with the help of the eagles. At the end Dwarves, Elves, and Men are victorious, and their differences are reconciled. Bilbo is also reconciled with Thorin and the other Dwarves. Thorin's dying words pay tribute to Bilbo's courage but also to his humane qualities.

> "There is more in you than you know, child of the kindly West. Some courage and some wisdom, blended in measure. If more of us valued food and cheer and song above hoarded gold, it would be a merrier world. But sad or merry, I must leave it now. Farewell."

Through all this Bilbo retains his humility and good sense, scarcely needing Gandalf's reminder at the end of the story.

> "You are a very fine person, Mr. Baggins, and I am very fond of you: but you are only quite a little fellow in a wide world after all."

"Thank goodness," said Bilbo, laughing, and handed him
the tobacco-jar.

We will see all of Bilbo's virtues again in the Hobbits in *The Lord
of the Rings*, but it is worthwhile to pause here and sum up what we
have learned from Tolkien's first story. Bilbo is not a "natural" hero: his
life up to the beginning of the story has not demanded heroism. He
needs to be bullied into adventure by Gandalf and at first does little
more than allow himself to be pushed into dangerous situations by
the Dwarves, who have a tendency to let Bilbo, the outsider, do the
dirty work. (The Dwarves are not only united as Dwarves but are all
members of one extended family.) However, Bilbo does do his best
when in these dangerous situations, and with each small and partial
success his confidence grows.

To a certain extent Gandalf functions as a parental figure,
pushing Bilbo to get him started but then stepping back to let Bilbo
struggle and learn on his own. After Bilbo's discovery of the ring and
his success in escaping from Gollum and the Goblins on his own,
Gandalf soon removes himself entirely and lets Bilbo gradually take
his place as leader and protector of the Dwarves.

In taking on this responsibility, Bilbo gradually grows fond of
his grumbling, ungrateful companions and exhibits loyalty to them
in situations in which they do little to deserve his loyalty. Gradually
Bilbo assumes the parental role in place of Gandalf until, as we have
seen, "he had become the real leader in their adventures."

The Dwarves never entirely acknowledge this fact explicitly,
however, and when lust for the treasure overcomes them, they soon
rebel against Bilbo's attempts to make a sensible peace. So Bilbo has
little chance to develop a swelled head or become autocratic. However,
he does receive praise from the Elf king, from Gandalf, and eventually
from the Dwarves, and keeps his modest and sensible attitude despite
it. So the characteristic virtues of Bilbo might be summed up as
courage, loyalty, and humility—courage toward dangers and enemies,
loyalty and love to friends, humility with regard to his own qualities
and achievements.

These characteristics also apply to the Hobbits we encounter in *The
Lord of the Rings*, but they are found to a greater extent in Sam than in
any of the other characters, This may seem surprising, for at the begin-

ning Sam seems only a minor, comic character, and Frodo seems to be the "hero" of the tale. Nor is this impression entirely mistaken: Frodo is the Ring-bearer and in one sense the most important character in the story. But in another way Sam is the central character, as some of Tolkien's comments in letters tell us. When *The Lord of the Rings* was still being written, he wrote to his son Christopher:

> Sam is the most closely drawn character, the successor to Bilbo of the first book, the genuine hobbit. Frodo is not so interesting, because he has to be high-minded, and has, as it were, a vocation. The book will probably end up with Sam. Frodo will naturally become too ennobled and rarified by the achievement of the great Quest and will pass West with all the great figures but Sam will settle down to the Shire and gardens and inns.

In the event, this is just how *The Lord of the Rings* ends—with Frodo passing to the West and Sam returning home to the Shire. At one point in a later letter, Tolkien refers to Sam as the "chief character" of the story.

However, at first the focus is certainly on Frodo. The magic ring that Bilbo has found in *The Hobbit* has turned out to be *the* Ring, the Ring of Power into which Sauron, the Dark Lord, has put a good deal of his own power, the ring that rules the other magical rings held by Men and Elves. Bilbo is persuaded by Gandalf to leave this ring to Frodo, his nephew, when Bilbo leaves the Shire, the land of the Hobbits. We find Bilbo later in the story living at Rivendell, one of the last outposts of the Elves in Middle-earth. Frodo is warned by Gandalf that he is accepting a dangerous gift, but he accepts it to relieve Bilbo of a burden and because he trusts the wisdom of Gandalf.

At first we see Gandalf as again a parent figure and Frodo as a child figure. At first he merely reacts to events, leaving Bilbo's home, now his, for a remote part of the Shire and then fleeing to Rivendell as emissaries of the Dark Lord pursue him, trying to capture the Ring. The weaknesses he shows at this stage are childish ones—putting off his departure despite Gandalf's warnings, giving away information by "showing off" at Bree. After this incident, he finds another parent figure, Aragorn, the descendant of the ancient kings of the land, who helps him on the next stage of his journey.

However, by the time he gets to Bree, he has had to do some growing up already. Instead of slipping away quietly and alone, he finds himself with three companions, his servant Sam and his friends Merry and Pippin. The little band is a help but also a responsibility. They are loyal to him but not subservient to him.

> "It all depends on what you want [Merry says] . . . . You can trust us to stick to you through thick and thin—to the bitter end. And you can trust us to keep any secret of yours—closer than you keep it yourself. But you cannot trust us to let you face trouble alone, and go off without a word. We are your friends, Frodo. Anyway; there it is. We know most of what Gandalf has told you. We know a great deal about the Ring. We are horribly afraid— but we are coming with you—or following you like hounds.

So Frodo, like Bilbo earlier, finds himself thrust into a position of responsibility for others. His leadership is soon put to the test, for in the Wild Lands between the Shire and Bree, Frodo and his companions are captured by undead creatures who live in great burial mounds from the past, the Barrow-wights. Frodo awakes to find himself laid out like the corpse of a king, with his companions near him sleeping or entranced. Frodo is tempted to abandon his companions and win free with the aid of the Ring.

> A wild thought of escape came to him. He wondered if he put on the Ring whether the Barrow-wight would miss him, and he might find some way out. He thought of himself running free over the grass, grieving for Merry, and Sam, and Pippin, but free and alive himself. Gandalf would admit that there had been nothing else he could do.

Frodo resists the temptation and escapes with his companions, but the temptation is by no means simple. Which is more important—his mission to keep the Ring out of the power of the Dark Lord or his loyalty to his friends? At a later point he is to face this decision in another form.

After he has resisted the temptation to flee and fought off one attack by a Barrow-wight, Frodo calls on and is rescued by Tom

Bombadil, a comical but powerful being who has rescued the Hobbits from an earlier danger. The two incidents together are rather like Bilbo's early adventure with the Trolls: Frodo is rescued by a powerful outside force rather than by his own efforts. The childlike aspect of Frodo and the other Hobbits is emphasized at this point in the story when Tom Bombadil after his rescue tells them to take off the ancient garments the Barrow-wights have clothed them in and run naked in the grass. This is partly to dispel the enchantments that hold them by the power of the natural forces (such as sun and wind) that Tom is akin to and to some extent personifies. But it is also like the way one might treat a child after a terrifying experience: "Run and play in the sun, forget what happened."

When they arrive at Bree, where Men and Hobbits live together in friendship, Pippin lets down his guard and begins to talk too much in the common room at the inn. In an effort to silence him, Frodo stands up and makes a speech thanking the company for their welcome. Then, at a loss what to do next, he responds to requests to sing a song. Singing and drinking put Frodo off his guard, and he "accidentally" puts the Ring on his finger and disappears, betraying more than Pippin would have by his words.

The Hobbits are now helped by Aragorn, descendant of the ancient kings and member of a band of Men who protect the peaceful lands by fighting the evil things in the Wild Lands on their borders. The Hobbits win through to Rivendell despite several attacks by the forces of evil: Frodo shows courage but largely lets himself be guided and guarded by Aragorn.

Safe in Rivendell, Frodo must make a vital decision: whether to hand over the Ring to others, or continue to be the Ring-bearer, at peril of death or enslavement to the Dark Lord. For the decision of the wisest enemies of evil is that the only course is to take the Ring into the Dark Lord's stronghold of Mordor and destroy it in the fires in which it was made. The Ring cannot be safely used against the Dark Lord, for it contains not just power but the evil power of the Dark Lord. Even if this power could be turned against its owner, the one who wielded the Ring to defeat him would eventually become evil.

The idea that those who use evil means to destroy evil become like the enemy they are fighting is central to Tolkien's thinking and writing. During World War II he wrote to his son about some ways in which the defenders of freedom seemed to be aping their Nazi adversaries and drew a moral from his own work, "You can't fight the Enemy with his own Ring without turning into an Enemy, but unfortunately Gandalf's wisdom seems long ago to have passed with him into the True West."

At several points in the story, good and powerful characters, Gandalf among them, refuse to take the Ring, aware that they might be tempted to use it and fall into its trap. One of Frodo's qualifications for the task of Ring-bearer is his knowledge of his own limitations: up to the very end, he is aware that he is not great or powerful enough to take the Ring and wield it against its maker. As with Bilbo, part of Frodo's strength is humility.

Frodo does volunteer to carry the Ring to Mordor to destroy it, and his offer is accepted. He sets off with eight companions, and though he faces many dangers, he has both Aragorn and Gandalf with him and can be a follower rather than a leader. But in the Mines of Moria Gandalf is lost to them, seemingly killed in defending the others from a powerful evil being. The remainder of the Fellowship find rest and refuge and almost forget their grief for Gandalf in the beauty and wonder of Lothlórien, the greatest remaining stronghold of the Elves on Middle-earth.

But when they leave Lothlórien, disagreements begin about which route to take, and Boromir, a prince of the Men of Gondor, falls prey to the temptation of the Ring and tries to take it from Frodo. Frodo also feels the force of the Dark Lord's mind probing, searching for the Ring. Frodo escapes Boromir, fights off the impulse to submit to the Dark Lord, and sets off alone to carry out his mission. At the last moment Sam joins him, but Frodo is the leader—on his own at last.

His motive for going on alone is not pride, or even the feeling that one or two might escape notice where a larger group would not. Rather, he feels that the corrupting power of the Ring is responsible for the disagreements among the Fellowship and for Boromir's attempt to seize the Ring.

> A great weariness was on him, but his will was firm and his heart lighter. He spoke aloud to himself, "I will do now what I must," he said. "This at least is plain: the evil of the Ring is already at work even in the Company and the Ring must leave

them before it does more harm. I will go alone. Some I cannot
trust, and those I can trust are too dear to me."

In other words, his motive for going on alone is the same as his
motive for taking the Ring in the first place: to help those he loves
and because he feels that the responsibility has fallen on him. It is
interesting that he mentions as those "too dear to me" the three other
Hobbits and Aragorn, who has helped and defended him in the
past. Boromir has "fallen into evil," as he says, and the Elf Legolas
and the Dwarf Gimli do not come to his mind as among those too
dear to him to risk. Frodo loves the Elves and likes the Dwarves, but
his greatest love is for his own folk, the Hobbits, and for a few like
Gandalf and Aragorn who have been quasi-parental figures to him.
This is just to say that Frodo is a limited being, not God. Christ in
traditional Christian theology dies for all human beings individually;
Frodo is willing to lay down his life for all those threatened by evil,
but especially for his own folk and his own friends.

Yet in many ways Frodo's journey to Mordor is an echo, conscious
or unconscious on Tolkien's part, of Christ's journey to Golgotha.
One preparation for the Way of the Cross imagery in the last part of
the story is the re-introduction of Gollum, whom Bilbo met long ago
in the caverns of the Goblins. We have learned earlier that Gollum
was originally a Hobbit named Sméagol, who accidentally found
the Ring long years ago, killed a friend to get possession of it, and
has been possessed and obsessed by it ever since. Now he is tracking
Frodo in hopes of recovering the Ring, which he calls his "Precious."
But Gollum is also being used as a tool by the Dark Lord, a hunting
animal that may be allowed to snatch the Ring from Frodo but will
not be allowed to keep it.

When Frodo finally meets Gollum face to face, he uses the power
of the Ring to establish an ascendancy over him but also treats him
with kindness, so that Gollum is torn between a growing love for
Frodo and his ravenous desire for the Ring. Sam is both mistrustful
of Gollum and jealous of him: one of Tolkien's very perceptive moral
insights in the book is in his account of the way in which Sam's own
devotion to Frodo is the innocent means of aborting Gollum's possible
reformation. Tolkien speaks of "the tragedy of Gollum who . . . came
within a hair of repentance—but for one rough word from Sam" and

elsewhere of "Gollum's failure (just) to repent when interrupted by Sam: this seems to me really like the *real* world in which the instruments of just retribution are seldom themselves just and holy and the good are often stumbling blocks."

Partly, the attachment of Gollum to Sam and Frodo as their guide and helper is a preparation for the final betrayal by Gollum: to taste the depths of suffering, Frodo must be betrayed by one in whom he put his trust, as Christ was betrayed by Judas. Gollum also serves as a warning: if Frodo or Bilbo allowed themselves to yield to the power of the Ring, they would become like Gollum, enslaved by it rather than becoming its Master.

Indeed, Tolkien may intend to suggest that in a sense the Dark Lord himself is the slave rather than the master of his own evil power. For evil is in the end a rejection of *every* good, including freedom: the lustful man or woman becomes a slave of lust; the vengeful become slaves of their hatred; and so on. The romantic picture of evil that some have seen in Milton's *Paradise Lost* is an illusion. Evil says, "Better to reign in hell than serve in heaven," but in hell, no one but the Prince of Evil ever seems to reign, and that reign is an illusion too. Every one of the servants of Sauron, the Dark Lord, is a slave, and in the end Sauron himself is a slave to his own fear and hate.

As Frodo comes closer to Mordor, he is led into a trap by Gollum and rendered unconscious by the bite of a giant spider, then captured by the ones who guard Mordor. His physical sufferings parallel those of Christ: he is imprisoned, stripped of his garments, mocked, and whipped. Even after Sam rescues him and they resume their journey to the fires of the Crack of Doom to destroy the Ring, Frodo's sufferings continue. He is terribly weary, and the Ring becomes a more and more intolerable burden. Frodo's journey now powerfully recalls Christ's carrying of the cross.

Whether this is intentional on Tolkien's part is hard to say. As a Catholic of a rather traditional kind, Tolkien would have been familiar with the Rosary, a form of prayer in which beads and spoken prayers occupy the body and the surface of the mind while the person praying meditates on various "mysteries"—incidents from the life of Christ and his mother, Mary. The five "sorrowful mysteries" are Christ's agony of mind in the Garden of Gethsemane, his whipping by the Roman soldiers and their crowning of him with thorns, the carrying of the cross, and Christ's crucifixion and death. These are natural images of sacrificial suffering for any Catholic, but they also represent all the basic kinds of suffering: mental anguish, physical pain, being mocked, wearily carrying a burden, death in agony. Almost any great suffering will involve most of these in some way: all of them could be distinguished, for example, in the suffering of the Jews in Nazi concentration camps. So it is not clear if Tolkien consciously intended the reminder of Christ's suffering or merely tried to convey archetypal agony.

Frodo, of course, does not die. More surprisingly, he does not persevere to the end: at the last moment his will fails, and he is saved only by a seeming accident from undoing all the good of his mission. This is so important a point that we will have to discuss it at length in the next chapter. But to sum up the discussion of "Hobbits and heroism": both Bilbo and Frodo are examples of ordinary persons rising to heroism when it is demanded of them. The original motive of their heroism is loyalty and love of friends. Their realization of their own limitations, their common sense and humility, keeps them from the rashness that is the excess of the virtue of courage, the megalomania that is the downfall of some more conventionally heroic figures such as Boromir. Their courage is moral as well as physical: Bilbo is willing to bear the reproaches of his friends to try for a just peace. Frodo rejects the seemingly good advice of Sam and others and forgives and trusts Gollum. And in the last analysis, their self-sacrificing love rises to such heights as to be comparable to the greatest love the world has known.

A MAN FOR ALL SEASONS (ROBERT BOLT)

"The Hero as Rebel:
Robert Bolt's *A Man for All Seasons*"
by Scott Walters,
University of North Carolina at Asheville

Sir Thomas More, the Renaissance English writer, statesman, and philosopher whose final years serve as the subject of Robert Bolt's 1961 drama *A Man for All Seasons*, has long been revered within Roman Catholic circles as a martyr and a saint and, as such, a moral hero. However, to examine a literary character such as Bolt's More in terms of the hero's journey, the first question we must address is whether the character is, in fact, an archetypal hero at all. Bolt, a self-identified agnostic, refers to the deeply religious More as a "hero of selfhood" (xiv), a phrase that refers to the ideas of twentieth-century French existentialist philosopher Albert Camus as an exemplar of this orientation. In fact, it is this type of existentialist hero, more than the archetypal hero figure, that More represents in *A Man for All Seasons*.

Joseph Campbell, whose classic book *The Hero with a Thousand Faces* definitively described the archetypal hero's journey, defined the actions of a hero:

> *A hero ventures forth from the world of common day into a region of supernatural wonder: fabulous forces are there encountered and a decisive victory is won; the hero comes back from this mysterious*

123

adventure with the power to bestow boons on his fellow man.
(Campbell 30; italics author's)

If we accept this definition, even without the fantastical qualities, we must admit that More is not a traditional hero in Campbell's sense. He doesn't "venture forth" to do battle, for instance, with the "fabulous force" of King Henry VIII, whose desire to have his marriage to Queen Catherine annulled is the source of the play's conflict. In fact, More's primary tactic is to *avoid* direct conflict with Henry through the strategic and continual use of silence. It is difficult to regard such tactics as in any way similar to a "battle" with a "decisive victory," even if More succeeded in accomplishing his goals.

But More fails in his efforts to avoid conflict, and despite his silence, King Henry and his ministers not only remain unconquered, but More himself is routed. He not only fails to slay the "dragon," King Henry, but he is ultimately slain *by* him. As a result, everything More resisted through his silence comes to pass: Henry abolishes papal supremacy and declares himself head of the newly established Church of England, his marriage to Catherine is thus annulled, and he marries Anne Boleyn (the first of many such marriages, although in the future Henry forgoes divorce in favor of the simpler beheading), whose heirs are declared the legitimate successors to the throne. In all practical respects, More's actions, or inactions, result in complete failure. His death is for naught, and the only boon to be distributed to his fellow men is an image of courage in the face of death. In short, there is little evidence to support viewing More as a hero in Campbell's sense.

But there are other definitions of hero that more accurately apply to More. Aristotle, in his *Poetics*, defines tragic heroes (and certainly More's death at the end of the play qualifies him for the tragic label) very simply as "people who are better than the average" (52), and Campbell himself writes that "the composite hero of the monomyth is a personage of exceptional gifts" who is frequently "honored by his society" (37). Both of these more general descriptions can comfortably be applied to More with little further discussion. We might run into more trouble with critic Lionel Trilling's definition of a hero as "a man who commits an approved act of unusual courage" (85); after all, at least at first blush, More's courage is less an act than a refusal to act, and his courage is most unwilling. Interestingly, Trilling goes on to say that the hero's "virtue is such that [he] wears the crowning perfection of *megalopsychia*, 'great-souledness' or 'aristocratic pride,' [which] is to be recognized by the way he comports himself, by his slow gait, his low-pitched voice, his measured diction, his conscious irony in dealing with inferiors." More as played by Paul Scofield, who won both a Tony Award for the Broadway performance and an Academy Award for his film version, fit Trilling's description like a glove. Trilling finishes by saying, "The hero is one who looks like a hero: the hero is an actor—he acts out his own high sense of himself" (85). Bolt himself seems to see a bit of the performer in More as well. "What's amazing about More," Bolt marveled in an interview, "is the perfection of his behavior—both in detail and overall. A nearly faultless performance ... a breathtaking performance as a human being ..." (qtd. in Harben 172). By which Bolt means More maintained his sense of personal integrity and courage in the face of intense pressure and death.

This brings us to an alternate version of heroism that might be more obviously applicable to the case of Sir Thomas More: martyrdom. One might persuasively argue that More's hero's journey is not that of a warrior hero as per Joseph Campbell but rather that of a martyr, which usually is defined less as a journey of action and more a refusal to act, a refusal to compromise one's most deeply held religious beliefs. Martyrs are victims and as such are acted upon. Indeed, the traditional martyr story centers on those who, as the description of the seventeenth-century Dutch book *Martyr's Mirror* says, were "willing to stand alone for a simple, obedient faith" and who pay for this stand with their lives. This is certainly true of More, whose religious beliefs pit him against the assembled power of an absolutist state, which ultimately leads to his death.

Nevertheless, if a martyr is by definition called to "stand alone," More willingly embraces only the second half of that equation, the solitary part, while at the same time taking, he says himself, "every path my winding wits would find" to avoid having to undertake the first part at all (Bolt 159). Indeed, when More is confronted with a letter from the king of Spain expressing his "admiration for the stand you ... have taken over the so-called divorce of Queen Catherine," More adamantly insists, "I have taken no stand!" and refuses to accept the letter (108). For much of the play, More embraces silence as a means of providing himself "safety under the law" (95), using passive aggression—resistance to authority through what is *not* done rather than what is done—as a means of defiance. This is a well-worn and respected tactic that has often been used by martyrs who are suffering under torture and who nevertheless refuse to grant the torturers what they want. More uses silence for the same purpose of refusal, but does so as a way of *avoiding* torture. More's focus is as much on the protection of himself and his family as it is on the protection of his integrity and eternal soul.

In essence, More seeks invisibility. His ideal outcome, once he has resigned his chancellorship and retired into humble private life near the beginning of Act 2, is that Henry and his ministers forget he exists at all and that they thus allow him to slip back into domestic anonymity, releasing him from the necessity of taking a public stand on the issue of Henry's divorce. He is not desirous of bringing his own personal morality to bear on the public, as he would be if he were a warrior hero; rather, this is a matter of his soul, and his soul is his own private affair separate from the rest of the world. Indeed, when his son-in-law, William Roper, suggests More take a public stand against the parliamentary act that requires the administering of an oath concerning Henry's marriage, More retorts that "God made the *angels* to show him splendor," not humankind. More feels no need for posturing or evangelizing but rather sees his responsibility to God as being to "serve him wittily" and, when threatened, to use that same wit to escape harm if at all possible. He goes on, in an explanation of what likely seems cowardice to Roper (and perhaps to those who subscribe to Joseph Campbell's definition of heroism):

> If [God] suffers us to fall to such a case that there is no escaping, then we may stand to our tackle as best we can, and yes, Will, then we may clamor like champions . . . if we have the spittle for it. And no doubt it delights God to see splendor where He only looked for complexity. But it's God's part, not our own, to bring ourselves to that extremity! Our natural business lies in escaping . . . (126)

This is an unlikely hero. It is only when More fails to escape, when his wit fails in the face of betrayal and he faces the scaffold, that he rises from lawyerly complexity to simple splendor in accepting his fate. By the time More condemns the "Act of Parliament which is directly repugnant to the Law of God" (159), his declaration is a dramatic anti-climax of the first order. However, his main moral claim to innocence, as he faces those who have condemned him, centers on the right to privacy within one's soul so long as it does not do damage to others. "I do none harm, I say none harm, I think none harm," he asserts. "And if this be not enough to keep a man alive, in good faith I long not to live . . ." (160). The king's representatives, save for More's friend Norfolk, are happy to oblige. When, at the end of the play, he ascends to the scaffold alone, he does so with quiet calm, confidently enjoining the Headsman to "be not afraid of your office. You send me to God" (162). In doing so, he is the perfect picture of a martyr.

One might be tempted to stop there, declaring More a martyr and a saint and *A Man for All Seasons* simply as a religious pageant written to provide an inspirational message for believers and a testimonial for nonbelievers. Yet Bolt's reference to More as a "hero of selfhood," written in the introduction to the published version of the play, sticks in the mind. What does Bolt mean by this? Is a hero of selfhood different than the traditional hero? Is it different than a martyr? And if so, how does More exemplify this different model?

"I think the paramount gift our thinkers, artists, and for all I know, our men of science, should labor to get for us," Bolt writes, "is a sense of selfhood without resort to magic" (xiv), or as he puts it elsewhere, a "transcendental explanation" (Harben 172). In other words, as a writer Bolt created a character whose actions are less about faithfully following the dictates of a higher power—in this case God, and God's representative on earth, the pope—than of staying true to one's personal values and beliefs. "Though few of us have anything in ourselves like an immortal soul which we regard as absolutely inviolable," Bolt writes, revealing the agnosticism that informs his, if not his central character's, worldview, "yet most of us still feel something which we should prefer, on the whole, not to violate" (xiv). This "something" is what he, echoing Camus, a "writer I admire in this connection" (xiv), calls the "self," which he sees standing inviolate. In this sense, Bolt stands less as a martyr than as an existential rebel, at least as defined by Camus.

"What is a rebel?" Camus asks in the first sentence of his stirring book *The Rebel: An Essay on Man in Revolt*. He answers, "A man who says no . . ." (13). What the rebel means with his no, Camus goes on, is "'up to this point, yes, beyond it no,' 'you are going too far,' or, again, 'there is a limit beyond which you shall not go.' In other words," Camus concludes, "his no affirms the existence of a borderline" (13). Yet can More's silence, his refusal to say anything at all concerning the matter of his king's marriage or claiming of the title of head of the English church, be seen as actually saying no? His prosecutors certainly think so. During his trial, Thomas Cromwell angrily asserts that "silence can, according to circumstances, speak" (Bolt 151), whereas More repeatedly asserts that "Silence is not denial" (150) and even hints that the "maxim of the law is . . . 'Silence gives consent'" (152). Yet Cromwell insists that, in More's case, silence speaks louder than words. "[I]s there a man in this court, is there a man in this country, who does not *know* Sir Thomas More's opinion of the King's title? Of course not! But how can that be? Because his silence betokened—nay, his silence *was* not silence at all but a most eloquent denial" (152).

To some extent, this might seem, despite the life-and-death ramifications, like legal hairsplitting. Indeed, More seems to take almost mischievous glee in forcing his persecutors to focus their energy on this point of legal minutiae. As audience members, there certainly is as little doubt in our own minds as there is in Cromwell's concerning More's beliefs, and along with More we are entertained by his intellectual game of "I've got a secret." What lies at the center of this titanic struggle, however, is a matter much larger than whether silence legally implies consent or denial but rather whether societal demands take precedence over individual integrity. Cromwell sees the issue politically, and he sees More's refusal to take the oath as an attempt to undermine temporal political authority. More, on the other hand, sees the issue personally, and he sees his refusal as an attempt to save his own eternal soul.

Whereas initially More's silence was a means of protecting himself and his family, once Cromwell introduces an oath as a way to force compliance, he raises the stakes to a point where More, like Camus's rebel, has no choice but to say no and "affirm the existence of a borderline." His soul—his self—is in peril. For More, "when a man takes an oath . . . he's holding his own self in his own hands.

Like water .... And if he opens his fingers *then*—he needn't hope to find himself again" (140). He makes explicit the ramifications of this statement when he explains that "In matters of conscience, the loyal subject is more bounden to be loyal *to* his conscience than to any other thing," including the state. When Cromwell, fast losing his composure, calls this a "frivolous self-conceit," More counters that it is "very and pure necessity for respect of my own soul." To which Cromwell shoots back, "Your own self, you mean!" And More, in a sentence whose brevity belies its centrality to the play, replies, "Yes, a man's soul is his self!" (153).

It is now that Bolt's portrayal of More as a "hero of selfhood" becomes clear, and Campbell's definition of a hero rejoins the discussion. For Bolt's More, once brought to trial for his rebellious silence, *does* "venture forth from the world of common day into a region of supernatural wonder" (Campbell 30), where he battles for the highest stakes a man can encounter—not his own life but his own soul. Cromwell is the force with which he must contend, and while More loses his life, ultimately a decisive victory is in fact won, for despite all the efforts of his foes, More's soul remains pure and whole to the last. His final words of the play, after Thomas Cranmer, one of his persecutors, marvels enviously at his confidence that the headsman will be sending him to God, are: "He will not refuse one who is so blithe to go to him" (Bolt 162). To be blithe is to be heedless and carefree, which is the attitude of a victor, of a man who has faced the worst the world has to offer and emerged unscathed.

More's equating of the soul and the self may seem to Bolt, who doubts the existence of an immortal soul, to require an "explanation and apology" for seemingly converting a "Christian saint" into an existential hero (xiv). However, More's statement that a man's soul is his self is, logically speaking at least, an equivalence in that the word "is" points to an identity shared by both soul and self. Thus, while a man's soul is his self, as More says, it is equally true that his self is his soul. More's protection of his soul, therefore, forges a continuity between earth and heaven, time and eternity, humans and angels. The treasure that a traditional hero acquires because of his earthly battles in More's case is the ultimate one: eternal life. Without his faith in that eventuality, and despite Bolt's agnostic disclaimer, More's victory would be pyrrhic and most likely dramatically unsatisfying for an audience. While most people, as Bolt states, "feel something that we should prefer, on the whole, not to violate," it is arguable that we would feel it strongly enough to give up our lives rather than violate it. Even Bolt's way of saying it implies a certain lukewarm quality that hardly lends itself to heroism. But to defend one's eternal soul—that is truly a hero's journey. Thus, from the viewpoint that More loses his life, he is a martyr; but from the perspective that he wins his battle for his soul, for his self, he is a hero—a hero who says no, a hero who is a rebel.

WORKS CITED

Campbell, Joseph. *The Hero with a Thousand Faces*. Princeton University Press, 1972.

Camus, Albert. *The Rebel: An Essay on Man in Revolt*. New York: Vintage Books, 1956.

Harben, Niloufer, ed. *Twentieth-century English History Plays: From Shaw to Bond*. Totowa, N.J.: Barnes & Noble Books, 1987.

Pearson, Carol S. *The Hero Within: Six Archetypes We Live By*. HarperOne, 1998.

Radice, Betty, ed. *Aristotle Horace Longinus/Classical Literary Criticism*. Penguin, 1970.

Trilling, Lionel. *Sincerity and Authenticity*. Harvard University Press, 2006.

MIDDLEMARCH
(GEORGE ELIOT)

"Middlemarch and the Hero's Journey"
by Merritt Moseley,
University of North Carolina at Asheville

Middlemarch (1871–72) is, as its title hints, about middling or moderate matters. Set in the middle of England in the middle of the nineteenth century among middle-class people, it features moderate, unspectacular deeds and states of being. It could hardly be further from the kind of setting and plot readers that find in *The Iliad* or *Moby-Dick*. It approaches heroism in a way more appropriate to the realist novel than the epic poem or tragic drama. Nevertheless, it demonstrates the possibilities of heroism in an essentially private life and even the domestic sphere. During her journey, Dorothea Brooke shows a resolve and courage that match those of the more famous, more spectacular heroes of literary history.

Middlemarch is one of the greatest novels of the nineteenth century. It is also a high point for achievement in serious prose fiction and especially important as a model of the genre, a work that has had lasting importance. As Harold Bloom describes, "If there is an exemplary fusion of aesthetic and moral power in the canonical novel, then George Eliot (real name Marianne or Mary Anne Evans) is its best representative, and *Middlemarch* is her subtlest analysis of the moral imagination" (298). George Eliot's masterpiece not only calls for comparison with the supremely long, ambitious, multiplot novels of social realism written by her compatriots—Dickens's *Our Mutual Friend* (1864–65), Thackeray's *Vanity Fair* (1847–48), or Trollope's *The Way We Live Now* (1874–75)—but surpasses them in its wisdom of human motives and behavior. Perhaps only Tolstoy's *Anna Karenina* (1873–77) is the closest model.

It is difficult to pinpoint just one clear hero in the novel. In fact, the subtitle of *Middlemarch* almost vehemently *denies* a focus on single heroism or even a strongly narrative intention: "A Study of Provincial Life." The best example is the character Dorothea Brooke, and her heroism is of a sort that would be unrecognizable to a traditional hero, a Roland or an Odysseus. Moreover, her journey is a mental, moral, and emotional one rather than a physical one. Though she has been educated at Lausanne, Switzerland, before the action of the novel begins and spends an unhappy honeymoon in Rome, for the most part she is fixed in Tipton, then after marriage at Lowick, five miles away. These two villages are near the somewhat larger manufacturing town of Middlemarch, though Dorothea and her circle seldom go there because they are country gentry and have little to do with its population of manufacturers, businessmen, bankers, and other middle-class aspirants to genteel status. The county is Loamshire, a region in the middle of England.

Indeed, *Middlemarch* provides an exhaustive survey of life in the middle of the country in the early 1830s. But *Middlemarch*, as Alison Booth points out, "in spite of the strong alternate plots, 'reads' as Dorothea's story" (195). This seems to be a nearly universal reaction for good reasons. The first of its eight books is called "Miss Brooke." The first chapter begins, "Miss Brooke had that kind of beauty which seems to be thrown into relief by poor dress," and the last lines of the book are about her, too (5). This foregrounding of Dorothea is partly a result of the divided origins of the novel, which resulted from Eliot's decision to combine a story she had begun, called "Miss Brooke," with another, already called *Middlemarch*, which would have been a study of provincial life (Beaty 3–42). The result is that characteristically Victorian subgenre, the multiplot novel. In his study of the form, Peter K. Garrett comments on Eliot's "experiments with parallel and converging narrative lines" in her earlier works, declaring that the multiplot novel "became a means of pursuing some of her most important artistic purposes and articulating some of her deepest imaginative concerns" (135). It is important to emphasize the "parallel and converging" narrative lines. Eliot's success lies largely in the way she launches a number of different and originally separate stories, develops each in its own way and with its own independent sources of interest, and yet makes them all part of a larger system—or, to use her metaphor, a web—that gives the long and multifarious book an intricate unity.

If Dorothea's is the main plot, then the second plot is that of Tertius Lydgate, a high-born physician newly arrived in Middlemarch. Bearing what Eliot calls "spots of commonness"—features that ultimately mar his chances for heroism despite his noble intentions—Lydgate marries badly to a pretty but silly woman and spoils his life's promise; he is hampered by convention, by debt, by marriage, and by the prejudices of small-minded people. Once a man with heroic ambitions—to become a "discoverer," one of the "great originators," and to "do good small work for Middlemarch, and great work for the world"—he dwindles to a fashionable resort physician, whose contribution to medical knowledge has to do not with discovering the primitive tissue of all life, as he hoped, but with an improvement in the treatment of gout (108, 110). Lydgate fails at heroism through a combination of social pressures and his own character.

But Dorothea is different. William Deresiewicz, who attributes the difference to gender, writes:

> *Middlemarch* is generally regarded as an antiheroic novel. Dorothea's failure to perform "some long-recognizable deed," and even more, that of Lydgate, are seen as implicit arguments against the possibility of heroism in any grand sense and for a heroism of small measures, even of resignation.... Of course the novel clearly does assert the impossibility of heroism for a woman like Dorothea, but it just as clearly does not extend that claim to men. (723)

Nevertheless, Eliot understands the possibility of female heroism, at least in times past (the bourgeois nineteenth century may be different). Her prelude begins with a consideration of Saint Theresa, whose "passionate, ideal nature demanded an epic life: what were many-volumed romances of chivalry and the social conquests of a brilliant girl to her?" (3). What does this have to do with *Middle-march*? It prepares us for the limited scope of heroic action available to Dorothea, despite her noble ambitions:

> Many Theresas have been born who found for themselves
> no epic life wherein there was a constant unfolding of far-
> resonant action; perhaps only a life of mistakes, the offspring
> of a certain spiritual grandeur ill-matched with the meanness
> of opportunity; perhaps a tragic failure which found no sacred
> poet and sank unwept into oblivion. (3)

The narrator suggests explanations for why such potential Theresas, fired by ardor (a trait insistently attributed to Dorothea), achieved so little: perhaps the conditions of life, perhaps the indefinite natures of woman, perhaps domestic reality. "Here and there is born a Saint Theresa, foundress of nothing, whose loving heart-beats and sobs after an unattained goodness tremble off and are dispersed among hindrances, instead of centering in some long-recognizable deed" (4).

It is worth remembering that every significant character in *Middlemarch* falls short of his or her aspirations. Rosamund Vincy marries Lydgate but never enters England's aristocracy; Bulstrode, the banker, wishes to expiate a criminal past without baring his guilt; Lydgate aspires to make a dramatic scientific breakthrough; Will Ladislaw, Dorothea's second husband, longs to bring about a radical reform of England; Edward Casaubon, her first husband, is almost laughable and pathetic as he attempts to discover "the Key to all Mythologies." Nobody is smart enough, or good enough, or pretty enough, or forceful enough, or single-minded enough, or lucky enough, and besides, the world is too complicated, the web of complications too intricate and confining. This is the sense in which *Middlemarch* is antiheroic.

Yet the novel invites us to contemplate heroism, most often in connection with Dorothea, via allusions and comparisons. In Chapter 19, Dorothea is on her honeymoon in Rome and already discovering the misery of marriage to Casaubon. In the Vatican she is the object of admiration by a German artist, who is initially struck by the contrast between the marble voluptuousness of a sculpture of Ariadne and the demure and melancholy Dorothea. Later, in conversation with

Ladislaw, he says: "If you were an artist, you would think of Mistress Second-Cousin as antique form animated by Christian sentiment—a sort of Christian Antigone—sensuous force controlled by spiritual passion" (141). What is the force of this allusion? It refers to Antigone, the daughter of Oedipus, a self-sacrificing young woman with a rather lightweight sister named Ismene, who may be the counterpart to Dorothea's Celia. But Antigone was the hero of a Greek tragedy who faced down civil authority in defense of the higher-law obedience that she would not compromise, was condemned to death, and died by her own hand.

Gerhard Joseph writes that:

> the character of Antigone is profoundly relevant to a "modern" life, providing one of the mythic types against which Dorothea's soul making asks to be measured. But what of the action of the play, which was after all the focus of [Matthew] Arnold's judgment? . . . Eliot all but seconds Arnold's charge that the action is obsolescent, although her grounds differ. The distance between the heroic, larger-than-life context of Thebes and the prosaic reality of Middlemarch is too great. (27)

Is the function of heroic allusions—to Saint Theresa, the Virgin Mary, Antigone, John Milton, King Arthur—only to point out, with repetitive insistence, that Dorothea Brooke is not one of these heroes and cannot be? That every time we measure her soul against one of the mythic types, we get the same result: She comes up short?

That is one way of reading the book, and it accords with Eliot's devotion to realism, her artistic fidelity to the ordinary dimensions of human life. Northrop Frye classified literary modes by the nature of the hero and stipulated that if the character is:

> superior neither to other men nor to his environment, the hero is one of us: we respond to a sense of his common humanity, and demand from the poet the same canons of probability that we find in our own experience. This gives us the hero of the *low mimetic* mode, of most comedy and of realistic fiction. . . . On this level the difficulty in retaining the word "hero" . . . occasionally strikes an author. (34)

Antigone is superior to other men though not her environment and thus belongs to the *high mimetic* mode of epic and tragedy. By this reading, Dorothea's failure to achieve a long-recognizable deed is due not to her character, nor the conditions of the society in which she finds herself, but to the genre of the book in which she is a character.

Dorothea's failure to understand her own limitations may be a character flaw. Dorothea is introduced as a passionate young woman, with a "nature altogether ardent, theoretic, and intellectually conse-quent" and with "an exalted enthusiasm about the ends of life" (21). The surprising means to reach those exalted ends is to make an unlikely marriage with an unprepossessing, older (forty-five years old to her nineteen), ugly, self-centered, desiccated shell of a scholarly clergyman. She is the one person who cannot see the folly of her choice, in part because of her Saint Theresa-like desire for a greatness of life (and, perhaps, because she is terribly naïve about marriage). Her reasoning deserves to be quoted at length:

> "I should learn everything then," she said to herself, still walking quickly along the bridle road through the wood. "It would be my duty to study that I might help him the better in his great works. There would be nothing trivial about our lives. Everyday-things with us would mean the greatest things. It would be like marrying Pascal. I should learn to see the truth by the same light as great men have seen it by. And then I should know what to do, when I got older: I should see how it is possible to lead a great life here—now—in England." (21)

This initial delusion prepares her for the frustrating life she will lead. Her marriage to Mr. Casaubon is increasingly miserable. Not only is he, as Sir James Chettam (admittedly, a disappointed rival) fumes, "no better than a mummy!" but also Casaubon lacks the largeness of mind to appreciate Dorothea. Casaubon suspects her motives, and when she finally realizes that he is a failure as a scholar (he knows no German, for instance), he resents her more for this (43). His jealousy of his cousin Will Ladislaw, who is in love with Dorothea, leads him to churlish behavior. Thus even his death does not grant her complete release.

But what if Dorothea had been *correct* about Mr. Casaubon's greatness? Can one marry heroically? *Middlemarch* suggests that the answer may be yes. Dorothea badly misses the mark with her first marriage. But she marries again, to Will Ladislaw. Doing so requires her to forfeit her legacy from Mr. Casaubon, and in putting her love above her material interests and a certain amount of negative publicity, she certainly behaves in a disinterested and principled, if not positively heroic, fashion. But in the finale, the narrator refers oddly to marriage as "the beginning of the home epic" and emphasizes its heroic aspects when she writes: "Some set out, like Crusaders of old, with a glorious equipment of hope and enthusiasm, and get broken by the way, wanting patience with each other and the world" (608). Dorothea's role is to give her husband, who is now in Parliament, "wifely help" (611). Those who knew Dorothea's personality "thought it a pity that so substantive and rare a creature should have been absorbed into the life of another, and be only known in a certain circle as a wife and mother" (611).

This discontent, if felt by Dorothea's contemporaries in the 1830s, has been increasingly felt by more modern readers. Gertrude Himmelfarb sums up the dissatisfaction:

> Why does Dorothea, who carries the moral burden of the book and who has, more than any other character, attained a state of moral maturity, have to find her own moral purpose in being a wife—first to Casaubon and then to Ladislaw, both of whom are clearly her moral inferiors? Why does she have to marry at all? Or if she does choose to marry, why does she have to be merely the helpmate in that marriage? (580)

In explaining why a fate inconsistent with feminist beliefs befell Dorothea, Himmelfarb explains that Eliot was not much of a feminist. Furthermore, Himmelfarb states, Eliot believed in marriage, though one based on love and reverence. Dorothea's hero's journey, as Himmelfarb says, has brought her to a "state of moral maturity" (580).

If fulfilling her heroic aspirations by marrying and becoming a helpmate strikes many modern readers as insipid and disappointing, then Dorothea's other kind of heroic accomplishment will probably be no more exciting. That is, she is heroically *good;* much of her goodness consists in passive and self-abnegating behaviors. She tolerates life with Mr. Casaubon and treats him with kindness he does not "deserve," caring for him in his illness and reading to him tirelessly long after she realizes that she does not love him and he cannot love her. Her marriage is a torment to her. Her passionate nature cannot receive any encouragement from the dry-as-dust, probably impotent Casaubon, and he slights her mind as well. But she is, in the strongest sense the words can carry, a good wife to Casaubon. She is a caring sister to Celia, a kind aunt to little Arthur, a good landowner, and a philanthropist.

Late in the novel she learns of Lydgate's troubles—he is in debt, and being in debt involves him unwittingly in a scandalous entanglement with Bulstrode. Lydgate unburdens himself to her, and she undertakes, fearlessly, to counteract his bad reputation, even going to appeal on his behalf to his wife, whom she does not know. The narrator's language creates a sense of moral heroism: "The presence of a noble nature, generous in its wishes, ardent in its charity, changes the lights for us: we begin to see things again in their larger, quieter masses, and to believe that we too can be seen and judged in the wholeness of our character" (558). Lydgate thinks of Dorothea's compassion, as he "had for many days been seeing all life as one who is dragged and struggling amid the throne." As he rides home, Lydgate reflects:

> "This young creature has a heart large enough for the Virgin Mary. . . . She seems to have what I never saw in any woman before—a fountain of friendship towards men—a man can make a friend of her. . . . Well—her love might help a man more than her money." (563)

Her love does help Lydgate—it doesn't heal his marriage, for that sort of heroism belongs to romance, not the realistic novel—and it even helps his wife to emerge briefly from her shell of narcissism and self-absorption to perform the only selfless act of her life.

The finale of *Middlemarch* recalls the preface and draws together the strands of what Alison Booth calls "everyday heroism" (200). Dorothea is heroic in a different way from the typical historical or mythical heroes to whom she has been compared. She is an unsung hero.

A new Theresa will hardly have the opportunity of reforming a conventual life, any more than a new Antigone will spend her heroic piety in daring all for the sake of a brother's burial: the medium in which their ardent deeds took shape is for ever gone. . . . Her full nature, like that river of which Cyrus broke the strength, spent itself in channels which had no great name on the earth. But the effect of her being on those around her was incalculably diffusive: for the growing good of the world is partly dependent on unhistoric acts; and that things are not so ill with you and me as they might have been, is half owing to the number who lived faithfully a hidden life, and rest in unvisited tombs. (Eliot 612-13)

WORKS CITED

Beaty, Jerome. *Middlemarch from Notebook to Novel: A Study of George Eliot's Creative Method*. Urbana: University of Illinois Press, 1960.

Beer, Gillian. *George Eliot*. Bloomington: Indiana University Press, 1986.

Bloom, Harold. *The Western Canon*. New York: Harcourt and Brace, 1994.

Booth, Alison. "Little Dorrit and Dorothea Brooke: Interpreting the Heroines of History," *Nineteenth-Century Literature* 41 (September 1986): 190–216.

Deresiewicz, William. "Heroism and Organicism in the Case of Lydgate," *Studies in English Literature, 1500-1900,* 38 (Autumn 1998): 723–740.

Eliot, George. *Middlemarch*. 1871–72. Boston: Houghton Mifflin, 1956.

Frye, Northop. *Anatomy of Criticism: Four Essays.* (Princeton: Princeton University Press, 1957.

Garrett, Peter K. *The Victorian Multiplot Novel: Studies in Dialogical Form* New Haven: Yale University Press, 1980.

Himmelfarb, Gertrude. "George Eliot for Grown-Ups," *The American Scholar* 63 (Autumn 1994): 577–581.

Joseph, Gerhard. "The Antigone as Cultural Touchstone: Matthew Arnold, Hegel, George Eliot, Virginia Woolf, and Margaret Drabble," *PMLA* 96 (January 1981): 22–35

MOBY-DICK
(HERMAN MELVILLE)

"Moby Dick"
by William Ellery Sedgwick,
in *Herman Melville: The Tragedy of Mind* (1944)

INTRODUCTION

William Ellery Sedgwick sees Ahab's quest for truth as a "tragedy of mind," contrasting Ahab's myopic gaze with Ishmael's panoramic vision of the world. As Sedgwick argues, Ishmael's heroic fate lies in the way he confronts and resolves his inner conflicts, ultimately embracing a "spiritual balance" he finds along the journey.

Ahab pursues the truth as the champion of man, leaving behind him all traditional conclusions, all common assumptions, all codes and creeds and articles of faith. Although the universe of sea and sky opens around him an appalling abyss, and although the abyss seems the visible apprehension of his mind that the truth will prove that there is no truth, still he sails on. He will at any rate have the universe show its cards, so that a man may know how it stands with him, whether or not there is anything beyond himself to which he can

---

Sedgwick, William Ellery. *"Moby Dick." Herman Melville: The Tragedy of Mind.* Cambridge, Mass.: Harvard UP, 1944. 82–136.

entrust his dearest, hopes, and then bear himself accordingly. "I feel deadly faint," he says, "faint, bowed, and humped, as though I were Adam staggering beneath the piled centuries since Paradise."

Ahab is nobly mad. Yet there are ambiguities about his conduct that this madness does not explain. Something else must be taken into account. We must discriminate in this matter of his madness. He says himself, "They think me mad—Starbuck does; but I'm demoniac, I am madness maddened!" That is just it. On his last trip, as the result of his mutilation, he fell prey to a terrible monomania. In all that he suffered in forty years of seafaring that injury affected him as nothing else. It was like Job's plague of boils that of all his humiliations touched nearest the quick. For "no turbanned Turk, no hired Venetian or Malay" could have smitten Ahab with more seeming malice. "Small reason was there, to doubt then, that ever since that almost fatal encounter, Ahab had cherished a wild vindictiveness against the Whale, all the more fell for that in his frantic morbidness he at last came to identify with him, not only all his bodily woes, but all his intellectual and spiritual exasperations. The White Whale swam before him as the monomaniac incarnation of all those malicious agencies which some deep men feel eating in them, till they are left living on with half a heart and half a lung. That intangible malignity which has been from the beginning; to whose dominion even the modern Christians ascribe one-half of the worlds; which the ancient Ophites of the East reverenced in their statue devil;—Ahab did not fall down and worship it like them; but, deliriously transferring its idea to the abhorred White Whale, he pitted himself, all mutilated against it. All that most maddens and torments; all that stirs up the lees of things; all truth with malice in it; all that cracks the sinews and cakes the brain; all the subtle demonisms of life and thought; all evil, to crazy Ahab were visibly personified, and made practically assailable in Moby Dick."

His monomania could hide itself, if necessary, to serve its own ends. His absence while the *Pequod* was preparing for the voyage did not trouble the owners. "I don't know exactly what's the matter with him," says Peleg, "but he keeps close inside the house; a sort of sick and yet he don't look so." But out at sea it would be manifested when "with glaring eyes Ahab would burst from his state-room, as though escaping from a bed that was on fire." While Ahab slept, then, sometimes "the eternal living principle or soul in him" would dissociate itself from Ahab's scorched mind, so that what seemed Ahab was divorced from "the common vitality ... was for the time but a vacated thing, a formless, somnambulistic being." His monomaniac's purpose "by its own sheer inveteracy of will" had fixed itself into a self-assumed, mechanical being of its own. "God help thee, old man, thy thoughts have created a creature in thee; and he whose intense thinking thus makes him a Prometheus; a vulture feeds upon that heart forever; that vulture the very creature he creates."

Without impairing his strength of mind and purpose, Ahab's monomania has all but possessed itself of Ahab. His noble madness still has its own consciousness and ends in view. But it is horribly disfigured and perverted by his monomania which held it like a vise. "Ahab's full lunacy subsided not, but deepeningly contracted.... But as in his narrow-flowing monomania not one jot of Ahab's broad madness had been left behind; so in that broad madness, not one jot of his great natural intellect had perished. That before living agent, now became the living instrument. If such a furious trope may stand, his special lunacy stormed his general sanity, and carried it, and turned all its concentrated cannon upon its own mad mark."

The White Whale is all evil to Ahab. Nevertheless it is wrong to say, as do almost all the critics of *Moby Dick*, that Melville intended him to represent evil. The White Whale has a tremendous power to do harm. But unless the word is so denatured as to be synonymous with harmful or dangerous, he cannot be called evil. If a man sees evil in him, then it is his own evil which is reflected back at him.

The chapter called "The Doubloon" makes Melville's meaning here perfectly clear. Ahab has had the great gold coin nailed to the main-mast, the reward for the first man who hails Moby Dick. "The ship's navel," Pip calls it. One day it happens that, one after another, Ahab, the three mates and members of the crew walk up to the coin and study the design of three mountain peaks stamped on the face of it. Each interprets it according to his own nature. For instance, Ahab makes out "three peaks as proud as Lucifer," while Starbuck makes out three "heaven-abiding peaks that almost seem the Trinity." Pip has been watching all this and when the last man has gone by he steals up to the coin. Now Pip has gone quite mad but "man's insanity is heaven's sense; and wandering from all mortal reason, man comes at last to that celestial thought, which, to reason, is absurd and frantic; and weal or woe, feels then uncompromised, indifferent as his God." Reflecting on what he has just seen, Pip speaks the wonderful indifference of heaven's sense. "I look, you look, he looks; we look, ye look, they look." The words, oddly remembered from Pip's negligible schooling, sound like gibberish, yet they sum up what has just transpired. The object is indifferent, the subject is all that is needed because the subject always sees himself. This is Pip's version of the solipsism of consciousness, a theme which Melville continually broaches in *Moby Dick*. Here, for certain, is the clue to Melville's meaning with respect to the White Whale. He stands for the inscrutable mystery of creation, as he also stands for what man sees in creation of himself.

Ahab's noble madness sprang from an excess of humanity. His monomania on the contrary is identified with mutilation. Truly a monomania, wherever it looks it sees only itself. It sees its evil in the White Whale. And Ahab's hate does not rest there. Be the White Whale agent or be he principal, Ahab will wreak his hate upon him. It was hardly in his nature not to believe in a divine power above creation. There must be a creator beyond his creation. There, too, Ahab saw his own hate reflected back at him. His soul and his religious sense could not but believe in God. His monomania, intruding itself, revealed a Satanic god.

Ahab's monomania is evil. It demands the ruthless sacrifice of love and preys on his common humanity. It implicates Ahab in "the heartless voids and immensities of the universe." He has leagued himself with them. Or, to show the tragic aspect, which is so close to the aspect of evil in Ahab's case, we may put it this way: when Ahab thrust his harpoon into the flanks of Moby Dick, at that awful moment which came after nearly forty years of facing the interlinked wonders and terrors of the sea, just then the universe got its barbs into him. His human front broke down at last and the inscrutable inhumanity of the universe passed into him. Noble Ahab stood in mortal danger of being abased to the condition of such an insensate thing as the ship's carpenter, a human semblance to bedeck the inhuman voids.

While the story of Ahab's pursuit of Moby Dick goes forward to its end, a drama of inner conflict is unfolded. A victim of his own nature, a victim of the tragedy of mind, Ahab would have been torn asunder (like Babbalanja, as "by wild horses") under any circumstances. His tragedy is far more bitter and more terrible because, finally, his own hand is raised against himself. His monomania has all but possessed itself of his noble madness. Therefore, his humanity is all but hideously perverted as well as otherwise maimed. Viewed outwardly, Ahab is like a figure in an old morality play, standing between a good and a bad angel and each suing for his soul. Starbuck is his good angel. His bad angel is Fedallah, "tall and swart, with one white tooth evilly protruding." But the drama of inner conflict I speak of is deeper; it is the struggle of Ahab's humanity—stout even in this extremity—to free itself from the fell clutches of his evil monomania.

Ahab's first words show the unkindness that his hate has wrought in him. "Down, dog, and kennel," he says outrageously to Stubb. In the great scene on the quarterdeck when he makes his purpose known he is in the image of his monomania. He clubs down Starbuck's reluctance, elevates over Starbuck the pagan harpooners and binds the crew with satanic rites. But presently his humanity speaks out. His anguish is profoundly human. "This lovely light, it lights not me; all loveliness is anguish to me." Pointed south, the *Pequod* sails into milder weather; there "more than once did he put forth the faint blossom of a look, which, in any other man, would have soon flowered out into a smile." The painful isolation to which the mysterious laws of his being have brought him is driven home by the desolation of the seas beyond Good Hope. A school of harmless little fish has been following the *Pequod*. Ahab observes that they forsake the *Pequod* to follow in the wake of a passing vessel, homeward bound. In a tone of deep and helpless sorrow Ahab murmurs, "Swim away from me, do ye?" His is like King Lear's anguish, "The little dogs and all, Tray, Blanch, and Sweet-heart, see, they bark at me." Another ship is hailed, "'Well, now, that's cheering,'" says Ahab, "while whole thunder clouds swept aside from his brow." For some time the *Pequod* has been becalmed and now it is reported that the stranger ship brings a breeze with her. "Better and better," Ahab says; then, showing that the deepest fountains of his being are not sealed up, "Would now St. Paul would come along that way, and to my breezelessness bring his breeze!"

I have said that in spite of everything Ahab's noble madness keeps its own ends in view. In the chapter "The Candles" we see his titanic defiance. But we see more. His soul and his religious sense are equal to his defiance. "I own thy speechless, placeless power," he shouts to the lightning that forks from the masts of his ship, "but to the last gasp of my earthquake life will dispute its unconditional, unintegral mastery in me. In the midst of the personified impersonal, a personality stands here. Though but a point at best; whenceso'er I came; whereso'er I go; yet while I earthly live, the queenly personality lives in me, and feels her royal rights." The whole strength of his being is coiled in words which cannot fail to recall the words of Job: "Though Thou slay me, yet shall I worship Thee, but I shall maintain my own ways before Thee." Then at once we see the broader slopes of his humanity again: "But war is pain, and hate is woe. Come in thy lowest form of love, and I will kneel and kiss thee."

All this time the *Pequod* is in danger of immediate destruction. Starbuck has ordered the ends of the chains thrown into the sea so as to draw off the lightning. Ahab countermands the order. "Avast," he cries, "let's have fair play here, though we be the weaker side ... out on all privileges." And not only this; while condescending to it, in virtue of something superior in him, he also pities the lightning. "There is some unsuffusing thing beyond thee, thou clear spirit, to whom all thy eternity is but time, all thy creativeness mechanical.... Oh, thou foundling fire, thou hermit immemorial, thou too has thy incommunicable riddle, thy unparticipated grief ... defyingly I worship thee." Like Prometheus, once more, Ahab scales the ramparts of inhuman heaven. Infuriated courage carries him along, but it is as if he carried, to plant upon those ramparts, a banner bearing the names of the highest emblems of humanity—love, compassion, justice. However, such are the paradoxes of human greatness in general and of Ahab's predicament in particular, that hardly has he reached this high pinnacle than he falls as low.

In order to gauge this catastrophe we should refer to the last paragraph in *White Jacket*. "Oh, shipmates and world-mates, all round! we the people suffer many abuses. Our gun-deck is full of complaints." Vain to appeal from lieutenants to captains or—"while on board our world frigate"—to "the indefinite Navy Commissioners." "Yet the worst of our evils we blindly inflict upon ourselves.... From the last ills no being can save another; therein each man must be his own saviour. For the rest, whatever befall us, let us never train our murderous guns inboard; let us not mutiny with bloody pikes in our hands." There is much in the passage which bears on Ahab. What is most pertinent at the moment is the earnest invocation at the end, expressing the loyalty and high-mindedness which it is the nature of Ahab's monomania to discard. That has been true of his monomania all along. Now the truth is borne out dramatically. In no uncertain terms Ahab trains murderous guns inboard. The celestial, mechanical lightning now forks from Ahab's own harpoon, at which Starbuck raises his protesting voice. "God, God is against thee, old man; forbear! 'tis an ill voyage," and he moves to bring the ship about and point her homeward. The panic-stricken crew instantly follows his lead. But Ahab interposes. He seizes his burning harpoon and waves it among them, "swearing to transfix with it the first sailor that but cast loose a rope's end. Petrified by his aspect, and still more shrinking from the fiery dart that he held, the men fell back in dismay, and Ahab again spoke," recalling them to their oath to hunt the White Whale—to the death.

The drama of Ahab's inner conflicts does not end there. It resumes when, not long afterwards, Ahab begins to take notice of Pip. Between him and Pip there is a bond of madness, the same in both, although they have come by it in opposite ways; the one from strength, the other from weakness. At any rate, Ahab begins to feel sympathy with and for Pip. If suffered to grow and ramify this feeling might cast out Ahab's hateful monomania and restore him to his humanity. Ahab sees the point. He says to Pip, "There is that in thee ... which I feel too curing to my malady ... and for this hunt my malady becomes my most desired health," and orders him to his own cabin.

"No, no, no!" Pip pleads, "ye have not a whole body, sir; do ye but use poor me for your one lost leg; only tread upon me, sir; I ask no more, so I remain a part of ye." "Oh! spite of million villains, this makes me a bigot in the fadeless fidelity of man!—and a black! and crazy!—but methinks like-cures-like applies to him too; he grows so sane again. ... If thou speakest thus to me much more, Ahab's purpose keels up in him. I tell thee no; it cannot be."

The situation here is akin to that between King Lear and his fool in the storm scenes:

> My wits begin to turn,
> Come on, my boy. How dost, my boy? Art cold?

> I am cold myself ... Come, your hovel.
> Poor fool and knave, I have one part in my heart
> That's sorry yet for thee.

His sympathy with his fool is like a cordial to keep his madness off. It takes his mind from his own exasperation, and leads him to a broader fellow feeling with his kind.

The crisis in Ahab's spiritual drama follows in the chapter called "The Symphony" which occurs just before the White Whale is sighted and the chase begins. For Ahab's salvation it is necessary that his sympathies, renewed by Pip, should reach out to embrace the great community of men—the common continent of men—represented in Starbuck. And for a moment this seems on the point of consummation. It is a lovely mild day; a day such as seems "the bridal of the earth and sky." The stepmother world, Melville writes, which had so long been cruel, "now threw affectionate arms round his stubborn neck, and did seem to joyously sob over him, as if over one, that however wilful and erring, she could yet find it in her heart to save and to bless." Ahab's mood relents, and Starbuck observing this draws up to him. Then Ahab's sympathies flow forth, drawing him deeper and deeper into their common humanity. "Close! stand close to me, Starbuck; let me look into a human eye; it is better than to gaze into the sea or sky; better than to gaze upon God. By the green land, by the bright hearthstone! this is the magic glass, man; I see my wife and my child in thine eye." Starbuck abundantly rejoins, "Oh, my captain! my captain! noble soul! grand old heart, after all! ... Away with me! let us fly these deadly waters! let us home! Wife and child, too, are Starbuck's—wife and child of his brotherly, sisterly, play-fellow youth; even as thine, sir, are the wife and child of thy loving, longing, paternal old age! Away! let us away!—this instant let me alter the course!" Ahab continues to mingle his sympathies with Starbuck's landward thoughts. But, of a sudden, his mind takes off in its endless speculation; the sea-instinct surges up in him, and, almost simultaneously, his maniacal hate bares its visage. "Look! see yon albicore! who put it into him to chase and fang that flying-fish? Where do murderers go, man? Who's to doom, when the judge himself is dragged to the bar?" He looks up for Starbuck's answer, but "blanched to a corpse's hue with despair, the mate had stolen away." Ahab "crossed the deck to gaze over on the other side; but started at two reflected, fixed eyes in the water there. Fedallah was motionlessly leaning over the same rail."

By separating himself from Starbuck, Ahab has cut himself off from the common continent of man. He is doomed. The whole inward truth is reflected in the outward circumstances of his death. His boats all smashed, the rest of his men, all save two, have managed to climb aboard the *Pequod*, and she, her sides stove in by the Whale, begins to sink. Ahab dies alone, cut off, as he says, "from the last fond pride of meanest shipwrecked captains." Long before he had said to Starbuck about Moby Dick, "He tasks me; he heaps me." In "The Symphony" he had said, "What is it, what nameless, inscrutable, unearthly thing is it; what cozening, hidden lord and master . . . commands me; that against all natural lovings and longings, I so keep pushing, and crowding, and jamming myself on all the time?" The whole inward truth, as I say, is reflected in the manner of his death. On the previous day, the second in the three-day battle, Fedallah had disappeared. On the third and last day his corpse reappeared lashed round and round to the Whale's back. Then Ahab, stabbing his harpoon into the Whale, at the same moment gets caught up in his own line and is dragged after him, with his last breath shouting, "Toward thee I roll, thou all-destroying but unconquering whale; to the last I grapple with thee . . . while chasing thee, though tied to thee, thou damned Whale! Thus, I give up the spear!"

Yet we have one more glimpse of him. "Oh, lonely death on lonely life! Oh, now I feel my topmost greatness lies in my topmost grief," he cries at the end. His nobility is reaffirmed in these words. He speaks here as the noble victim of the tragedy of mind.

He dies in the grip of his own evil, his heart racked by hate. His "most brain-battering fight" has availed him nothing. The problem of evil, the responsibility for suffering, these mysteries have eluded him in the end. "How can the prisoner reach outside except by thrusting through the wall? To me, the White Whale is that wall shoved near to me." "The dead blind wall butts all enquiring heads at last," says Ahab another time, hopeless of getting any answer to his final questions. The most terrifying aspect of Moby Dick in the last encounter is the featureless, wall-like countenance he presents to his assailants.

Still, defeated as he is in these respects, Ahab does not acknowledge defeat. So far as he can see he retains his sovereignty. Then by sheer strength of will he transcends all the considerations, which had driven him on, all the considerations arising from his "queenly personality," except its royalty.

In Ahab we come to feel the same tremendous act of will which is required for a tremendous act of forgiveness, although the act itself has another form than forgiveness. He accepts fate. "This whole act's immutably decreed. 'Twas rehearsed . . . a billion years before this ocean rolled." Yet this act has a more positive force than resignation. His is "a prouder, if a darker faith." He reverses himself to take his station in the eternal, impersonal order of things, which is beyond right or wrong, justice and injustice, and to which all the forces of which a man has outward knowledge are the obedient servants. If this is surrender or abdication, it is in terms of absolute equality with all the known forces of creation.

Only Ishmael survived. It so happened that on the last day he was asked to take the part of bowsman in Ahab's boat, left vacant when Fedallah disappeared the day before. In the commotion of the battle he was tossed and left floating on the margin of the final scene, where he just escaped being sucked in after the sinking *Pequod*. All that remained to him was his own lifebuoy and by that means Ishmael kept himself afloat, until picked up by a vessel that chanced to come his way.

This lifebuoy had been a coffin made for Queequeg when he thought himself dying. Upon his recovery Starbuck ordered the carpenter to make it over to serve in the opposite capacity. Observing the transformation, Ahab is given pause; "A life-buoy of a coffin! Does it go further? Can it be that in some spiritual sense the coffin is, after all, but an immortality preserver! I'll think of that. But no. So far gone am I in the dark side of earth, that its other side, the theoretic bright one, seems but uncertain twilight to me." Ishmael escaped then by means of the coffin life preserver which Ahab had rejected as a possible symbol of faith.

The truth we come at by way of Ishmael's story is the final truth about *Moby Dick*,—the truth, I might add, that made it whole. At the beginning, Ishmael explains that he is suffering one of his fits of hypochondria; "a damp, drizzly November" in his soul. His misanthropic hypos are getting the best of him. Therefore—his usual remedy for this condition—he decides to go to sea. That is his substitute for "pistol and ball. With a philosophical flourish Cato throws himself upon his sword; I quietly take to the ship. There is nothing surprising in this. If they but knew it, almost all men . . . some time or other, cherish very nearly the same feelings towards the ocean with me." When, some days later, on the little boat that takes him from New Bedford to Nantucket, he first catches sight of open water, his soul leaps up in him. "How I snuffed the Tartar air!—how I spurned the turnpike earth!—that common highway all over dented with the marks of slavish heels and hoofs; and turned me to admire the magnanimity of the sea which will permit no records." In Nantucket, Ishmael chooses the garish and outlandish *Pequod* as the ship for himself and Queequeg. What he gleans about Captain Ahab when he goes on board to sign affects him deeply; "I felt a sympathy and a sorrow for him, but I don't know what, unless it was the cruel loss of his leg." It is worth noticing that Ishmael is the only one of those who sailed with Ahab on the *Pequod* who caught sight of shadowy Fedallah being sneaked on board. Of what he felt when Ahab announced his purpose we already know something: "Who does not feel the irresistible arm drag?" "I, Ishmael, was one of that crew; my shouts had gone up with the rest; my oath had been welded with theirs; and stronger I shouted, and more did I hammer and clinch my oath, because of the dread in my soul. A wild, mystical, sympathetical feeling was in me; Ahab's quenchless feud seemed mine."

That is sufficient to show Ishmael's danger. His story turns on his mortal need to maintain himself against the strong drag he feels towards Ahab.

Since there is nothing on which Melville digresses that does not serve his meaning, Ishmael's jeopardy can be put in the picturesque language of the fishery as Melville explains it under the headings, "Fast-Fish and Loose-Fish." A fast-fish is a whale who has been stuck and who, presumably, can be brought alongside and made fast to the ship whose harpoon has caught him. A loose-fish is still fair game for anybody: he is still free for anybody to have, himself first of all. Ahab is a fast-fish. The universe has got its barb in him. His humanity is transfixed. Ishmael, on the contrary, is a loose-fish. Will he keep himself so? Or will he like Ahab impale himself on the exasperating inscrutability of things? Will he cease to stand up a "sovereign nature (in himself) amid the powers of heaven, hell and earth"?

"If any of those powers choose to withhold certain secrets, let them; that does not impair my sovereignty in myself; that does not make me tributary." But that, directly and indirectly, is what did impair Ahab's sovereignty.

The chapter called "The Whiteness of the Whale" begins with Ishmael saying, "What the White Whale was to Ahab has been hinted; what, at times, he was to me, as yet remains unsaid.... It was the whiteness of the Whale that above all things appalled me."

Thereupon he proceeds to follow the meaning of whiteness, tracking it down through all its associations in man's mind from time out of mind—as they appear in pageantry, story and ritual. Whiteness enhances beauty. It is associated with royalty and with royal preeminence, the same in kings and which, among peoples, gives "the white man ideal mastership over every dusky tribe." Whiteness is associated with gladness, with innocence, with the holy of holies. Yet, for all these associations, there is an ambiguity about whiteness; the same ambiguity that in the connotations of the sea seem to identify death with glory, bleached bones and desecration with spirituality. "Is it," Ishmael asks, "that by its indefiniteness it shadows forth the voids and immensities of the universe, and then stabs us from behind with the thought of annihilation, when beholding the white depths of the Milky Way? Or is it, that as in essence whiteness is not so much a colour as the visible absence of colour, and at the same time the concrete of all colours; is it for these reasons that there is such a dumb blankness, full of meaning, in a wide landscape of snows—a colourless, all-colour of atheism from which we shrink? And when we consider that other theory of the natural philosophers, that all other earthly hues—every stately or lovely emblazoning—the sweet tinges of sunset skies and woods; yea, and the gilded velvets of butterflies, and the butterfly cheeks of young girls; all these are but subtle deceits, not actually inherent in substances, but only laid on from without; so that all deified Nature absolutely paints like a harlot, whose allurements cover nothing but the charnel-house within; and when we proceed further, and consider that the mystical cosmetic which produces every one of her hues, the great principle of light, forever remains white or colourless in itself, and if operating without medium upon matter, would touch all objects, even tulips and roses, with its own blank tinge—pondering all this, the palsied universe lies before us a leper; and like wilful travellers in Lapland, who refuse to wear coloured and colouring glasses upon their eyes, so the wretched infidel gazes himself blind at the monumental white shroud that wraps all the prospect around him."

Under the spell of Ahab, yet going his own way, Ishmael catches sight or, better, has a "sensational presentiment" of the cleavage in creation which sprang up an active principle, in Ahab. Not "the time is out of joint" but the very underpinning of creation. "Oh, cursed spite,"—there lies the source "of all those malicious agencies which some deep men feel eating in them. . . . That intangible malignity which has been from the beginning. . . . All that maddens and torments . . . all truth with malice in it" and, "the instinct of the knowledge of the demonism in the world."

The horror of whiteness, is it the soul's fear of death, the fear of extinction after death? Yes, but it goes beyond that. It is more fearful because more intimate. It is the soul's fear of itself. For in its own conscious self lies the seed of its destruction. The preoccupation with truth, with ideality, with "ideal mastership," with "spiritual things," nay, with the Deity itself, which are of the conscious soul, these are of the light principle, which "great principle of light, forever remains white or colourless in itself." In the white light of the soul's preoccupation with truth all its earthly satisfactions seem illusory—all stale, flat and unprofitable. The vital needs of its own earth born humanity are but "coloured and colouring glasses." Refusing to wear these kindly glasses, the soul finds itself in a void. It sees everywhere, as was seen in the White Whale, when he faced the staggering *Pequod*, its own featurelessness, its own colorlessness.

Ishmael felt himself on the verge of the abyss which he saw outwardly in Ahab's lurid light. In that extremity he felt within himself the source of all the tormenting ambiguities of life. What is life to one side of the soul is death to the other, and death at last to both.

Strong as his attachment to Ahab is, Ishmael is open to contrary influences. He is reluctant to share a bed with Queequeg at the inn at New Bedford, but the next morning brings a change. Ishmael is glad to accept Queequeg's offer of friendship and they share a pipe over it. Then Queequeg, according to the custom in his country, makes him a gift of half his possessions in silver and tobacco. Ishmael feels himself restored. He is in the position that Ahab is in, much later, with Pip. Ishmael, however, goes the full length of his more kindly emotions; "I began to be sensible of strange feelings. I felt a melting in me. No more my splintered heart and maddened hand were turned against the wolfish world. This soothing savage had redeemed it."

While Ahab's hunt for the hated White Whale gets hotter, Ishmael's land sense struggles to preserve itself. Whereas Ahab curses "that mortal inter-indebtedness" which makes a man dependent on his fellows, Ishmael submits to the fact that it is "a mutual, joint-stock world, in all meridians." Two thirds of the way through the book comes the chapter, "A Squeeze of the Hand." Ishmael describes the operation of squeezing down lumps of sperm into a delicious aromatic milk. The work is done in tubs, and since many hands are at work in each tub, they often squeeze each other by mistake. "Squeeze! squeeze! squeeze!" cries Ishmael, himself melting down again. "I declare to you, that for the time I lived as in a musky meadow; I forgot all about our horrible oath. . . . I felt divinely free from all ill-will, or petulance, or malice, of any sort whatsoever. . . . Would that I could keep squeezing that sperm forever! For now, since by many prolonged, repeated experiences, I have perceived that in all cases man must eventually lower, or at least shift, his conceit of attainable felicity; not placing it anywhere in the intellect or the fancy; but in the wife, the heart, the bed, the table, the saddle, the fireside, the country; now that I have perceived all this, I am ready to squeeze case eternally."

In the next chapter but one Ishmael's drama reaches its climax. It is night and he is taking his turn at the helm. The rest of the crew are employed in boiling blubber and have gathered around two vast cauldrons under which fires have been kindled. From his place in the stern Ishmael looks on, while "the wind howled on, and the sea leaped, and the ship groaned and dived, and yet steadfastly shot her red hell further and further into the blackness . . . ." While he was watching it came over Ishmael that "the rushing *Pequod*, freighted with savages, and laden with fire . . . and plunging into that blackness of darkness, seemed the material counterpart of her monomaniac commander's soul." Then something happens. There just fails of being a fiery welding between his soul and Ahab's. He is conscious that something is very wrong. He cannot see the compass. There is nothing in front of him but a pit of gloom, "now and then made ghastly by flashes of redness. Uppermost was the impression, that whatever swift, rushing thing I stood on was not so much bound to any haven ahead as rushing from all havens astern. A stark, bewildered feeling, as of death, came over me.... My God! what is the matter with me? thought I. Lo! in my brief sleep I had turned myself about.... In an instant I faced back, just in time to prevent the vessel from flying up into the wind, and very probably capsizing her. How glad and how grateful the relief from this unnatural hallucination of the night, and the fatal contingency of being brought by the lee!"

"Look not too long in the face of the fire, O man!" Fire is idiosyncratic. It has a capricious, distorting intensity. It is the light of personal feelings, that take the universal sorrow of life as personal grievance, and reason for personal rage. And "that way madness lies." "There is a wisdom that is woe; but there is a woe that is madness. And there is a Catskill eagle in some souls that can alike dive down into the blackest gorges, and soar out of them again and become invisible in the sunny spaces."

The freedom of spirit, alike to plunge and to soar. Here we come upon the significance of Ishmael's escape in the coffin life-preserver, which is more directly rendered when Ishmael, or rather Melville, taking a suggestion from the vapour that hangs about a whale's head "as you will sometimes see it—glorified by a rainbow, as if heaven itself had put its seal upon his thoughts"—writes, "And so through all the thick mists of the dim doubts in my mind, divine intuitions now and then shoot, enkindling my fog with a heavenly ray. And for this I thank God; for all have doubts; many deny; but doubts or denials, few along with them have intuitions. Doubts of all things earthly, and intuitions of some things heavenly; this combination makes neither believer nor infidel, but makes a man who regards them both with equal eye."

THE ODYSSEY
(HOMER)

"The Man of Many Turns"
by Albert Cook,
in *The Classic Line: A Study in Epic Poetry* (1966)

INTRODUCTION

In "The Man of Many Turns," Albert Cook discusses Odysseus' character in relation to the chaotic events that befall him on his journey homeward. Cook asserts Odysseus' complexity lies in the "varieties of experience" he recounts. From this perspective, Odysseus' heroism, adaptability, and intelligence determine his fate; his journey tests his skills and enables him to fulfill his destiny. Thus, the many turns Odysseus navigates reflect the many sides of his character.

Homer managed the complexity of the *Iliad* by coordinating an entire society at war. This achievement was unique, and since it was, it could not serve him for a poem which presents a like complexity in the sequential experience of a single hero.

Achilles stands at the center of the *Iliad*, but his world measures him. Odysseus, however, measures his world as he moves through it.

Cook, Albert. "The Man of Many Turns." *The Classic Line: A Study in Epic Poetry.* Bloomington, Ind.: Indiana University Press, 1966. 120–137.

And it does not alter him; he remains the same from first to last, not only in the actual time span of the poem, but also, essentially, over the twenty years of his wanderings.

In his dominance of the action he resembles Beowulf, Roland, and the Cid. But their experience is also single, while Odysseus goes through varieties of experiences that intimately mirror his complexity while testing his mind and emotions. In its characteristically light and subtle way, the *Odyssey* exhibits a hero whose experience is internalized; whose psyche is plumbed. So the heroes of the best epic poems after Homer—Aeneas, Dante, Adam—resemble Odysseus more closely than they do Achilles. And Pound has taken Odysseus in *The Cantos* for the persona most fit to mirror his varieties of experience.

The actual fable (*logos*) of the *Odyssey* is short, as Aristotle points out. And yet the poem is complexly interwoven (*peplegmenon*). This is because we have recognition (*anagnorisis*) throughout, he says, and this simple term serves as well as any other to describe Homer's mediation between his single hero and the hero's manifold experience.

The poem insists on this singleness, and this complexity, in its very first line:

Andra moi ennepe, Mousa, polutropon, os mala polla

Tell me, Muse, about the man of many turns, who many . . .

Man, the first word. Complexity is named twice, in *polutropon*, "of many turns," and also in *polla*, "many."

Odysseus' situation deepens in time, and the situation of the poem deepens as it progresses; yet Odysseus' adequacy remains everywhere the same in all its aspects (*polutropos*). Only by a kind of alteration of the substance of the poem can we accept Cedric Whitman's reading of a developing self for Odysseus. His wholeness appears from the beginning in the memory of friends and comrades about him, in the persistence of his return, in his adroitness at meeting the enigmas of societies so variable that beside them the forms of Proteus which Menelaus must master seem simple indeed.

Through all the "change" of the poem—the term is Whitman's—
Odysseus, by intelligence and striving (as the opening tells us) copes
consistently with minds and peoples:

> Tell me, Muse, about the man of many turns, who many
> Ways wandered when he had sacked Troy's holy citadel;
> He saw the cities of many men and he knew their thought.

The variations of scene in the *Odyssey* involve a progression
from the young to the mature (Telemachus to Odysseus), from the
old to the new (Ithaca to a Phaeacian present), from the single to
the complex (Nestor to Menelaus; Calypso to and through Circe),
from the hostile to the hospitable (Ciconians to Phaeacians), from
the natural to the fantastic (Ciconians to Hades, to the Oxen of the
Sun groaning on the roasting spits), from the known Troy far from
home to the remote Phaeacia whence Odysseus may soon sail for
Ithaca.

Underlying these progressions is the psyche of the hero, broad
because we have narrow ones (Nestor, Telemachus) for comparison.
And since everyone's experience is appropriate for his character, the
experience becomes a figure of the extent and complexity and subtlety
of his inner life.

Applying this principle of congruence between a man's self and
his destiny to the smaller characters, to the other peoples, we may
apply it *a fortiori* to Odysseus. In this principle lies the canon of unity
for the whole poem. Character in the *Iliad* is a given affirmation of
a man's stable situation. In the *Odyssey* the situation is in flux, which
means not that character changes, but that the flux of situation itself
is seen to rest obscurely on the predisposition of the person or persons
involved, character as fate.

The heroes return from war on voyages that are revelatory to us of
their very selves. The simple Nestor had a straight return, the proud
Agamemnon a disastrous one. The subtle and elegant Menelaus, a
slighter of the gods, finds a return which tests his subtlety. Prompted
by a nymph, he must first grapple with Proteus' sleepy noon disguises
on lonely Pharos; then sacrifice in Egypt to the gods. Far more various
are the wanderings of Odysseus, and consequently far more famous
is Odysseus himself. He is outstanding in all virtues (IV, 815: *pantoies*

aretesi kekasmenon).[1] And the fullness of his humanity is mirrored in his wanderings.

Telemachus, too, voyages to learn to become like his father, to overcome his excessive respect (*aidos*, III, 24). He already has too much of what Achilles had too little. As the disguised goddess of wisdom says to him:

> Few are the sons who are equal to their fathers;
> Most are worse, but few are better than their fathers.
> If you would not be a coward hereafter, and senseless,
> If the counsel of Odysseus has not forsaken you wholly,
> Your hope in that case is to bring these deeds to pass. (II, 276–280)

Telemachus passes over into his manhood; it is through him, as he moves into the present of the poem, that the narrative begins, evoking both memory and futurity in the longing for Odysseus, and also the dim sense that the father who has been gone so long may have come to his mortal end.

Telemachus, risking a voyage to learn the facts about his father, learns that no simple facts are forthcoming, because facts undergo the alteration of memory; the glorious Trojan war that Nestor tells about, in which he and Odysseus were equal counsellors, does not seem the exploit that subtle Helen and Menelaus remember, focusing as it does on the deceptions of the wooden horse.

How a man sees things depends on who he is; Intelligence is the presiding goddess. These gods are not objective, standing for the unknown-and-visible, as in the *Iliad*. They are clear in the *Odyssey*, and yet they too vary according to the observer, who is then himself objectively presented in the foreground of the poem. To Menelaus they are beings who must be propitiated. Nestor sees them as stubborn (III, 147), Helen as capable of great favor (IV, 220–222), the Phaeacians as always benign. At the same time this particular people takes the gods with sophisticated familiarity and humor, laughing at Demodocus' tale about Ares and Aphrodite; adultery occasions mirth for them—the very evil that Penelope has been avoiding for twenty years.

Character is fate: who a man is also determines how far he goes, how widely he is tested, what sort of a home he has made his own. In this

sense men get exactly what they deserve, a moral transparently presented
at the very outset in Zeus' speech to Athene and the other gods:

> Well now, how mortal men do accuse the gods!
> They say evils come from us, yet they themselves
> By their own recklessness get pains beyond their lot.

The Phaeacians are near to the gods (V, 35); they dwell far away
from other mortals, having been close to the challenging Cyclops.
Their location and their way of life are taken altogether for a total character that compasses Odysseus at this stage, but does not absorb him.

Each man is closed in the world of his own perceptions, and so is
each people. Each place visited is an episode for the variable Odysseus, as in a lesser way for his searching son. Nestor lives a simple life,
his boys doing his work for him. It is a comfortable life, too; there are
smooth stones before his palace. Beyond his imagination, overland
from his territory, lies the elegant court of Menelaus, come upon
characteristically in the midst of a wedding celebration. In that court
there is a dominance of ceremoniousness all but total. But neither of
Telemachus' hosts exhibits any trait so surprising as the near-super-
naturalism of the Phaeacians, who also marry their cousins; or the
out-and-out incest of the forever dining children of Aeolus.

Pain[2] befalls man, but the gods have taken pain away from the
Phaeacians. With pain, the gods have taken away the sort of wholeness exemplified, as always, by Odysseus, who lands naked and hungry
on *their* shore just before finally going home. Nestor can face pain in
nostalgia, but Menelaus can stand little pain. His "heart breaks," he
tells us, when he learns from Proteus that he must sail the relatively
little distance from Pharos to Egypt. And he has small patience for
combat, as his words imply:

> quick is the glut of cold lamentation. (IV, 103)

Helen passes to her guests a drink with a nepenthe in it, to make the
drinker so forget all his pain that:

> He would not shed a tear down his cheeks the whole day
> long,

Not if his mother and his father were both to die,
Not if right in front of him his brother or his dear son
Were slaughtered with bronze, and he saw it with his own eyes.
(IV, 224–7)

Through the formality of Helen and Menelaus there is felt a
certain coldness. And to Odysseus the Phaeacians display a childish
eagerness, for all their own elegance. Menelaus has the servants bathe
Telemachus, a task Nestor assigned to his own daughter. Anxious
about their cleanliness, Menelaus orders the bath as soon as they
arrive; Nestor has had it done as a send-off. Such coldness, in this
poem of heartfelt pain and joy, may evidence cruelty. Menelaus
mentions casually that if Odysseus should care to settle nearby, he
would gladly sack and depopulate a city for his old friend.

Each character, of place and society, becomes objectified in
the comparing eye of the visitor; Telemachus, like his father, can
compass the varieties by encountering them. Home is the norm, and
Ithaca—unlike Aeaea or Ogygia or Phaeacia or Pylos or Argos—has
no special features other than the chaos into which it has fallen.

Odysseus discovers himself on his way home. The wideness of
the way, the wideness of the character destined for so much turning,
becomes apparent by comparison with the briefer ways of others, and
by the more circumscribed societies, each of which objectifies a whole
moral attitude and destiny: a character (*ethos*) of the sort Aristotle
asserted this poem to be woven from (*peplegmenon*).

Ithaca lacks the heightened felicity of Lacedaemon and Phaeacia, their ordered painlessness and easy delight. Subject to pain and
chaos, it is the more rooted in the human variety known and sought
by its absent overlord, and it stands waiting in memory, changing in
reality, for his rearrival. When he does arrive, his reinstitution must
be so deliberate as to take nearly half the poem. While Odysseus
wanders, Ithaca stands in unseen relation to him, though from the
beginning it is portrayed in its changed reality. Perpetually the poem
holds his biased and unswaying nostalgia in a comparison, often
unexpressed, between home and the place of sojourn. Explicitly he
declares that Calypso surpasses Penelope in appearance and form,
but such ideal excellence pales before the real rootedness of his
mortality. Telemachus, in refusing Menelaus' gift of horses, admits

that Ithaca affords poor pasturage; but he persists in his superlative praise of the island:

> In Ithaca there are no broad courses or any meadow;
> It has pasture for goats and is pleasanter than a horse pasture.
> But none of the islands that lie by the sea has good meadows
> Or a place for driving horses, and Ithaca surpasses them all.
> (IV, 605–8)

So he feels; and so does his father, enough to strain his ingenuity to return there.

This epic hero substitutes supple intelligence for the courage and prowess of the Cid, Beowulf, and Achilles. He follows not a code but the course of his own longing, an inner canon the poem sets out as equally to be trusted. Consistently, then, he does not gather all he knows in order to face the unknown. He acts on hunches (Lestrygonians) or social canniness (Phaeacia) or a surfaced feeling (Calypso) or luck (Circe) or improvised plan (Cyclops). In a sense there is nothing he can rely on as known, because he always copes with a wholly new situation in utter ignorance:

> For I have arrived here as a long suffering stranger
> From afar, from a distant land; so I know no one
> Of the men who conduct this city and its fields. (VII, 22–25)

He faces not the unknown but the new, not death but transience. Transience, itself a consequence of mortality and a kind of figure for it, replaces death in the imaginative vision of this epic. Longing for permanence drives the resourceful Odysseus round the changing seas and years.

Home itself changes, in the relentless metamorphosis of a third of a life-time. Permanence and change, satisfaction and longing, joy and pain, foresight and happenstance—these never get fixed in hard opposition because Odysseus moves too fast and copes too variously. His fable allows him to embody all these complexities without setting one stiffly against another; without overembroiling himself in any, and also without slighting the real difficulty or allure of a single one.

It is not death he must face. From the present time of the poem on, that risk is slight. In this epic, a life rounds itself out by return to an original mature circumstance that the very course of life has altered.

Change brings pain, and yet the joy of changelessness among the lotus eaters or the Phaeacians lacks the fullness of changeful life. Death may be taken as a fearful circumstance and at the same time as bland fact. The death of his mother Anticleia is spoken of matter-of-factly (XIII, 59) in a salutation wishing joy.

In the seeming universality of transience, arrival seems forever debarred, and Odysseus comes back a second time to Aeolus, who will not help him; to Circe, who greets him with a warning. Back again he comes, also, to Scylla and Charybdis. Death lies as a test in the future. Though the hero's own death is vague and remote, he must risk it and pass its country in order to return. Odysseus can get back only by visiting the dead, all the way past the eternally shrouded Cimmerians. Even then it takes the escort of the Phaeacians, who are near to gods, to get him back. The Phaeacian vessel, moving like a star, unerringly and effortlessly swift, bears Odysseus in a sleep "most like to death" (XIII, 879–92) to the home he has not been able to sight for twenty years.

Odysseus has changed so much himself, and Ithaca has become so remote to him, that he does not know where he is when he wakes up there. Of the disguised Athene he asks a question at once obvious and profound: are the inhabitants hospitable or wild?

All is old, and all is new. If Odysseus did not recognize old elements in any new situation, he could not exercise his many wiles. If he did not have to confront the new, there would be less need for any wiles at all.

The need dwindles at the end, but it has not disappeared. At the end of his life he must undertake another journey across the sea and set up a tomb to Poseidon among men who do not know the sea (IX, 120 ff).

Odysseus stands midway between the easier returners, achievers of a simpler permanence, Menelaus and Nestor, and those who have died on the return, the victims to change, Agamemnon and Ajax, not to mention all his own followers.

Permanence brings joy, transience pain. The living sustain a subtle balance between permanence and transience, and so between joy and pain. The sea is sparkling but treacherous; to the solitary Odysseus

Ogygia is joyful for its unearthly beauty but painful for its not being home. Pain coalesces with joy, or else a life is shown to lack the epic wholeness: if pain becomes total, one is to die; if joy fully dominates, one enters the lifeless permanence of the Lotus Eaters and the Phaeacians, whom Odysseus' long tale of suffering fills not with tears like his own but with a feeling of charm, the poem twice says (*kelethmos*: XI, 334; XIII, 2).

To return brings joy but causes pain. It is of the joy of return that Agamemnon speaks (IV, 522)—he who least of all would have cause to remember that joy. Yet the pain of becoming reinstated in a changed home offsets, precedes, and intensifies, the joy of restitution.

In his coping, Odysseus works his way through contrarieties; pain and suffering he names at once when he is asked what his wanderings have brought.

[. . .]

In all the alterings of circumstance, in all the pains, the hero's self remains wholly adequate in its adaptability (*polutropos*)—and without being defined. To take Odysseus' wanderings as deepening him, the way Cedric Whitman does, involves reading the significance of the places he visits as allegory or symbol. They do have the ring of archetype, and they do figure a total spiritual condition, each of them, mysteriously. Yet to read their significance as symbol or allegory is to pierce the veil of mystery. The depth is all on the surface, a sunlit mystery. No totality glides like a Moby Dick in the darkness beneath these waters. To interpret the surface of this poem metaphorically is to translate the surface as gaining significance from some depth; but the significances are all there on the surface, embodied simply in landscape and lightness of gesture.

Achilles develops and realizes his manhood. Odysseus moves ahead with his into time, changing only as he ages, while events at once tax and fortify him. He simply exists. No coordinated social world can deepen him; there is only the series of unpredictable surfaces, each complete and partial in itself, which he shows himself capable by meeting, and whole by transcending. Intelligence attends him from first to last, and the manifestation of Athene at his landing on Ithaca attests no special consideration, no final success, but only a momentary embodiment, as the world of his striving has actualized itself under his feet without his being aware of it.

When Odysseus speaks to himself, as he does after having set out from Ogygia (V, 299ff), the soliloquy explores no motive but merely develops and estimates the incidence of misfortune. Once again, it is all on the surface: the depth inheres in the irony with which it is presented, an irony so slight as to seem transparent, vanishing at a breath.

The irony may at numerous moments emerge into event. Odysseus slights Calypso in his account to Arete, falsifies his contact with Nausicaa, and delicately implies a refusal of Alcinous' marriage offer by mentioning in the course of his narrative how he has often refused such offers elsewhere. Menelaus, who had to wander years because he had slighted the gods, gives Telemachus a libation bowl! So, the poem hints, he has learned his lesson. Athene sacrifices to her enemy Poseidon. But the events need not be ironic; they may be deadly serious, and irony is still conveyed in the uniform tone of the verse.

Without the *poetry*, the flexible Odyssean hexameter, the humor would be episodic, and so would the nostalgia. The variety of incident would then merely add up to a superficial romance of the picaresque with some fine detail and occasional lyric moments, rather like the *Lusiads*. But in the *Odyssey* nostalgia comments on humor. Humor and nostalgia blend but do not fuse in the epic unity of this poem, lighter than the *Iliad*, but no less profound.

Suffering, even the dark terror of Cyclops or Odysseus' wholesale slaughter of the suitors, is kept serenely in vision, as it is not in even so equanimous a comedy as the *Tempest*. Only loosely can the *Odyssey* be called a comedy, or even a comic epic. It is an epic whose lightness compasses comic events, and also tragic; that allows of both tragic and comic events without inventing a whole philosophic relation for them (or a Dantesque justification) beyond the unitary tonal feeling of myth and verse.

NOTES

1. The plural here forbids our reading *arete* in anything like a Platonic sense.
2. George Dimoff finds pain the pervasive theme of the *Odyssey*, deriving Odysseus' name from the verb for suffering.

A PORTRAIT OF THE ARTIST AS A YOUNG MAN (JAMES JOYCE)

"On *A Portrait of the Artist as a Young Man*" by Dorothy Van Ghent, in *The English Novel: Form and Function* (1953)

INTRODUCTION

The hero of Joyce's book is Stephen Dedalus; we see his journey unfold from childhood into adulthood. At every turn, Stephen struggles with language and its potential to make meaning. Thus, he is a kind of epic hero whose journey unfolds in his would-be creation: the novel itself. While we never see Stephen write his book, the subjects he explores all hinge, as in Freudian psychology, on the use and understanding of words. In her landmark book *The English Novel: Form and Function*, Dorothy Van Ghent explores language as a primary theme in *A Portrait of the Artist as a Young Man*. Calling *Portrait*, like *Don Quixote*, "an extensive investigation of the creative effects of language," Van Ghent sees Stephen Dedalus as a heroic artist who insists "on the objectivity of the wholeness, harmony, and meaning, and on the objectivity of the revelation—the divine showing-forth." Stephen's epiphanies pull together disparate pieces of reality, creating a sense of wholeness. Thus, Stephen is

---

Van Ghent, Dorothy. "On *A Portrait of the Artist as a Young Man*." *The English Novel: Form and Function*. New York: Rinehart & Co., 1953. 263–76.

a kind of priest or prophet whose destiny lies in "naming the names." As one engaged in a kind of religious quest, Stephen imagines spiritual fulfillment as coming through words, the poem we see him write, the diary entries that end the book, and the way the young artist wields language as a weapon and as a tool with which to seek enlightenment.

༺༂༺

One of the oldest themes in the novel is that language is a creator of reality. There is this theme in *Don Quixote*. Quixote is supremely a man animated by "the word"; and as the words he has read in books send him into action—creating reality for him by determining what he sees and what he feels and what he does—so Quixote in turn has a similar effect upon other people, subtly changing their outlook, creating in them new forms of thought and activity. *Don Quixote* may be looked on as an extensive investigation of the creative effects of language upon life. Joyce's *Portrait* is also an investigation of this kind; appropriately so, for the "artist" whose youthful portrait the book is, is at the end to find his vocation in language; and the shape of reality that gradually defines itself for Stephen is a shape determined primarily by the associations of words. We follow in the circumstances of the boy's life the stages of breakdown and increasing confusion in his external environment, as his home goes to pieces, and the correlative stages of breakdown in his inherited values, as his church and his nation lose their authority over his emotions. Very early the child's mind begins to respond to that confusion by seeking in itself, in its own mental images, some unifying form or forms that will signify what the world *really* is, that will show him the *real* logic of things—a logic hopelessly obscure in external relations. His mental images are largely associations suggested by the words he hears, and in intense loneliness he struggles to make the associations fit into a coherent pattern.

To the very young child, adults seem to possess the secret of the whole, seem to know what everything means and how one thing is related to another. Apparently in command of that secret, they toss words together into esoteric compounds, some words whose referents the child knows and many whose referents are mysterious; and the context of the familiar words guides him in his speculation about the unfamiliar ones, the unfamiliar ones thus taking on their meaning for him in a wondrously accidental and chaotic fashion. These accidents of context, however bizarre, build up his notion of reality and deter- mine his later responses and the bias of his soul. There is the story that Stephen's father tells him about a cow coming down along a road. There is the song about the wild rose blossoming on the green place. He, Stephen, is evidently the "nicens little boy" toward whom the cow designs its path, and he, Stephen, can make the wild rose into a green one by a transposition of adjectives. The world's form, then, is apparently shaped toward him and out from him as its center. But how to put the story and the song intelligibly together, in a superior meaningful pattern of reality, with his father's hairy face looking at him through a glass? or with the queer smell of the oil sheet? or with Dante's two brushes? or with Eileen, the neighbor girl, who has a different father and mother? or with some shadowily guilty thing he has done for which he must "apologize," else eagles will pull out his eyes? In this extremely short sequence at the beginning of the book, the child's sense of insecurity, in a world whose form he cannot grasp, is established—and with insecurity, guilt (he must apologize) and fear (the horrible eagles). With these unpromising emotional elements established in him, the maturing child will try again and again to grasp his world imaginatively as a shape within which he has a part that is essential to its completeness and harmoniousness and meaningfulness.

Immediately there is a transition to the children's playground at Clongowes Wood, the child's earliest experience of a commu- nity other than that of the home. Again the auditory impression is predominant—sounds heard, words spoken—and the life-directed attempt of the young mind is to understand their meaning in rela- tion to each other and in relation to a governing design. There are the "strong cries" of the boys and the "thud" of their feet and bodies; then comes a quick succession of references to special oddnesses in the names of things. To the child's laboring apprehension, which assumes all names to have intimate and honest connections with reality, the name "dog-in-the-blanket" for the Friday pudding must represent something about the pudding which is real and which other people know but which is obscured from him; it may

have more than one meaning, like the word "belt," which means a
strap on a jacket and also "to give a fellow a belt"; or it may have
complex, mysterious, and terribly serious associations with destiny,
understood by others but dark and anxious to himself, like his own
name, Stephen Dedalus, which Nasty Roche says is "queer" with a
queerness that puts the social status of Stephen's father in doubt.
Through words the world comes to Stephen; through the words he
hears he gropes his way into other people's images of reality. Doubts
and anxieties arise because the words and phrases are disassociated,
their context frequently arbitrary, like that of the sentences in the
spelling book:

> Wolsey died in Leicester Abbey
> Where the abbots buried him.
> Canker is a disease of plants,
> Cancer one of animals. (249)

The sentences in the spelling book at least make a rhythm, and a
rhythm is a kind of pattern, a "whole" of sorts; they are therefore
"nice sentences" to think about. But the threatening, overwhelming
problem is the integration of all the vast heap of disassociated
impressions that the child's mind is subjected to and out of which
his hopeful urgency toward intelligibility forces him, entirely lonely
and without help, to try to make superior rhythms and superior
unities.

The technique of the "stream of consciousness," or "interior
monologue," as Joyce uses it, is a formal aspect of the book which
sensitively reflects the boy's extreme spiritual isolation. There is a
logical suitability in the fact that this type of technique should arise
at a time of cultural debacle, when society has failed to give objective validation to inherited structures of belief, and when therefore
all meanings, values, and sanctions have to be built up from scratch
in the loneliness of the individual mind. When an author assumes
the right to enter his novel in his own voice and comment on his
characters—as Fielding does or George Eliot does—we are able to
infer a cultural situation in which there are objective points of reference for the making of a judgment; the author and reader enter into
overt agreement, as it were, in criticizing and judging the character's

actions; and where there is this assumption of agreement, we are in a relatively secure social world. The "gregarious point of view" used by the older novelists reflects a world, comparatively speaking, of shared standards. As the technical point of view adopted by the novelist more and more tends to exclude the novelist's own expression of opinion from his book, the world which he represents tends more and more to be one whose values are in question; and we have, for instance, in the later work of Henry James, a work such as *The Ambassadors*, where the subjective point of view of the main character is dominant, a concentration on a process of mind in which values are reshifted and rejudged from top to bottom, all in the loneliness of an individual's personal experience. The technique of the "interior monologue" is a modification of the subjective point of view. It is not a departure from traditional convention, for even Fielding used this point of view when he wanted to show "from the inside" how a character's mind worked; but it is an employment of the subjective point of view throughout the entire novel—instead of sporadically, as in the older English novel—and it follows more devious and various paths of consciousness than traditional novelists were concerned with. Joyce's concern, in the *Portrait*, is with the associative patterns arising in Stephen's mind from infancy into adolescence. What we need to emphasize, however, is that he is concerned with these only as they show the dialectical process by which a world-shape evolves in the mind. The process is conducted in the absolute solitude of the inside of the skull, for Stephen has no trustworthy help from the objective environment. The technique of the interior monologue is the sensitive formal representation of that mental solitude.

"By thinking of things you could understand them," Stephen says to himself when he arrives at the conclusion that the epithet "Tower of Ivory," in the litany of the Blessed Virgin, means what Eileen's hand felt like in his pocket—like ivory, only soft—and the "House of Gold" means what her hair had looked like, streaming out behind her like gold in the sun (286). Shortly before, he has been puzzling over the fact that Dante does not wish him to play with Eileen because Eileen is a Protestant, and the Protestants "make fun of the litany of the Blessed Virgin," saying, "How could a woman be a tower of ivory or a house of gold?" (278). Who was right then,

the Protestants or the Catholics? Stephen's analytical quandary
is resolved by the perception of the identity between the feel of
Eileen's prying hand and the meaning of "Tower of Ivory." In the
same way, by the same dialectical process, his flooding impressions
reach a stage of cohesion from moment to moment, a temporary
synthesis in which he suddenly sees what they "mean." As Stephen
matures, there is mounted on the early association between the
Virgin and Eileen an identification between his dream—Mercedes
(ideal girl in a rose-cottage) and a whore. By extension, this association holds in it much of Stephen's struggle between other-worldli-
ness and this-worldliness, for it has identified in his imagination
flesh and spirit, while his intellect, developing under education,
rebels against the identification.[1] Thus "the word"—Tower of Ivory,
House of Gold—creates by accident and at random the reality of
suffering and act.

   Those moments in the dialectical process when a synthesis is
achieved, when certain phrases or sensations or complex experiences suddenly cohere in a larger whole and a meaning shines forth
from the whole, Joyce—who introduced the word into literary
currency—called "epiphanies." They are "showings-forth" of the
nature of reality as the boy is prepared to grasp it. Minor epiphanies
mark all the stages of Stephen's understanding, as when the feel of
Eileen's hand shows him what Tower of Ivory means, or as when the
word "Foetus," carved on a school desk (339), suddenly focuses for
him in brute clarity his "monstrous way of life." Major epiphanies,
occurring at the end of each chapter, mark the chief revelations of
the nature of his environment and of his destiny in it. The epiphany
is an image, sensuously apprehended and emotionally vibrant, which
communicates instantaneously the meaning of experience. It may
contain a revelation of a person's character, brief and fleeting, occurring by virtue of some physical trait in the person, as the way big
Corrigan looked in the bath: "He had skin the same colour as the
turf-coloured bogwater in the shallow end of the bath and when he
walked along the side his feet slapped loudly on the wet tiles and
at every step his thighs shook a little because he was fat" (299). In
this kind of use, as revelation through one or two physical traits of
the whole mass-formation of a personality, the epiphany is almost
precisely duplicable in Dickens, as in the spectacle of Miss Havisham

leaning on her crutch beside the rotten bridecake, or of Jaggers flourishing his white handkerchief and biting his great forefinger. The minor personalities in the *Portrait* are reduced to something very like a Dickensian "signature"—as Heron with his bird-beaked face and bird-name, Davin with his peasant turns of speech, Lynch whose "long slender flattened skull beneath the long pointed cap brought before Stephen's mind the image of a hooded reptile" (470). Or the epiphany may be a kind of "still life" with which are associated deep and complex layers of experience and emotion. In the following passage, for instance, the sordor of Stephen's home, the apprehensive and guilty image of the bath at Clongowes, and the bestiality he associates with the bogholes of Ireland, are illuminated simultaneously by a jar of drippings on the table. "He drained his third cup of watery tea to the dregs and set to chewing the crusts of fried bread that were scattered near him, staring into the dark pool of the jar. The yellow dripping had been scooped out like a boghole, and the pool under it brought back to his memory the dark turf-coloured water of the bath at Conglowes" (434).

Here the whole complex of home, school, and nation is epitomized in one object and shot through with the emotion of rejection. The epiphany is usually the result of a gradual development of the emotional content of associations, as they accrete with others. Among Stephen's childish impressions is that of "a woman standing at the halfdoor of a cottage with a child in her arms," and "it would be lovely to sleep for one night in that cottage before the fire of smoking turf, in the dark lit by the fire, in the warm dark, breathing the smell of the peasants, air and rain and turf and corduroy . . ." (258). The early impression enters into emotional context later with the story Davin tells him about stopping at night at the cottage of a peasant woman, and Stephen's image of the woman is for him an epiphany of the soul of Ireland: "a batlike soul waking to the consciousness of itself in darkness and secrecy and loneliness" (444–445; 488). The epiphany is dynamic, activated by the form-seeking urgency in experience, and itself feeding later revelations. At the point of exile, Stephen feels, "under the deepened dusk, the thoughts and desires of the race to which he belonged flitting like bats, across the dark country lanes, under trees by the edges of streams and near the pool mottled bogs" (508).

The major epiphanies in the book occur as the symbolic climaxes of the larger dialectical movements constituting each of the five chapters. As Hugh Kenner has pointed out, in his essay "The Portrait in Perspective,"[2] each of the chapters begins with a multitude of warring impressions, and each develops toward an emotionally apprehended unity; each succeeding chapter liquidates the previous synthesis and subjects its elements to more adult scrutiny in a constantly enlarging field of perception, and develops toward its own synthesis and affirmation. In each chapter, out of the multitude of elements with which it opens, some one chief conflict slowly shapes itself. In the first, among all the bewildering impressions that the child's mind entertains, the deeper conflict is that between his implicit trust in the authority of his elders—his Jesuit teachers, the older boys in the school, his father and Mr. Casey and Dante—and his actual sense of insecurity. His elders, since they apparently know the meaning of things, must therefore incarnate perfect justice and moral and intellectual consistency. But the child's real experience is of mad quarrels at home over Parnell and the priests, and at school the frivolous cruelty of the boys, the moral chaos suggested by the smugging in the square and the talk about stealing the altar wine, and the sadism of Father Dolan with his pandybat. With Stephen's visit to the rector at the end of the chapter, the conflict is resolved. Justice is triumphant—even a small boy with weak eyes can find it; he is greeted like a hero on his emergence from the rector's office; his consolidation with his human environment is gloriously affirmed.

The second chapter moves straight from that achievement of emotional unity into other baffling complexities, coincident with the family's removal to Dublin. The home life is increasingly squalid, the boy more lonely and restless. In Simon Dedalus' account of his conversation with the rector of Clongowes about the incident of the pandying, what had seemed, earlier, to be a triumph of justice and an affirmation of intelligent moral authority by Stephen's elders is revealed as cruel, stupid indifference. In the episode in which Stephen is beaten for "heresy," the immediate community of his schoolfellows shows itself as false, shot through with stupidity and sadism. More importantly, the image of the father is corroded. On the visit to Cork, Simon appears to the boy's despairing judgement as besotted, self-deluded, irresponsible—and with the corruption of the father-image his whole picture of society suffers the same ugly damage. On the same visit, Stephen's early dim apprehension of sin and guilt is raised into horrible prominence by the word "Foetus" which he sees inscribed on the desk at Queen's College and which symbolizes for him all his adolescent monstrosity (the more monstrous in that Simon looks with obscene sentimentality on the desk carvings, thus condemning the whole world for Stephen in his own sickened sense of guilt). Meanwhile, his idealistic longings for beauty and purity and gentleness and certitude have concentrated in a vaguely erotic fantasy of the dream-girl Mercedes in her rose-cottage. Again, at the end of the chapter, Stephen's inner conflict is resolved in an emotional unity, a new vision of the relationships between the elements of experience. The synthesis is constituted here by a triumphant integration of the dream of Mercedes with the encounter with the whore. It is "sin" that triumphs, but sublimated as an ideal unity, pure and gentle and beautiful and emotionally securing.

As Hugh Kenner has observed, in the essay cited above, the predominant physical activity in the *Portrait* that accompanies Stephen's mental dialectics, as he moves through analysis to new provisional syntheses, is the activity of walking; his ambulatory movements take him into new localities, among new impressions, as his mind moves correspondingly into new spiritual localities that subsume the older ones and readjust them as parts of a larger whole. Living in Dublin, his walks take him toward the river and the sea— toward the fluid thing that, like the "stream" of his thoughts, seems by its searching mobility to imply a more engrossing reality. At first, in Dublin, the boy

> contented himself with circling timidly round the neighbouring square or, at most, going half way down one of the side streets; but when he had made a skeleton map of the city in his mind he followed boldly one of its central lines until he reached the Custom House. . . . The vastness and strangeness of the life suggested to him by the bales of merchandise stocked along the walls or swung aloft out of the holds of steamers wakened again in him the unrest which had sent him wandering in the evening from garden

> to garden in search of Mercedes . . . . A vague dissatisfaction
> grew up within him as he looked on the quays and on the
> river and on the lowering skies and yet he continued to
> wander up and down day after day as if he really sought
> someone that eluded him. (312–313)

On his visit to Cork with his father, in his wanderings in the
brothel section of Dublin, on his seaward walk at the end of the
fourth chapter when his chief revelation of personal destiny comes to
him, on his later walks between home and the university, on his walk
with Lynch during which he recapitulates his aesthetics, and with
Cranly when he formulates his decision not "to serve"—on each of
these peripatetic excursions, his mind moves toward more valid orga-
nizations of experience, as his feet carry him among other voices and
images and into more complex fields of perception.

In the third chapter of the book, the hortations to which he is
exposed during the retreat pull him down from his exaltation in sin
and analyze his spiritual state into a multitude of subjective horrors
that threaten to engulf him entirely and jeopardize his immortal soul.
The conflict is resolved during a long walk which he takes blindly
and alone, and that carries him to a strange place where he feels
able to make his confession. A new synthesis is achieved through his
participation in the Mass. Chapter 4 shows him absorbed in a dream
of a saintly career, but his previous emotional affirmation has been
frittered and wasted away in the performance of pedantically formal
acts of piety, and he is afflicted with doubts, insecurities, rebellions.
Release from conflict comes with a clear refusal of a vocation in the
church, objectified by his decision to enter the university. And again
it is on a walk that he realizes the measure of the new reality and the
new destiny.

He has abandoned his father to a public house and has set off
toward the river and the sea.

> The university! So he had passed beyond the challenge of the
> sentries who had stood as guardians of his boyhood and had
> sought to keep him among them that he might be subject to
> them and serve their ends. Pride after satisfaction uplifted
> him like long slow waves. The end he had been born to serve

yet did not see had led him to escape by an unseen path; and
now it beckoned to him once more and a new adventure was
about to be opened to him. It seemed to him that he heard
notes of fitful music leaping upwards a tone and downwards
a diminishing fourth, upwards a tone and downwards a major
third, like triple-branching flames leaping fitfully, flame
after flame, out of a midnight wood. It was an elfin prelude,
endless and formless; and, as it grew wilder and faster, the
flames leaping out of time, he seemed to hear from under the
boughs and grasses wild creatures racing, their feet pattering
like rain upon the leaves. Their feet passed in pattering tumult
over his mind, the feet of hares and rabbits, the feet of harts
and hinds and antelopes, until he heard them no more and
remembered only a proud cadence from Newman: "Whose
feet are as the feet of harts and underneath the everlasting
arms." (424–425)

The imagery is that of mobile, going things, increasingly passionate
and swift—first slow waves, then fitful music leaping, then flames, then
racing creatures. A phrase of his own making comes to his lips: "A day
of dappled seaborne clouds." The dappled color and the sea movement
of the clouds are of the same emotional birth as the images of music
and flames. All are of variety and mobility of perception, as against
stasis and restriction. Physically Stephen is escaping from his father—
and the public house where he has left Simon is the sordid core of that
Dublin environment whose false claims on his allegiance he is trying
to shake off; at the same time he is realizing a "first noiseless sundering"
with his mother, a break that is related to his decision against accepting
a vocation in the church. Dublin, the tangible and vocal essence of his
nationality, and the Roman Church, the mold of his adolescent intellect,
have failed to provide him with a vision of reality corresponding with
his experience, and he thinks in terms of a movement beyond these—
toward another and mysterious possible synthesis. "And underneath the
everlasting arms": the phrase from Newman implies an ultimate unity
wherein all the real is held in wholeness. Toward this problematic divine
embrace Stephen moves, but it is only problematic and he can approach
it only by his own movement. The epiphany which confronts him in
this moment on the beach is a manifestation of his destiny in terms of

a winged movement. He hears his name, Dedalus, called out, and the name seems to be prophetic.

> ...at the name of the fabulous artificer, he seemed to hear the noise of dim waves and to see a winged form flying above the waves and slowly climbing the air...a hawklike man flying sunward above the sea, a prophecy of the end he had been born to serve and had been following through the mists of childhood and boyhood, a symbol of the artist forging anew in his workshop out of the sluggish matter of the earth a new soaring impalpable imperishable being.... (429)

The ending of Chapter 4 presents this new consciousness in terms of an ecstatic state of sensibility. It is marked by the radiant image of the girl standing in a rivulet of tide, seeming "like one whom magic had changed into the likeness of a strange and beautiful seabird ... touched with the wonder of mortal beauty" (431–432), while his own life cries wildly to him, "To live, to err, to fall, to triumph, to recreate life out of life!" (432) The girl is a "wild angel" that has appeared to him, to "throw open before him in an instant of ecstasy the ways of error and glory." The batlike woman-soul of his race, flitting in darkness and secrecy and loneliness, has given place to this angelic emissary from "the fair courts of life," of strange seabird beauty, inviting him to exile across waters and into other languages, as the sun-assailing and perhaps doomed Icarus. And it is in the flights of birds that Stephen, standing on the steps of the university library, in the last chapter, reads like an ancient haruspex the sanction of his exile.

With Chapter 5, Stephen's new consciousness of destiny is subjected to intellectual analysis. Here, during his long walks with Lynch and Cranly, all the major elements that have exerted emotional claims upon him—his family, church, nation, language—are scrutinized dryly, their claims torn down and scattered in the youthfully pedantic and cruel light of the adolescent's proud commitment to art. Here also he formulates his aesthetics, the synthesis which he has contrived out of a few scraps of medieval learning. In his aesthetic formulation, the names he borrows from Aquinas for "the three things needed for beauty"—*integritas, consonantia, claritas*—are names for those aspects of reality—wholeness, harmoniousness, significant character—that he has been seeking all his life, from earliest childhood. His aesthetic formulation is thus a synthesis of the motivations of his psychological life from the beginning; and the vocation of artist which he has chosen is the vocation of one who consciously sets himself the task of apprehending and then representing in his art whatever wholeness, harmony, and meaning the world has.

In an earlier version of the *Portrait*, called *Stephen Hero*, it is said that the task of the artist is to "disentangle the subtle soul of the image from its mesh of defining circumstances most exactly and 're-embody' it in artistic circumstances chosen as the most exact for it in its new office . . ." (*SH*, 78).

The "new office" of the image is to communicate to others the significant character of a complete and harmonious body of experience. The artist is a midwife of epiphanies. Joyce's doctrine of the epiphany assumes that reality does have wholeness and harmony— even as Stephen as a child premises these, and with the same trustfulness—and that it will radiantly show forth its character and its meaning to the prepared consciousness, for it is only in the body of reality that meaning can occur and only there that the artist can find it. This is essentially a religious interpretation of the nature of reality and of the artist's function. It insists on the objectivity of the wholeness, harmony, and meaning, and on the objectivity of the revelation—the divine showing-forth.

At Clongowes Wood, there had been a picture of the earth on the first page of Stephen's geography, "a big ball in the middle of clouds," and on the flyleaf of the book Stephen had written his name and "where he was."

> Stephen Dedalus
> Class of Elements
> Clongowes Wood College
> Sallins
> County Kildare
> Ireland
> Europe

The World
The Universe (255)

His ambulatory, dialectical journey is a quest to find the defining unity, the composing harmony, and the significant character of each of these broadening localities containing Stephen Dedalus, and the intelligible relationships making each functional in the next. It is an attempt, by progressive stages, at last to bring the term "Stephen Dedalus" into relationship with the term "The Universe." Through the book he moves from one geographical and spiritual orbit to another, "walking" in lengthening radius until he is ready to take up flight. As a child at Clongowes it had pained him that he did not know what came after the universe.

> What was after the universe? Nothing. But was there anything round the universe to show where it stopped before the nothing place began? It could not be a wall but there could be a thin thin line there all round everything. It was very big to think about everything and everywhere. Only God could do that. He tried to think what a big thought that must be but he could think only of God. God was God's name just as his name was Stephen. *Dieu* was the French for God and that was God's name too; and when anyone prayed to God and said Dieu then God knew at once that was a French person that was praying. But though there were different names for God in all the different languages in the world and God understood what all the people who prayed said in their different languages still God remained always the same God and God's real name was God. (255–256)

At the end of the book Stephen is prepared at least to set forth on the "dappled, seaborne clouds" (426) that float beyond Ireland and over Europe. His search is still to find out "what came after the universe." The ultimate epiphany is withheld, the epiphany of "everything and everywhere" as one and harmonious and meaningful. But it is prophesied in "God's real name," as Stephen's personal destiny is prophesied in his own name "Dedalus." It is to be found in the labyrinth of language that contains all human revelation vouchsafed by divine economy, and to be found by the artist in naming the names.

NOTES

1. Irene Hendry points this out in her admirable essay "Joyce's Epiphanies," in *James Joyce: Two Decades of Criticism*, Seon Givens, ed. (New York: Vanguard Press, 1948).
2. *Ibid.*

PRIDE AND PREJUDICE
(JANE AUSTEN)

"Pride and Prejudice:
Jane Austen's 'Patrician Hero'"
by Kenneth L. Moler,
in *Studies in English Literature,*
1500–1900 (1967)

INTRODUCTION

In ancient Rome, the patrician class consisted of wealthy, elite families. In the English-speaking world, we tend to use the word *patrician* to indicate a member of the upper class who has most often inherited wealth and is, from the perspective of the common person, an elitist. Yet, although we tend to see such people as elitist, we also tend to expect them to use their wealth, power, and prestige to do socially responsible things. In *"Pride and Prejudice*: Jane Austen's 'Patrician Hero,'" Kenneth L. Moler focuses on "Jane Austen's rather unusual treatment of a popular eighteenth-century character-type"—the "patrician hero"—as "represented in the novels of Richardson and Fanny Burney." By "unusual," Moler refers to the way Austen parodies this character type in the first half of

---

Kenneth L. Moler. "*Pride and Prejudice:* Jane Austen's 'Patrician Hero.'" *Studies in English Literature, 1500–1900*, Vol. 7, No. 3, Restoration and Eighteenth Century. (Summer 1967), 491–508.

the novel, only to justify this character's (Mr. Darcy's) existence later in the novel, the result of his growth and his (and our) ability to change. Additionally, Moler shows us how this derivative character type helps to understand the theme of "art vs. nature" in Jane Austen and other 19th-century authors' works. According to Moler, the patrician hero is part of a symbolic relationship that encompasses the antithesis between "art" and "nature." Darcy and Elizabeth form such a relationship, a dramatic union in which "two complex, sensitive and often blindly wrong-headed 'intricate characters' . . . progress toward a better understanding of one another, the world, and themselves." Thus, the heroic journey the two undertake is a testimony to our ultimate mutability, our ability to understand more about each other, and our ability to change.

❧

It is generally agreed that *Pride and Prejudice* deals with a variant of the "art-nature" theme with which *Sense and Sensibility* is concerned. *Sense and Sensibility* primarily treats the opposition between the head and the heart, between feeling and reason; in *Pride and Prejudice* Elizabeth Bennet's forceful and engaging individualism is pitted against Darcy's not indefensible respect for the social order and his class pride. Most critics agree that *Pride and Prejudice* does not suffer from the appearance of one-sidedness that makes *Sense and Sensibility* unattractive. Obviously neither Elizabeth nor Darcy embodies the novel's moral norm. Each is admirable in his way, and each must have his pride and prejudice corrected by self-knowledge and come to a fuller appreciation of the other's temperament and beliefs. Ultimately their conflicting points of view are adjusted, and each achieves a mean between "nature" and "art." Elizabeth gains some appreciation of Darcy's sound qualities and comes to see the validity of class relationships. Darcy, under Elizabeth's influence, gains in naturalness and learns to respect the innate dignity of the individual.[1]

One of the few features of *Pride and Prejudice* to which exception has been taken is Jane Austen's treatment of the character of her Mr. Darcy. It is said that the transition between the arrogant young man of the early chapters of the novel and the polite gentleman whom Elizabeth Bennet marries is too great and too abrupt to be completely credible.[2] Reuben A. Brower and Howard S. Babb have vindicated Jane Austen to some extent, showing that much of Darcy's early conversation can be interpreted in various ways, and that our reactions to him are often conditioned by the fact that we see him largely through the eyes of the prejudiced Elizabeth.[3] Still there remain grounds for objection to Jane Austen's handling of Darcy. His remark about Elizabeth at the Meryton assembly is almost unbelievably boorish, and we have no reason to believe that Elizabeth has misunderstood it. We hear with our own ears his fears lest he should be encouraging Elizabeth to fall in love with him, and the objectionable language of his first proposal. Such things remain stumbling blocks to our acceptance of Darcy's speedy reformation.

This essay is concerned with Jane Austen's rather unusual treatment of a popular eighteenth-century character-type and situation. Mr. Darcy bears a marked resemblance to what I shall call the "patrician hero," a character-type best known as represented in the novels of Richardson and Fanny Burney; and it is rewarding to investigate the relationship between Darcy and his love affair with Elizabeth Bennet and the heroes of Richardson's and Fanny Burney's novels and their relations with their heroines. Jane Austen's treatment of her patrician hero has a marked relevance to the theme of the reconciliation of opposites that plays such an important part in *Pride and Prejudice*. And a study of Darcy's possible origins helps to account for those flaws in his character for which Jane Austen has been criticized.

[. . .]

Jane Austen must have been as much amused by the all-conquering heroes and too humble heroines of the day as many other readers have been, for in the juvenile sketch entitled "Jack and Alice" she reduces the patrician hero to absurdity with gusto. Charles Adams, in that sketch, is the most exaggerated "picture of perfection" conceivable. He is incredibly handsome, a man "of so dazzling a Beauty that none but Eagles could look him in the Face."[4] (The continual references in "Jack and Alice" to the brilliance of Charles's countenance are probably specific allusions to *Sir Charles Grandison*: Richardson repeatedly describes Sir Charles in similar language.[5])

But the beauties of Charles's person are nothing to those of his mind.
As he tells us himself:

> I imagine my Manners & Address to be of the most polished
> kind; there is a certain elegance, a peculiar sweetness in them
> that I never saw equalled. . . . I am certainly more accomplished
> in every Language, every Science, every Art and every thing
> than any other person in Europe. My temper is even, my
> virtues innumerable, my self unparalleled. (VI.25)

The superciliousness and conceit that readers cannot help attrib-
uting to Sir Charles Grandison or Orville becomes the very essence of
Charles Adams's being. The kind of praise that Richardson and Fanny
Burney heap on their heroes is most liberally bestowed by Charles on
himself. And just as Charles is a burlesque version of the too perfect
Burney-Richardson hero, so he is provided with two heroines who are
ten times more inferior, and twenty times more devoted to him than
Evelina and Harriet Byron are to their heroes. Charles is the owner
of the "principal estate" in the neighborhood in which the lovely Lucy
lives, and Lucy adores him. She is the daughter of a tailor and the
niece of an alehouse-keeper, and she is fearful that Charles may think
her "deficient in Rank, & in being so, unworthy of his hand" (VI.21).
Screwing up her courage, however, she proposes marriage to him.
But to her sorrow, she receives "an angry & peremptory refusal" from
the unapproachable young man (VI.21). Alice Johnson, the titular
heroine of the novel, is also infatuated with Charles. Although, like
the rest of her family, Alice is "a little addicted to the Bottle & the
Dice," she hopes, after she has inherited a considerable estate, to be
found worthy of Charles. But when Alice's father proposes the match
to him, Charles declares that she is neither "sufficiently beautifull,
sufficiently amiable, sufficiently witty, nor sufficiently rich for me—."
"I expect," he says, "nothing more in my wife than my wife will find in
me—Perfection" (VI.25–26). Fortunately, Alice is able to find consolation in her bottle. "Jack and Alice," I believe, was not Jane Austen's
only attack on the patrician hero. There is a good deal of Charles
Adams in her Mr. Darcy.

Darcy's actual circumstances are not an exaggeration of those of
the patrician hero, as Charles Adams's are. In fact Jane Austen seems

at times to be uncritically borrowing the popular Burney-Richardson character type and situation in *Pride and Prejudice*—altering them, if at all, only by toning them down a bit. Mr. Darcy is not the picture of perfection that Sir Charles Grandison is, but he shares many of the advantages of Sir Charles and Lord Orville. He has, for instance, a "fine, tall person, handsome features, noble mien . . . and ten thousand a year" (II.10). He has mental powers that command respect. He is not as powerful and important as Sir Charles Grandison, but he is the owner of a large estate and a giver, and withholder, of clerical livings. He marries a woman who, like Evelina, is embarrassed by the inferiority of some of her nearest connections, although even Mrs. Bennet can scarcely approach the supreme vulgarity of Madame Duval.

But Darcy is a Charles Adams in spirit, if not in circumstances. It is his exaggerated conception of the importance of his advantages, his supercilious determination "to think well of myself, and meanly of others" who are not so fortunate that causes him at times to sound very much like a caricature of the Burney-Richardson hero. He may not expect to have to address "an angry & peremptory refusal" to a fawning, lovelorn Elizabeth Bennet; but during Elizabeth's visit at Netherfield he is anxious lest, by devoting so much of his conversation to her, he may have been encouraging her to hope for the honor of his hand. On the eve of her departure from Netherfield, we are told: "He wisely resolved to be particularly careful that no sign of admiration should now escape him, nothing that could elevate her with the hope of influencing his felicity. . . . Steady to his purpose, he scarcely spoke ten words to her through the whole of Saturday" (II.60). The idea of a proposal which is humiliating to a heroine may come from Cecilia. But the language of Darcy's first proposal to Elizabeth sounds like something that might have come from Charles Adams's lips, rather than the gallant, ardent language of a Delvile. During Darcy's proposal, we are told that "his sense of her inferiority" was "dwelt on with a warmth which seemed due to the consequence he was wounding, but was very unlikely to recommend his suit" (II.189). And when Elizabeth rebukes him, he declares that he is not "ashamed of the feelings I related. . . . Could you expect me to rejoice in the inferiority of your connections? To congratulate myself on the hope of relations, whose condition in life is so decidedly beneath my own?" (II.192).

On two occasions, I believe, Darcy is specifically a caricature of Fanny Burney's Lord Orville. The scene at the Meryton assembly in which Darcy makes rude remarks about Elizabeth Bennet is a burlesque of Orville's unfavorable first impression of Evelina.[6] In *Evelina*, shortly after Orville and Evelina have had their first dance together, there is a conversation between Orville and Sir Clement Willoughby on the subject of Evelina's merits. Sir Clement says to Orville:

> "Why, my Lord, what have you done with your lovely partner?"
>
> "*Nothing!*" answered Lord Orville, with a smile and a shrug.
>
> "By Jove," cried the man, "she is the most beautiful creature I ever saw in my life!"
>
> Lord Orville … laughed, but answered, "Yes; a pretty modest-looking girl."
>
> "O my Lord!" cried the madman, "she is an angel!"
>
> "A *silent* one," returned he.
>
> "Why ay, my Lord, how stands she as to that? She looks all intelligence and expression."
>
> "A poor weak girl!" answered Lord Orville, shaking his head. (I, Letter XII, p. 42)

In Darcy's remarks about Elizabeth at the Meryton assembly, Orville's gentle mockery becomes supercilious rudeness. Mr. Bingley sounds Darcy on the merits of the various ladies at the assembly, hoping to persuade his friend to dance. Like Sir Clement Willoughby, Bingley praises the heroine: Elizabeth, he declares, is "very pretty, and I dare say, very agreeable"; and he proposes that Darcy ask her to dance. Darcy replies that Elizabeth is "tolerable; but not handsome enough to tempt *me;* and I am in no humour at present to give consequence to young ladies who are slighted by other men" (II.12).

And another ballroom scene in *Evelina* is burlesqued in *Pride and Prejudice*. At one point in *Evelina* Sir Clement Willoughby, who is determined to punish the heroine for pretending that Lord Orville is to be her partner in a dance for which Sir Clement wished to engage her, conducts her to Lord Orville and presents him with her hand.

[. . . Similarly,] Darcy, "all politeness," as Elizabeth ironically describes him, signifies his willingness to oblige Elizabeth Bennet with a dance when Elizabeth is placed in a similarly embarrassing situation at Sir William Lucas's ball.[7]

[. . .]

Mr. Darcy is a complex human being rather than a mere vehicle for satire such as Charles Adams. Nevertheless, I think it is likely that Darcy has somewhere in his ancestry a parody-figure similar to the ones in which Jane Austen's juvenilia abound. Such a theory is consistent with current assumptions about Jane Austen's habits of composition. Her first three novels are the products of reworkings of drafts written at a period much closer to the time when her juvenile parodies of fiction were written than to that at which *Sense and Sensibility* as we have it was published. Both *Northanger Abbey* and *Sense and Sensibility* contain marked traces of satiric originals, and it seems reasonable to assume that *Pride and Prejudice*, as well as the other two novels, grew, through a process of refinement, from a criticism of literature into a criticism of life. Moreover, the theory accounts for what is perhaps the most serious flaw in *Pride and Prejudice*: the vast difference between the Darcy of the first ballroom scene and the man whom Elizabeth Bennet marries at the end of the novel. We have seen that the most exaggerated displays of conceit and rudeness on Darcy's part—his speech at the Meryton assembly, his fears lest he should be encouraging Elizabeth to fall in love with him, and the language of his first proposal—could have originated as burlesques of the patrician hero. If we postulate an origin in parody for Darcy and assume that he was later subjected to a refining process, the early, exaggerated displays of rudeness can be explained as traces of the original purely parodic figure that Jane Austen was not able to manage with complete success.

[. . .]

In the early stages of the novel's development, I believe [. . .] Elizabeth Bennett was merely an anti-type to the Burney-Richardson sycophantic heroine; Darcy, a caricature of the patrician hero. Later, although she retained an element of ironic imitation, Jane Austen refined her characters, transforming them from mere vehicles for satire into human beings interesting in their own right as well as because of their relationship to their literary prototypes. And, as the remainder of this essay implies, she also changed her attitude toward her patrician hero and her anti-Evelina, and accordingly altered her treatment of Darcy drastically and made Elizabeth, as well as Darcy, a target for her irony. Theories about the development of the novel aside, however, the fact remains that *Pride and Prejudice* as we have it is not simply, as critics have suggested, an imitation of the work of Jane Austen's fellow-novelists. It is, in part at least, an attack on Richardson and Fanny Burney and their patrician heroes.

Jane Austen thoroughly humbles her patrician hero. Darcy is subjected to a series of "set-downs" at the hands of the anti-Evelina, Elizabeth Bennet, and through his love for Elizabeth and the shock he receives from her behavior, he comes to see himself as he really is, and to repent of his pomposity and pride. "By you, I was properly humbled," he admits to Elizabeth towards the end of the novel (II.369).

Interestingly enough, however, Jane Austen does not allow her anti-Evelina to rout her patrician hero completely. For once Darcy has been humbled, she turns her irony on Elizabeth Bennet. She shows that Elizabeth, in her resentment of Darcy's conscious superiority, has exaggerated his faults and failed to see that there is much in him that is good. Elizabeth proves to have been blind and prejudiced in her views on the relationship between Darcy and Wickham, too willing to accept Wickham's stories because they so nicely confirm her own feelings about Darcy. When she reads the letter that follows Darcy's first proposal, she is forced to admit that her resentment has led her to be foolish and unjust. Again, until Darcy's letter shocks her into self-knowledge, Elizabeth has seen Darcy's interference in the affair between Jane and Bingley only as an instance of cold-hearted snobbery on Darcy's part. Reading Darcy's letter, and considering Jane's disposition, Elizabeth is forced to admit that Darcy's view of the affair, his belief that Jane was little more than a complacent pawn in her mother's matrimonial game, is not unjustified. Darcy's interference, Elizabeth must admit, was motivated not merely by snobbery, but by concern for his guileless friend's welfare as well. With her eyes thus opened, Elizabeth comes to see later in the novel that Darcy's position and fortune, and his pride in them, can be forces for good as well as sources of snobbery and authoritarianism. Seeing Pemberley, and hearing his house-keeper's praise of Darcy's conduct as a brother and a landlord, she learns that Darcy's position is a trust and a responsibility, and that his not unjustifiable self-respect leads to a code of conduct worthy of admiration. And in his action in the Lydia-Wickham affair she is provided with an impressive and gratifying instance of his power to do good and his sense of responsibility. At the end of the novel Jane Austen's anti-Evelina is defending her patrician hero. "I love him," Elizabeth says of Darcy to the astounded Mr. Bennet. "Indeed, he has no improper pride" (II.376).

As many critics have pointed out, a pattern of "art-nature" symbolism in *Pride and Prejudice* added depth of suggestion, for Jane Austen's early nineteenth century audience, to the novel's love plot. I suggest that Jane Austen's continual allusions, through parody, to her fellow-novelists' treatment of an eighteenth century authority-figure served a purpose similar to that which the "art-nature" symbolism served. We cannot, of course, assume that Jane Austen thought of her Mr. Darcy as an "authority-figure," in our sense of the term, any more than we can assume that she considered *Pride and Prejudice* a treatise on the eighteenth-century "art-nature" antithesis. But we can be sure that she expected the novel-reading audience for which she wrote to respond to her work on the basis of their impressions of the insufferable Sir Charles Grandisons and Lord Orvilles, the sycophantic Evelinas and Harriet Byrons, of noveldom. At the beginning of *Pride and Prejudice* Darcy is a pompous Burney-Richardson aristocrat, with many of the most disagreeable attributes of his literary progenitors as well as a representative of "art" and excessive class pride. Elizabeth is a determined anti-Evelina as well as a symbol for "nature" and aggressive individualism. The marriage at the end of the story joins a "properly humbled" patrician hero and an anti-Evelina who has also undergone a partial reformation. This element of burlesque-with-a-difference co-operates with the novel's "art-nature" symbolism in broadening and deepening the significance of Elizabeth and Darcy's love story.

[...]

Pride and Prejudice is a story about two complex, sensitive and often blindly wrong-headed "intricate characters" and their progress toward a better understanding of one another, the world, and themselves. This drama of self-knowledge is played out in the context of a symbolism based on the antithesis between "art" and "nature," in the comprehensive eighteenth-century sense of those terms. It is also referred, at many points, to the fiction of Jane Austen's day—particularly to her fellow-novelists' handling of the figure that I have called the patrician hero. Jane Austen's first response to the patrician hero, I believe, was purely satiric. Later, I think, she refined, revised, and greatly complicated her treatment of him. At any rate, *Pride and Prejudice* is something more than a much-improved imitation of the novels Jane Austen knew. It is a work in which she tumbles an eighteenth-century authority-figure from the pedestal on which Richardson and Fanny Burney had placed him—and, with a gesture that distinguishes her also from some later novelists, then stoops to retrieve him from the dust.

NOTES

1. The most detailed study of *Pride and Prejudice* in terms of the "art-nature" dichotomy is Samuel Kliger's "Jane Austen's *Pride and Prejudice* in the Eighteenth-Century Mode," *UTQ*, XVI (1947), 357–370.
2. See, for example, the comments in Mary Lascelles's *Jane Austen and Her Art* (Oxford, 1939), pp. 22 and 162, and Marvin Mudrick's complaints about the change in Darcy in his *Jane Austen: Irony as Defense and Discovery* (Princeton, 1952), pp. 117–119.
3. See Brower's *The Fields of Light* (New York, Oxford University Press, 1951), pp. 164–181, and Babb's *Jane Austen's Novels: The Fabric of Dialogue* (Columbus, Ohio, 1962), pp. 115–118.
4. Jane Austen, *Works*, ed. R.W. Chapman (London, 1954), VI, 13. All references will be to this edition.
5. As E.E. Duncan-Jones points out in "Notes on Jane Austen," *N & Q*, 196 (1951), 114–116. Numbers of heroes in the minor fiction of the period, however, among them Lord C— in *The History of Sir William Harrington* and Mr. Charlemont in *The Lake of Killarney*, are similarly described.

6. In "A Critical Theory of Jane Austen's Writings," Part I, *Scrutiny*, 10 (1941–42), 61–87, Mrs. Leavis recognizes the similarity between the two scenes.
7. Of course, as Brower (*Fields of Light*, pp. 168–169) points out, we see this scene largely through the eyes of the prejudiced Elizabeth Bennet. Darcy is actually eager to dance with Elizabeth, although his manner of expressing himself is not very gallant.

SIR GAWAIN AND THE GREEN KNIGHT

"Sir Gawain's Unfulfilled/Unfulfilling Quest,"
by Michael G. Cornelius,
Wilson College

The fourteenth-century alliterative romance *Sir Gawain and the Green Knight* is a classic example of heroic questing literature and one of the finest medieval epic romances ever composed in the English language. Yet the anonymous author of *Gawain* disrupts the fulfillment generally found in questing tales. In defiance of custom, the heroic condition of both Gawain's society and the knight himself are not improved by Gawain's journey. However, this lack of fulfillment is precisely the purpose behind Gawain's quest in the first place. The *Gawain* author has designed his romance to demonstrate the inherent impossibility of the chivalric code that Gawain lives by, ensuring Gawain's failure. While this does not trouble Gawain's foes, the poet, or even the audience, it does weigh heavily on Gawain himself, and it is his lack of fulfillment, combined with the noncomprehending reaction of his own society to his disappointment, that results in the failure of Gawain's own heroic journey.

Gawain's expedition was never meant to be a triumph. As Shedd describes it, Gawain's quest, "constitutes a glaring violation of the traditional success-story pattern" specific to the genre (4). The quest was designed by Morgan le Fay to demonstrate the inherent shortcomings of the chivalric code: in short, the unfeasibility of living by a code that demands its practitioners to act in ways that are generally beyond the desires and capabilities of mere mortal humans. Piotr Sadowski writes that *Sir Gawain and the Green Knight* is "both a literary expression and critique of the chivalric ideal of its age" (53). Thus Gawain becomes Morgan's unknowing accomplice in personifying this critique; his failure ensures her success.

In describing the questing nature of *Gawain*, Sadowski writes, "the story of Sir Gawain as a particular literary manifestation of the standard epic heroic biography symbolically describes human life conceived as a pursuit of higher spiritual values, attained through a series of tests and trials of physical, psychological, and moral nature" (52). It is through these trials that the questing hero finds fulfillment. Aaron Steinberg argues that fulfillment is connected to the "content of [the] inner life" (191). Fulfillment thus adheres to a "psychological inner reality and structure," reflecting the fantasies, desires, fears, and motivations of the quester (Steinberg 188). Richard J. Collier, however, also notes that fulfillment is dependent upon external factors as well as internal. In works like *Gawain*, there exists an overseeing figure—in this case, Morgan le Fay, who "guided me . . . to your great hall / to put pride on trial"—and it is this figure who has essentially ordained the actions that are to follow (Armitage 2456–7). All that remains for Gawain to add to the chain of events is his own struggle toward an internal sense of fulfillment; thus both the external will, the fulfillment of Morgan le Fay's design by Bertilak the Green Knight, and the internal motivations of Gawain himself, must come together to create the quest Sadowski describes. However, because of the type of quest Morgan has created, and because of the motivations and fears of the very human knight at the center of the epic, the quest itself is doomed to failure—a failure predicated by the lack of both external fulfillment (the inability of Gawain to complete the quest as promised) and internal fulfillment (the quest fails to transform Gawain into the type of celebrated hero he imagines when he accepts the Green Knight's challenge at Camelot). Yet the quest's failure is what ultimately allows for the growth of the hero. In failure, Gawain finds only imperfection and the stunning recognition that he is only human.

It is perhaps a bit unfair to suggest that Gawain's quest is a resolute failure; after all, he does travel to the chapel of the Green

Knight, he does place his head on the block, and he does (finally) allow the Green Knight to have his return blow. Even the Green Knight himself declares Gawain's actions to be relatively honorable: "As a pearl is more prized than a pea which is white, / so, by God, is Gawain, amongst gallant knights" (2364-2365). Gawain, however, will not excuse himself so readily:

> Such terrible mistakes,
> and I shall bear the blame.
> But tell me what it takes
> to clear my clouded name. (2385-2388)

If Gawain overreacts (as Bertilak indicates he does in the subsequent line), it is because of the exacting nature of the chivalric code for knightly conduct. The genre of the medieval romance relies on such a code. As Dorothy Everett so astutely describes the genre and its code of conduct, "Medieval romances are stories of adventure in which the chief parts are played by knights, famous kings, or distressed ladies, acting most often under the impulse of love, religious faith, or, in many, mere desire for adventure" (3). Gawain, however, acts out of none of these but out of "knightly duty"; as Everett rightly adds, "all romance heroes must conform to medieval ideas of chivalric conduct" (5). Richard Hamilton Green enhances this description when he writes of medieval romances as depicting "an ideal society in a marvelous world where the virtuous hero represents the temporal and spiritual ideal," though Green is hesitant to suggest that Gawain ascribes to all of those conditions (122). Nonetheless, the chivalric code represents the "idealization of ordinary life," and the hero "does his duty whatever it may cost him" (Everett 8). Though Gawain's sacrifice at the end of his quest seems minor to a modern audience, he is saddled with the disheartening realization that his chivalric code is nearly impossible to live by and that his own society is determined to turn his failure into its success. As Shedd notes, the poet reveals through the "portrayal of Gawain and Arthur's court the weaknesses as well as the strengths of the knightly code. In doing so he reaffirms certain vital truths about the nature of man" (3-4). These truths, however, provide cold comfort to the poem's hero. Yes, Gawain survives his quest, but he survives unfulfilled.

The "tests and trials" Gawain endures most successfully demonstrate both the knight's need for and failure in achieving fulfillment. Throughout the poem, Gawain undertakes numerous challenges that are designed to test the essential characteristics of a chivalric knight: courage, honor, loyalty, and courtesy. These are the attributes the Green Knight challenges when he arrives at Arthur's palace:

> "So here is the house of Arthur," he scoffed,
> "whose virtues reverberate across the realm.
> Where's the fortitude and fearlessness you're so famous for?
> And the breathtaking bravery and the big-mouth bragging?
> The towering reputation of the Round Table,
> Skittled and scuppered by a stranger—what a scandal!" (Armitage
> 309–315)

The Green Knight's initial arrival creates a palpable shock throughout the court, not just because of his outward appearance, but also because of the blustery nature of the challenge he throws down among the assembled knights. Green calls this moment an "ominous intrusion of a figure from another world," and thus it seems we can forgive the knights for being stunned into momentary silence (124). It is Arthur himself who initially steps forward to confront the Green Knight. Many critics have suggested that Arthur's response is less than valorous, motivated more by wounded pride and embarrassment than by any more genuine chivalric ideal; however, the text does not necessarily bear this reading out. In fact, the opposite seems more likely true; once over his initial shock at the Green Knight's odd request, Arthur's reply, though not as commanding as the Green Knight's initial provocation, is bold and aggressive.

It is now that Gawain steps forward, to take the stead of his king and measure the might of the Green Knight. Critics have long suggested that Gawain's initial response to the Beheading Game is both apt and courageous, and indeed, Gawain's words to both his king and the Green Knight demonstrate his humility and courage. However, Gawain's initial motivation for undertaking the challenge has itself never been questioned. Though a knight is always supposed to perform his chivalric duty regardless of the potential danger to his person, Gawain's words suggest that he reacts to the Green Knight's challenge for reasons other than duty. Initially, upon witnessing his king step forward to take on the Green Knight, Gawain mutters to himself, "I stake my claim. / This moment must be mine" (341-342). Later, Gawain adds:

> I am the weakest of your warriors and feeblest of wit;
> loss of my life would be grieved the least.
> Were I not your nephew my life would mean nothing. (354–357)

Gawain's lack of hubris at the moment of undertaking the challenge demonstrates his proper humility as a chivalric and Christian knight. Yet it also underscores a motivation for his doing so: For a man with no particular deeds to boast of (something the Green Knight himself marks as important when he arrives at Arthur's palace), the Beheading Game offers Gawain a notable opportunity to further his own fame. The fulfillment being satisfied by this gesture is Gawain's desire for renown and a bold reputation. While internal fulfillment is significant to the quest, Gawain's desire to act out of reputation negates his sense of duty and chivalric honor.

The Beheading Game is at best a mixed success for Gawain. He does boldly answer the challenge of the Green Knight, but surely he does so believing that his response would bring him adulation. That the Green Knight survives his encounter with Gawain's axe-blow is a "wonder" to the assemblage, a word used several times in the original Middle English text to describe what the court witnessed (lines 17, 29, 148, 238, 467, 480, 496). Gawain likely never believed that the Green Knight would return the blow, presuming, no doubt, that he would not survive Gawain's own initial strike; yet once the Green Knight survives the challenge, Gawain realizes he has no choice but to keep his word and seek out the Green Knight in the fated year and a day. Though the journey fills him with "mourning," Gawain sets out on his unlikely quest with a humble if somewhat reluctant heart (Armitage 543).

Gawain's decision to keep his word and seek out the fatal visage of the Green Knight represents a choice between his life and his honor. Had Gawain remained behind or left Camelot and not sought the Green Knight, his life may have been assured, but his chivalry would forever be tarnished. For a knight of Gawain's stature, his honor is essentially his life, and thus Gawain truly has no choice in the matter. Nonetheless, the matter-of-fact and forthright manner in which Gawain seeks the Green Knight is laudable. Shedd writes, "when the time comes for the hero to depart in search of the Green Chapel and the return blow, we cannot help but be strongly affected by the spectacle of his unflinching honesty and bravery" (4). Shedd's sentiment is wholly correct; nonetheless, it is important to remember that Gawain truly had little choice in the matter. Gawain now acts, as Everett notes, out of duty and not out of any higher chivalric ideal.

Still, adherence to duty is an admirable trait in Gawain, who displays many more during the Exchange of Winnings game he engages in with Bertilak before heading off to the Green Chapel. The Exchange of Winnings game is predicated on a seemingly simple proposal between Gawain and his host:

> "Furthermore," said the master, "let's make a pact.
> Here's a wager: what I win in the woods will be yours,
> and what you gain while I'm gone you will give to me.
> Young sir, let's swap, and strike a bond,
> let a bargain be a bargain, for worse or for better." (1105–1109)

The Exchange of Winnings is perhaps the most obvious test placed before Gawain, an exchange that the medieval audience would instantly recognize as a trial of character. Both Gawain's loyalty and his honor are being challenged in the test: his loyalty to his host to abstain from romantic contact with his wife, and his honor to the wife to maintain his vow of fealty to her. Thus in keeping his vow to the lady, Gawain is offending the very characteristic in him the lady wishes to test. Nonetheless, during the first two days of the exchange, Gawain balances these twin pledges adequately; he finds a way to satisfy both the wife and his host without affronting either of them directly. Shedd continues: "Gawain simply cannot play the boor and tell his hostess to desist . . . given his reputation for refine-ment of manners—a point on which the lady has harped a number of times to his face—he must cope with the situation tactfully, while preserving the integrity of his relationship as Bertilak's guest" (6).

Gawain's playful banter with the lady—and his equally humorous return of the kisses to her husband—demonstrates not his loyalty but his tact and quick-wittedness, qualities the author of the text seems to prize, if not the chivalric code itself.

It is on the third day that Gawain falters. After refusing a golden ring from the lady, Gawain is offered something worth far more to him:

> For the body which is bound within this green belt,
> as long as it is buckled robustly about him,
> will be safe against those who seek to strike him,
> and all the slyness on earth wouldn't see him slain. (Armitage 1851–1854)

Gawain mulls over the offer before finally accepting; now that his salvation may be at hand, he refuses to give his winnings to Bertilak as agreed upon, thus breaking his oath of loyalty to this host.

Much has been made of Gawain's failure here, both in the form of condemnation and excuses. Green moralizes: "He breaks his faith as a knight to his host, to his fearful antagonist, and most of all to himself" (137). David Farley Hills is more forgiving: "In the circumstances who would have behaved as well?" (131). Shedd falls somewhere between the two: "By accepting the Girdle he gives in to fear, and by agreeing to the lady's request for silence he violates his sworn word to Bertilak vis-à-vis the exchange of winnings . . . [yet he] is a frightened, confused, fallible human being whose emotions dominate his reason and becloud his grasp of right and wrong" (8). Regardless, though, Shedd labels Gawain's action a "failure," a sentiment echoed by Green, Everett, and others. Yet it seems significant to point out that Gawain was supposed to fail this test, that the entire quest has been set up to elicit exactly this kind of failure. Thus while Gawain's failure ensures his own lack of both external and internal fulfillment, it does progress the external fulfillment of the quest itself as designed by Morgan le Fay.

Gawain faces one more test before arriving at the Green Chapel. Pausing before reaching the Green Chapel, Gawain's guide suggests to him, "So banish that bogeyman to the back of your mind, / and for God's sake travel an alternative track, / ride another road, and be rescued by Christ" (Armitage 2118–2120). Gawain, of course, refuses and proceeds on to the Green Chapel. Shedd suggests this scene demonstrates "the hero once more in command of himself—once more the familiar strong figure" (9). Yet what is the source of Gawain's strength? Is it his chivalric code? Is it a newfound resolve or a sense of acquiescence over his fate? Or is Gawain's mettle derived from the green sash he believes may preserve his life? By this point in the narrative Gawain's quest has already been lost; the true test—the test of his knightly codes—has already been decided. Certainly Gawain is courageous to continue forth, as he has no proof of the mantle's power. Yet the girdle must provide him with enough resolve and belief to offer him some hope of survival; otherwise, he would not have taken it in the first place.

As Bertilak never truly intends Gawain any physical harm, his conduct when returning the stroke made in the initial Beheading Game is almost cruel. Bertilak revels in Gawain's discomfort, taunting the knight with a feigned blow after Gawain flinches on the first. The conclusion to the Beheading Game suggests not so much another challenge for Gawain as a punishment: His humiliation at his own cowardice during the first blow, the aborted second blow, and the interminable fear of losing his life are designed to both chasten and censure Gawain. The quest has already failed, as has the quester; what follows is proper reparation before Bertilak explains how perfectly Gawain has played his part within the quest's ultimate design.

After Gawain is nicked by the third blow, he rises to his feet in a hasty, but joyous, reprieve. It is now that Bertilak explains that the entire quest has been a ruse designed to test Gawain's mettle and that Gawain's failure occurred not during this most recent challenge but earlier, during his conduct at the host's castle:

> Because the belt you are bound with belongs to me;
> it was woven by my wife so I know it very well.
> And I know of your courtesies, and conduct, and kisses,
> and the wooing of my wife—for it was all my work! (Armitage 2358–2361)

However, Bertilak finds little to fault in Gawain's conduct: "But a little thing more—it was loyalty that you lacked: / not because you're wicked, or a womanizer, or worse, / but you loved your own life; so I blame you less" (2366–2368). Gawain is not so kind to himself:

> "A curse upon cowardice and covetousness.
> They breed villainy and vice, and destroy all virtue."
> Then he grabbed the girdle and ungathered its knot
> and flung it in fury at the man in front.
> "My downfall and undoing; let the devil take it.
> Dread of the death blow and cowardly doubts
> meant I gave in to greed, and in doing so forgot
> the fidelity and kindness which every knight knows.
> As I feared, I am found to be flawed and false,
> through treachery and untruth I have totally failed," said Gawain. (2374–2383)

Shedd indicates that the Green Knight's jocular reaction to Gawain "is a compassionate recognition of the fact of human imperfection" and that "the most faultless of chevaliers is only human" (10, 12). The Green Knight's response reflects the quest's external sense of fulfillment; or, rather, it reflects the quest's external sense of impending failure. Morgan le Fay's grand design has met its own standard of success. She has proved the impossibility—or, at least, the strong improbability—that one could always live by the dictates of the chivalric code. Green observes that "the hero's claim to perfection . . . can only be confirmed by the success of the quest" (128). Morgan's tests have elicited pride, fear, cowardice, disloyalty, and dishonor from Gawain, traits that ensure he is far from perfect; though Bertilak reminds both the knight and the audience that, in reality, his faults are slight and his courage and conduct largely above reproach, the chivalric code does not enjoy the same reprieve.

This point is made emphatically when Gawain returns to Arthur's court. Upon his homecoming, Gawain calls himself a coward and notes, "For man's crimes can be covered but never made clean; / once entwined with sin, man is twinned for all time" (Armitage 2511–2512.) Gawain's recrimination reflects his own lack of internal fulfillment from the quest; the discovery of his fallible, human nature is cold comfort to the poor knight. The reaction of Arthur and court mirrors that of the Green Knight to Gawain's misery: laughter and kind words. Yet whereas the Green Knight was demonstrating the quest's larger point to Gawain, the "lords and ladies of the court, still somewhat *childgered* and given to pride, laughed loudly and decided amiably that the knights of the Round Table would wear the green lace in honor of Gawain. Amid the relieved laughter of the knights and ladies one sees the wry smile of the amiable poet: it is enough if some of the laughter is directed at themselves" (Green 139). Though the *Gawain* poet does not record Gawain's reaction to this, the reader can only imagine his chagrin and embarrassment at having had his failure turned into the court's success. After all, the great meaning of the quest for Gawain is "implicit in the failure of its hero" (Shedd 4). Through his failure, Gawain has achieved "self-discovery," and in this "self-discovery the hero made a beginning" (Green 138). Thus, the unfilled and unfulfilling nature of his great quest has perhaps taught Gawain a valuable and important lesson about the realities of human existence and the frailties of his own knightly code.

WORKS CITED

Armitage, Simon. *Sir Gawain and the Green Knight: A New Verse Translation.* New York: W.W. Norton, 2007.

Collier, Richard J. "The Action of Fulfillment in the York Corpus Christi Play." *Pacific Coast Philology* 11 (1976): 30–38.

Everett, Dorothy. "A Characterization of English Medieval Romance." In *Essays on Middle English Literature.* Ed. Patricia Kean. Oxford: Clarendon Press, 1955.

Green, Richard Hamilton. "Gawain's Shield and the Quest for Perfection." *ELH* 29.2 (1962): 121–139.

Hills, David Farley. "Gawain's Fault in *Sir Gawain and the Green Knight.*" *The Review of English Studies* 14.54 (1963): 124–131.

Sadowski, Piotr. *The Knight on His Quest: Symbolic Patterns of Transition in* Sir Gawain and the Green Knight. Newark: University of Delaware Press, 1996.

Shedd, Gordon M. "Knight in Tarnished Armour: The Meaning in 'Sir Gawain and the Green Knight.'" *The Modern Language Review* 62.1 (1967): 3–13.

Sir Gawain and the Green Knight. Ed. J.R.R. Tolkien and E.V. Gordon. Revised by Norman Davis. Second Edition. Oxford: Clarendon Press, 1967.

Steinberg, Aaron. "The Wife of Bath's Tale and Her Fantasy of Fulfillment." *College English* 26.3 (1964): 187–191.

To Kill a Mockingbird
(Harper Lee)

"'Stand up; your father's passing': Atticus Finch as Hero Archetype"
by Marlisa Santos,
Nova Southeastern University

Perhaps the question of why *To Kill a Mockingbird* has remained both popular and critically acclaimed for several generations can be answered by the nature of the reader's attraction to the character of Atticus Finch as the consummate hero. Joseph Campbell argued that the hero is "someone who has given his or her life to something bigger than oneself" (151), and this can certainly be said of Atticus. But the nature of his heroism is romantic—he manages to elevate local struggles, victories, and failures to global proportions, showing the reader the most fundamental kinds of ethical behavior and their great consequences.

Atticus Finch is made the moral center against which everything else in the novel is measured, as he exhibits individuality, bravery, and integrity against what seem insurmountable odds—and more importantly, sees the utmost importance of the value of passing these virtues to his children and community. Campbell's conceptualization of the hero as one who undertakes a journey is particularly applicable to Atticus, who travels through the various stages of test, trial, and revelation. Campbell argued that the complexity and speed of life make it difficult for modern society to identify or embrace heroes, adding that society nevertheless does need heroes "because it has to have constellating images to pull together all of these tendencies to separation, to pull them together into some intention" (163). Atticus serves this function in both his household and in the community. The majority of his lessons as a father focus on finding context for assumptions and synthesizing ideas and concepts into coherency for the children. He clarifies what it means to be "poor" for Scout as she struggles to understand the relationship to their lot in life vis-à-vis the Cunninghams and also how the inconsistencies she sees between her home life and her school life may be reconciled through "compromise." Scout thinks compromise is "bending the law," when it is actually "an agreement reached by mutual concessions" (36)—in this case, meaning that if Scout will continue to attend school, she and Atticus will continue to read at home, even though her new teacher said that Atticus was teaching Scout to read "all wrong" (34). Though Atticus respects law and societal order, he values individual experience and perspective even more—as long as both adhere to basic moral and ethical standards.

One of Atticus's most memorable lessons is the necessity to understand other human beings before judging them. Atticus explains to Scout that her teacher could not be expected to know all the ways of the community, because it was her first day teaching and being new to the school, adding that "you never really understand a person until you consider things from his point of view, . . . until you climb into his skin and walk around in it" (34). Atticus provides wider perspective to those things that people tend to assume or gloss over, such as quick judgments about the character and actions of others without due consideration. The ability to illuminate and educate is a hero's function, one that Jem and Scout largely take for granted until they see Atticus as heroic in a way that is more obvious to them: when he shoots the rabid dog. The drama of this scene is clear, including Jem's speechless reaction, but its importance lies more in the effects of the shooting. It is likely that Jem and Scout would not have understood so acutely the heroism in Atticus's court battle over Tom Robinson had they not seen him in this light; seeing him acting conventionally heroic lends more credence to the more subtle heroisms that Atticus enacts every day at home.

As a heroic father, Atticus conveys wisdom, yet this wisdom is anything but conventional, as is his unexpected shooting of the rabid dog. The act of Atticus dropping his slipping spectacles onto the street is symbolically powerful, casting a surprisingly virile light on Atticus and showing the children firsthand what he has been trying to teach them all along: that appearances can be deceiving. The children have concluded that because Atticus "was nearly fifty," he was "feeble," and he "didn't do anything. He worked in an office, not in a drugstore. Atticus did not drive a dump-truck for the county, he was not the sheriff, he did not farm, work in a garage, or do anything that could possibly arouse the admiration of anyone" (94). What he can do is "make somebody's will so airtight can't anybody meddle with it" (95), in addition to being the best checker player in town, an accomplished Jew's harpist, and, of course, "One-Shot Finch," the best shot in the county. Assuming that Atticus is a smart but weak man because he is too old to play football for the Methodists is faulty, as is the assumption that Atticus hesitates to let the children have guns until they are older because he does not understand anything about shooting.

Atticus also shows that there are many ways to fight without physical beating. His conversation with Scout forbidding her to fight, regardless of the reason, leads into a discussion of the reason for the fight: disparaging accusations against Atticus because he is defending Tom Robinson. Scout wants to know why he is doing it if so many people are against him, and he responds, "the main reason is that if I didn't, I couldn't hold my head up in town. I couldn't even tell you or Jem not to do something again" (80). Atticus's integrity as a parent—indeed as a person—is at stake, and he will not be a hypocrite. He is attempting to teach by example, showing that one doesn't lower oneself by a physical fight, as he exercises restraint on multiple occasions with Bob Ewell, even when Ewell spits in his face. By the same token, he is showing that one must not turn away from the more necessary—and often more difficult—fights that take place for the sake of justice and truth but are not fought with one's fists. Dean Shackelford argues that Atticus "seems oblivious to traditional expectations concerning masculinity (for himself) and femininity (for Scout)" (Shackelford 110). His admonishment to Scout has less to do with her being a girl than her being a human being, and he will not compromise his identity either for Jem, who believes, at least at the beginning of the novel, that being a man means physical prowess. And in the same way that Jem and Scout cannot understand their father's value right away, they also cannot understand that the things in life that they believe are frightening and threatening, like Boo Radley, are really illusory when compared to the things in life, like racism and injustice, that Atticus is trying to protect them from.

However, Atticus himself acknowledges that there is no shielding the children from the harsh truths of the world. The role of the hero, in fact, is not to block the harsh or dangerous consequences of the world entirely but to protect and, in so doing, reinforce fundamental values and recognition of truths. This is how Atticus plays a similar role in the community as he does at home. Campbell observes:

> A legendary hero is usually the founder of something—the founder of a new age, the founder of a new religion, the founder of a new city, the founder of a new way of life. In order to found something new, one has to leave the old and go in quest of the seed idea, a germinal idea that will have the potentiality of bringing forth that new thing. (167)

This is often the central quest of the hero: to venture into the wilderness in search of something meaningful to humanity, that will bring humanity to a new level. Campbell acknowledges that quite often, once the hero returns from his journey and its trials, the world rejects what he brings back, adding that "it isn't always so much that the world doesn't want the gift, but that it doesn't know how to receive it and how to institutionalize it" (173). It is not a foregone conclusion, then, that the world will embrace the hero. It is often quite the opposite, as the hero can seem to be a threatening figure when presenting foreign ideas to society, no matter how well intentioned or beneficial. This is precisely Atticus's position as he takes a stand in the Maycomb community to defend Tom Robinson, thereby bringing forth the radical-for-its-time concept that a black man is just as much of a human being as a white man, that injustice against a black man is just as reprehensible as injustice against a white man. Atticus is regarded with suspicion by many and with outright hatred by more.

Nevertheless, Atticus takes the high road in the trial, relying on logic and facts and, most importantly, relying on his belief, perhaps against all evidence of what he knows to be true about his community, that the jury will act in a logical, reasonable, and ethical manner. He takes the position that he knows the jury will not stoop to the level of mind that believes in all the racial stereotypes pointing against consideration of the facts. In his closing statement Atticus argues, "In this country, our courts are the great levelers. In our courts, all men are created equal. I'm no idealist to believe firmly in the integrity of our courts and of our jury system—that's no ideal to me. That is a living working reality!" (208). Most significantly, Atticus urges them, "In the name of God, do your duty" (208). But it may be of little use to urge men to do their duty when there are conflicting definitions of what their duty is. The jury ultimately believes that they are doing their duty by supporting the accusations of the white Mayella Ewell, regardless of how baseless those accusations are, and Atticus's propositions regarding equality and duty are rejected by the populace, who are not ready to hear them—or to live them.

This is why Atticus's defeat becomes akin to the hero's sacrifice. The fact that Atticus, according to Kathleen Murphy, "*acts* as though his hometown were peopled by rightminded folk, presenting himself to a jury of coveralled farmers as one who 'has confidence in you gentlemen'" may not make it so—at least not yet (20). A jury of Tom Robinson's peers does not judge him; his peers sit in the segregated gallery overhead, viewing, almost as a silent Greek chorus, the travesty below. Their little consolation is the gratitude they feel toward Atticus, as the courtroom clears of all but him; all the members of the gallery stand as he leaves. Reverend Sykes admonishes Scout to "Stand up. Your father's passin'," as they honor him in the only way that they can, the small, but significant, way that one honors everyday heroes (214). Atticus is defeated and demoralized for the day, in the name of a greater good that he may not even see in his lifetime. It is for this reason that Maudie, in consolation to Jem, who finally seems to understand the importance of his father's strength, says, "Some men in this world are born to do our unpleasant jobs for us. Your father's one of them" (218). These kinds of unpleasant jobs cannot be avoided if societies are to change and grow, and heroes like Atticus are the forces for such social change.

That Atticus clearly displays human frailties and weaknesses only highlights his heroic status. Though he finds incredible strength in spite of the challenges he faces, he is clearly troubled by the absence of his wife, dead four years by the time the story begins, and is resigned to suffer. Atticus is also quite human in the way that he misjudges the danger of Bob Ewell. He accurately realizes that the racism of Ewell and others like him presents the broadest danger possible to the community at large, but he thinks that, individually, the leering, posturing Ewell is best ignored. However, it becomes clear that there may be a great deal to fear from a man like Bob Ewell. His attack on Jem and Scout, especially when months have passed since the trial and Robinson was found guilty, comes as a shock and makes clear the level of ingrained racism in men like Ewell, who, despite his victory in court, cannot forget that a white man dared to defend a black man against a white woman. Such violence toward his own children was likely not something that Atticus anticipated and could not defend against.

Atticus is also humanly torn after the attack when he and Sheriff Heck Tate are discussing his discovery of Bob Ewell in the woods, stabbed with a kitchen knife. Atticus haltingly says, "Well, Heck . . . I guess the thing to do—good Lord, I'm losing my memory . . . it'll come before county court... Of course, it's a clear case of self-defense . . ." (275). Heck then argues that Bob Ewell fell on his knife, stating: "There's a black boy dead for no reason, and the man responsible for it's dead. Let the dead bury the dead this time Mr. Finch. Let the dead bury the dead" (278). There does not seem to be a question in either Heck's or Atticus's mind that it was necessary to kill Bob Ewell in order to save Jem and Scout, regardless of who stabbed him. The question becomes whether to bring the matter before the courts in strict accordance with the process of law. Atticus, though a passionate defender of the court system and law, acquiesces to Heck. Atticus does this in part perhaps because he has seen the courts fail in likely the worst way since he became a lawyer. But perhaps he also believes, as Heck voices, that to bring Boo Radley, "with his shy ways," into the limelight for such an ordeal after he has done a right and necessary thing would be "a sin," done for no good reason, like shooting a mockingbird. Boo, of course, is not the only mockingbird, far from the only victim in this story. But he may have the most to lose, as did Tom Robinson, by following the letter of the law. In the same way that Atticus teaches that you cannot be a full human being until you walk around in others' skins and understand their points of view, he acknowledges that morality and the law are not always in accord and that exceptions must be considered, weighed for greater good or ill. The law is only as good as the society that builds and upholds it, and though Atticus cites the Declaration of Independence regarding equality, he cannot ignore what are likely more important laws, such as those of Jim Crow, that govern his local community. The law, then, becomes to a certain extent fluid, a "new thing" that must evolve, catalyzed by the trials and revelation of the hero that create a higher purpose.

Harper Lee's story of Atticus Finch as a heroic single father was ahead of its time and presages the multitudes of parents and children who would find themselves in a similar situation. Everyday heroics are the most important kind because the extraordinary circumstances that promote change and growth arise out of the everyday assumptions and consequences that bring either complacency or action. As Atticus faces trials and makes sacrifices, Lee highlights the various issues of race, class, family, and social stagnation that make him an archetypal hero and *perhaps* the main reason for the book's endurance.

WORKS CITED

Campbell, Joseph. *The Power of Myth*. New York: Anchor, 1988.

Lee, Harper. *To Kill a Mockingbird*. New York, Warner, 1960.

Murphy, Kathleen. "The World in His Arms." *Film Comment* 28.2 (March 1992): 20–26.

Shackelford, Dean. "The Female Voice in *To Kill a Mockingbird*: Narrative Strategies in Film and Novel." *Mississippi Quarterly* 50 (Winter 1996–97): 101–13.

THE WOMAN WARRIOR: MEMOIRS OF A GIRLHOOD AMONG GHOSTS (MAXINE HONG KINGSTON)

"*The Woman Warrior* and the Hero's Journey"
by Lauren P. De La Vars,
St. Bonaventure University

When Maxine Hong Kingston's *The Woman Warrior* was published in 1976, it caused a sensation, mostly because of its unusual subject, but at least partly because critics could not easily classify it. It won the National Book Critics Circle Award for the best work of nonfiction in 1976, but the term nonfiction does not adequately describe its mix of fact and fantasy, dream and documentary. *What kind of book is this?* people wondered.

In some ways, *The Woman Warrior* is a realistic work dealing with an American life and an immigrant family: a memoir of childhood, a document of one family's experience in the 1940s and 1950s as Chinese immigrants to America, an autobiography of a girl's claiming her individuality amid the clamor of Chinese and American expectations for girls and women. But in other ways it is not at all American-realistic and certainly is not a conventional, chronological Western autobiography. First, the narrative has no one central narrator; only the last of the five chapters presents consistent first-person narration recognizable as Kingston's voice. Instead, most of the book mediates Kingston's own autobiography through her fictional or factual presentation of the stories of other women. In the second chapter, for instance, Kingston's first-person Chinese-American girl narrator transforms into a girl warrior in training in a fairy-tale Chinese past. The third chapter, the longest in the book, is not even about the narrator but is about her mother, Brave Orchid, in medical school long before the narrator was born. The fourth chapter is an exclusively third-person narrative about Brave Orchid and her sister Moon Orchid sometime during the narrator's teenage years. Many critics, Chinese-American and not, have argued over the book's anomalous generic status. Sau-ling Cynthia Wong surveys and analyzes the controversy over the nature of the book in a 1992 essay ("Autobiography as Guided Chinatown Tour? Maxine Hong Kingston's *The Woman Warrior* and the Chinese American Autobiographical Controversy").

Another way in which *The Woman Warrior* diverges from the mainstream of American-realistic autobiography is in its constant reference to "ghosts." The ghosts of the subtitle (*Memoirs of a Girlhood Among Ghosts*) are alien or foreign to ordinary Chinese life: the spirits of the unhappy dead like the drowned aunt; the heavy, hairy Sitting Ghost with whom Brave Orchid does a long night's battle in a haunted dormitory; the Ghost Teachers, Black Ghosts, Mail Ghosts, Meter Reader Ghosts, and Public Health Nurse Ghosts of the non-Chinese community in Stockton, California. Ghosts are the Other, feared and despised. The narrator's challenge is to maintain her identity against the threat of disintegration, cultural or personal, that the ghosts represent. The most disturbing ghosts of her childhood, because they are the most like her, are the "crazy women"—Moon Orchid, Crazy Mary, Pee-A-Nah—who were unable to adjust to life as Chinese Americans.

Kingston's deliberate thwarting of readers' expectations about the genres of fiction, autobiography, and even of anthropological analysis reflects the instability of her own growing up between two powerful and, to her adolescent mind, prescriptive and unforgiving cultures. *The Woman Warrior* traces these primary themes: the female hero or woman warrior; the complex relation of mothers and daughters; female silence; and the multifarious uses of storytelling.

The five chapters of *The Woman Warrior* interlock in structure, themes, and details chronicling the coming of age of a sullen, uncertain, culturally-conflicted, adolescent Chinese-American narrator, presumably Maxine Hong Kingston herself. Each chapter features a Chinese woman against whom the narrator, striving to understand what is Chinese and what is American, measures herself overtly or covertly. What will she grow up to be, a Chinese or a ghost? Will she be a passive pawn or will she be a woman warrior? Which "I" will she become: the complicated Chinese I, with "seven strokes, intricacies," or the self-assured American capital "I" (166), or the "Chinese word for the female *I*—which is 'slave'" (47)?

Is she like the no-name woman of the first chapter, her father's sister, who brought shame on her family and drowned herself and her illegitimate newborn daughter? Is she like Fa Mu Lan in the chapter called "White Tigers," the legendary swordswoman who dressed as a man to avenge her family, lead an army, and save all of China from the northern marauders? Is she like her mother, Brave Orchid, in the third chapter, "Shaman," whose resourcefulness won her a medical degree and who, to celebrate her diploma, bought a girl out of slavery? Is she like her mother's meek sister Moon Orchid, bullied and prodded by Brave Orchid to assert her rights as a first wife but finding peace only in madness, the madness that Kingston claims afflicts at least one woman in every Chinese-American family? Or is she like the mute girl in the final chapter, the one whom she bullies and prods to try to get her to speak?

The narrator presents her search for her own identity through re-presenting the actions and choices of these other Chinese women, some legendary, some her own relatives, some pitiable or selfish, some heroic. In the last pages of the work, the narrator marks her achievement: She has established an identity separate from her mother's but knotted into its traditions and equally capable of survival and success. Like her mother, she can use her anger, intelligence, strength, and force for good. When her family accepts a repulsive suitor for her and she sees that they are offering to cast her (out) as the family madwoman, she rebels in a two-page monologue of self-assertion:

> [M]y throat burst open. I stood up, talking and burbling. I looked directly at my mother and at my father and screamed, 'I want you to tell that hulk, that gorilla-ape, to go away. . . . I know what you're up to. . . . You think you can give us away to freaks. You better not do that, Mother. . . . If I see him here one more time, I'm going away. I'm going away anyway. I am.

Do you hear me? . . . I am not going to be a slave or a wife.
Even if I am stupid and talk funny and get sick, I won't let you
turn me into a slave or a wife. I'm getting out of here. . . . And
I don't want to listen to any more of your stories; they have no
logic. They scramble me up. You lie with stories. . . . I can't tell
what's real and what you make up. Ha! You can't stop me from
talking.' (201–202)

Kingston claims that *The Woman Warrior* was not her first choice of
title for this book (Brownmiller 175). Nevertheless, the image of the
powerful, dynamic, expressive female hero is central to understanding
the narrator's grown-up options: wife/slave or warrior woman? The
second-chapter story of the fabled swordswoman and general Fa Mu
Lan is fundamental, as is the third-chapter story of Brave Orchid's
successful negotiation of the perils of medical school:

> When we Chinese girls listened to the adults talk-story, we
> learned that we failed if we grew up to be but wives or slaves.
> We could be heroines, swordswomen. Even if she had to rage
> across all China, a swordswoman got even with anybody who
> hurt her family. . . . Night after night my mother would talk-
> story until we fell asleep. I couldn't tell where the stories left off
> and the dreams began, her voice the voice of the heroines in my
> sleep. . . . She said I would grow up a wife and a slave, but she
> taught me the song of the warrior woman, Fa Mu Lan. I would
> have to grow up a warrior woman. (19–20)

Fa Mu Lan's heroism is community directed. She is inspired not by
a selfish will to power but by the need to avenge the wrongs against
her family, to the point of allowing her father to carve the words of
the family's grievance into her back, so that even when she dies her
body will speak her family's history. Her "perfect filiality" (45) is the
hallmark of her heroism.

Against Fa Mu Lan's dutiful heroism, Kingston offers two
episodes of her young-adult life when she had a chance to avenge
the wrongs against the powerless and failed, both times when male
bosses were being crudely racist and Kingston spoke up weakly
and ineffectually in protest (48–49). Repeatedly, she underlines

the brokenness of her speaking voice even as an adult, her inability to assert herself in speech (165, 166, 169, 172, 192). Nevertheless, she is a writing warrior. "The swordswoman and I are not so dissimilar. . . . What we have in common are the words at our backs. The idioms for revenge are 'report a crime' and 'report to five families.' The reporting is the vengeance—not the beheading, not the gutting, but the words" (53). The difference, though, is this: Fa Mu Lan receives her back story from her father and carries it to her grave unread and unaltered. The narrator receives stories from her mother but selects, edits, embellishes, critiques, and interprets them before presenting them to us. She is truly a warrior of words.

Significant to the narrator's relationship with her mother is her belief that, when she was a baby, her mother sliced the membrane securing the underside of her tongue. "I don't remember her doing it, only her telling me about it. . . . 'Why did you do that to me, Mother?' . . . 'I cut it so that you would not be tongue-tied'" (164). The narrator is confused by this act: "Sometimes I felt very proud that my mother committed such a powerful act upon me. At other times I was terrified—the first thing my mother did when she saw me was to cut my tongue" (164). In one way, Brave Orchid is like Fa Mu Lan's father, scarring her daughter to emphasize the claims of family. In another way, she herself is a swordswoman, wielding her weapon to free a family member from restraint.

Daughters and mothers are intertwined in this book and not always in comfortable ways. The happiest mother-daughter pairs are the ones brought together by fate, not by biology. The illegitimate newborn girl joins her no-name mother drowning in the well. Fa Mu Lan's magical old foster mother teaches her survival skills and a joyous approach to life, while her real mother holds the basin to catch the blood when her father cuts into her back. Brave Orchid's clever girl slave is like a daughter to her, training as her nurse and inspiring jealousy in her daughter the narrator long after Brave Orchid left the slave behind in China. Committed to the state mental asylum, Moon Orchid adopts all the other inmates as her daughters and is blissfully happy in her insanity. "She was especially proud of the pregnant ones. 'My dear pregnant daughters.' She touched the women on the head, straightened collars, tucked blankets. 'How are you today, dear daughter?'" (160).

The narrator suffers agonies of resentment and rage because of her mother's high-handedness, her bossiness, and her inability to accommodate the American cultural differences her children are forced to accept at public school. Nevertheless, her abiding wish is to tell her mother the truth about herself:

> Maybe because I was the one with the tongue cut loose, I had grown inside me a list of over two hundred things that I had to tell my mother so that she would know the true things about me and to stop the pain in my throat. . . . If only I could let my mother know the list, she—and the world—would become more like me, and I would never be alone again. (197-198)

In every chapter, Kingston emphasizes that Chinese cultural attitudes dictate silence for women. A woman never speaks, nor is she spoken of, lest she become unspeakable, never named. "No Name Woman" never reveals the name of the man who impregnated her; her persecutors, who never question her, expect her reticence. The narrator reports her own mother's admonition: "Don't tell anyone you had an aunt. Your father does not want to hear her name. She has never been born" (15). The narrator cannily recognizes, though, that "there is more to this silence: they want me to participate in her punishment. And I have. In the twenty years since I heard this story I have not asked for details nor said my aunt's name; I do not know it" (16). She defies her family's insistence on silence both by recounting her mother's talk-story and by embroidering it through pages of speculation on the aunt's motivations, avenging her aunt through words.

Even the warrior woman Fa Mu Lan, though physically forceful, is obediently silent, not trusted to speak her revenge: Her father cuts words into her back to inscribe the family's grievances in her scars. Her body, not her words, becomes the text.

Nevertheless, women must speak in order to teach, even if silence and obedience are the lessons. "You must not tell anyone what I am about to tell you," says Brave Orchid to her daughter the narrator in the book's first sentence. The mother reserves the right to speak and to tell the daughter not to speak. Brave Orchid is a forceful and ingenious speaker throughout the book. She talks all night to the Sitting Ghost that finally releases her from the bed, and she instructs the other students in the exorcism. Bargaining shrewdly with the slave trader, she admires the girl slave who catches on to her game of words and plays along (80–82). She appropriates the voices of weaker women. For instance, she puts words in the mouths of her reluctant sister and her recalcitrant daughter, scripting Moon Orchid's ultimately inef-fectual confrontation with her wayward husband (124–127, 129–131, 143–144, 150–153) and dictating to the narrator the words she is to say in English to shopkeepers (82) and the bemused druggist (170). Even when the narrator bursts out of her silence and shouts at her parents for several hundred words, she reports, "My mother, who is champion talker, was, of course, shouting at the same time" (202).

For Kingston, female silence equals female invisibility; having no name means having no identity. The narrator is caught in a web of contradictions. Her Chinese culture values the silent, virtuous, passive woman, though it celebrates legends of avenging swords-women. Her mother is domineering and dynamic, trying to accul-turate her through talk-stories of family culture and trying to make her speak English as the mother would. Her American culture presents images of the desirable Chinese woman as whispery, exotic, and erotic. She and most of the other Chinese-American schoolgirls are silent in public school surrounded by "ghosts," noisy in Chinese school where they and their families are known. It is no wonder the narrator feels anxious about speaking and about claiming an iden-tity, a Chinese-American identity, separate from her mother's.

"If you don't talk, you can't have a personality" (180), says the narrator to the Chinese-American girl in the midst of a grueling scene of seven pages in which she pinches, shakes, yanks, and shouts at the girl in a frenzy to try to make her speak. "'Say 'Hi,' I said. 'Hi.' Like that. Say your name. Go ahead. Say it. Or are you stupid? You're so stupid, you don't know your own name, is that it? When I say, 'What's your name?' you just blurt it out, O.K.? What's your name?'" (177). She uses her mother's bewildering technique of simultane-ously prohibiting and demanding speech, telling the girl when not to speak, when to speak, and what to say: "'I'm doing this for your own good,' I said. 'Don't you dare tell anyone I've been bad to you. Talk. Please talk.'" (181). The narrator's rage at the soft, pretty, demure, and completely mute girl is rooted in her rage at the feminine constructs her cultures offer her and in her discomfort at recognizing this silent, stubborn girl as her double.

"The difference between mad people and sane people is that sane people have variety when they talk-story. Mad people have only one story that they talk over and over" (159). "Talk-story" is Kingston's verb for the kind of narrating done by her mother and the other elders of her Chinese-American community. "Talk-story" is story-telling, but it is neither strictly factual nor fairy-tale nor gossip nor history nor personal nor communal; it can be all of these at once. It accommodates the layered and shifting nature of present reality and the omnipresence of the past. The whole text of *The Woman Warrior* is "talk-story," Kingston's proof to herself and to her family that she is indeed a worthy inheritor, critic, and transmitter of the Chinese culture communicated to her in talk-story by her mother.

The book is also an act of defiant assertion of self, a stereotypically American act, in contrast to what Kingston portrays as the traditional Chinese submission of the individual to the claims of family and community. The first chapter opens with the sentence, "'You must not tell anyone,' my mother said, 'what I am about to tell you'" (3). Kingston defies her mother by not only repeating but reinventing that forbidden tale of a nameless aunt's punishment and revenge, imagining a range of empowering possibilities in the aunt's story.

As the book progresses, Kingston moves from retelling and commenting on the talk-stories her mother told her to telling her own talk-stories about her mother's life to telling her own talk-stories about her own life. Brave Orchid comes to acknowledge and respect her daughter's maturity as a teller of her own tales. "Here is a story my mother told me, not when I was young, but recently, when I told her I also talk story" (206), Kingston writes in introduction to the book's last story, the ancient tale of a Chinese poetess in a foreign land who would not be silent but sang unforgettably of her home even in an alien language.

WORKS CITED

Brownmiller, Susan. "Susan Brownmiller Talks with Maxine Hong Kingston, Author of *The Woman Warrior*." Wong 173–179.

Cheung, King-Kok. "'Don't Tell': Imposed Silences in *The Color Purple* and *The Woman Warrior*." *Reading the Literatures of Asian America*. Ed. Shirley Geok-lin Lim and Amy Ling. Philadelphia: Temple UP, 1992. 163–189.

Felski, Rita. *Literature After Feminism*. Chicago: U of Chicago P, 2003.

Grice, Helena. *Negotiating Identities: An Introduction to Asian American Women's Writing*. Manchester: Manchester UP, 2002.

Kingston, Maxine Hong. *The Woman Warrior: Memoirs of a Girlhood Among Ghosts*. 1976. New York: Vintage, 1989.

Lim, Shirley Geok-lin, ed. *Approaches to Teaching Kingston's The Woman Warrior*. New York: MLA, 1991.

Madsen, Deborah L. *Chinese American Literature*. Literary Topics series. Vol. 9. Detroit: Thomson Gale, 2001.

Trudeau, Lawrence J. "Maxine Hong Kingston." *Asian American Literature: Reviews and Criticism of Works by American Writers of Asian Descent*. Detroit: Gale, 1999. 209–231.

Svetich, Kella. "Maxine Hong Kingston." *The Oxford Encyclopedia of American Literature*. 4 vols. Ed. Jay Parini. Oxford: Oxford UP, 2004. 2:384–387.

Wong, Sau-ling Cynthia. "Autobiography as Guided Chinatown Tour? Maxine Hong Kingston's *The Woman Warrior* and the Chinese American Autobiographical Controversy." Wong 29–53.

———, ed. *Maxine Hong Kingston's* The Woman Warrior: *A Casebook*. New York: Oxford UP, 1999.

"THE WORN PATH"
(EUDORA WELTY)

"'The Worn Path' and the Hero's Journey"
by Jean Shepherd Hamm,
East Tennessee State University

First published in 1941, "The Worn Path" describes Phoenix Jackson's journey to a doctor's office in Natchez, Mississippi, where she acquires soothing medication for her ill grandson. Poor, black, and old, Phoenix must undertake the journey alone. Her route is long and difficult, but she finally reaches her destination, gets the medicine, and sets off on her journey home. There the story ends. Phoenix might be seen as the archetypal mother whose spirit remains undefeated even as she faces the hopelessness of her situation. Her path is worn not only because she has traveled it many times but also because it has been followed by countless self-sacrificing others. Yet Welty's story of an archetypal mother who perseveres also has sociological significance. Set in the Jim Crow South, "The Worn Path" portrays the struggles of women and African Americans who fight to survive in a world that denies them equality and humanity.

The protagonist's name alludes to the mythical Phoenix bird that regenerates itself from ashes. Welty admitted that she sometimes used myth to suggest "something perhaps bigger than ordinary life allows people to be" (Brans), and Phoenix's name suggests many possibilities as she is both renewed and brings new life to her sick grandchild each time she makes the journey. This journey also recalls the quest motif: the protagonist making a hazard-filled trek to obtain the prize that will bring new life. Phoenix's journey takes place at Christmas, a time for love and charity. Each person she encounters gives her help: the hunter, the lady on the street, and the doctor. Phoenix can also be seen as a Christ-like figure herself, traveling through a hostile world to bring salvation to her grandson.

Because readers know the narratives behind the story's allusions, we can be deceived into believing we know and understand the story. We are familiar with the Christmas story, Christian teachings, and the Phoenix myth, and we suppose "The Worn Path" is a simple retelling or restructuring of previous tales. Additionally, our shared understanding of literary conventions makes it hard to divorce ourselves from a careless reading, to look beyond the surface details and tackle the "subtle prose puzzle" that underlies the story (Bethea 32). In "The Reading and Writing of Short Stories," Welty says, "The finest writers seem to be . . . obstructionists" (qtd. in Pollack). Welty encourages us to find answers to our questions within the stories themselves; she encourages us to solve the puzzles of her fiction, puzzles that require more than surface reading. Critics such as Dean Bethea and Elaine Orr ask us to consider Welty's call to "resist the 'wornness' of old scripts" (Orr 57). "The Worn Path" makes full use of these old scripts, and readers can easily be led to accept them as affirmations of knowledge or beliefs they already hold. "Welty . . . has long been read for what she can offer of reassurance and the docile acceptance of what is given; she has been read as the avatar of a simpler world, with simpler values broadly accepted"(Heilbrun 14). However, Welty's body of work shows her to be a radical experimentalist in her writing, not one to follow the old scripts herself. Why then should we accept the old scripts as those that give meaning to her work?

In reading Phoenix's story for answers, we cannot ignore the socio-historical context. Her story would not be the same in another time and place. Welty said her characters "couldn't live" if you took them out of one story and put them in another. By writing about a black woman in the Jim Crow South, Welty positions her protagonist in a specific time and place. Yet according to Welty, she does not write "historically" but about "personal relationships" (Brans). What is of concern in "The Worn Path" is the relationship between Phoenix and each of the individuals she meets on her journey.

While the relationships are manifestations of historical and societal circumstances, each person Phoenix encounters has the ability to act in opposition to these conditions but does not. Each sustains the institutionalized racism found in southern Mississippi at the time, which Welty critiques.

Reading Phoenix with race in mind, we can see that the white characters believe they understand her. The white hunter says, "I know you old colored people! Wouldn't miss going to town to see Santa Claus!" "A charity case," the doctor's attendant announces without even learning Phoenix's name. Yet there is no true charity for this "charity case." The word has been perverted with connotations of disdain and racial superiority. Even though the hunter helps Phoenix out of the ditch, he has already laughed at her, lied about having no money to give her, and pointed his gun at her head. He no doubt could have given her the nickel, or more, or could have shared the birds he had killed with her. But he did neither, perhaps, since he knew "old colored people" or at least knew the stereotypes; he thought giving only encouraged dependence. In addition, although he says it is too far to walk to Natchez, he abandons Phoenix without any further help or comfort.

In town, though the nurse is willing to give Phoenix the medicine as the doctor has instructed, she admonishes Phoenix: "You mustn't take up our time this way." The doctor, who does not appear in the story, has placed conditions on the charity he extends to Phoenix and her grandson. She can have the soothing medicine for the sick child as long as she makes the difficult trip into Natchez to get it. Charity for these individuals has to be easy; it cannot cost them anything. In the Christmas season, ironically, the charity Phoenix receives is insincere and should challenge the reader's acceptance of these acts as motivated by love. Welty implies that true charity would not consist of tossing small favors to Phoenix, nor would it ignore her true needs. Furthermore, charity might involve questioning the social conditions that created Phoenix's need in the first place.

Alexandr Vaschenko also views Welty's stories as having more complexity than revealed on the surface. In spite of ordinary situations and "apparently insignificant" details, the "general mystery" of her narratives offers "a challenge for any critical mind" (9). Old Phoenix appears in the stereotypical dress of a black woman at the time, recalling the image of Aunt Jemima (a red rag tied around her head) and household workers ("a long apron of bleached sugar sacks"). For many years after the Civil War, it was the law in parts of the South that black women could not appear in public without an apron. Welty's fiction, with careful reading, can "come into focus as a photograph when" it is being developed (Pollack 505). As Pollack points out, when we consider Phoenix's clothing, she is obviously poorly dressed for the "frozen day" in December. Phoenix has no coat, and not one person she encounters in the story notices this fact. Even the seemingly kind lady who lays aside her Christmas parcels to tie "Grandma's" shoelaces does not really see the person before her. Each of the characters Phoenix meets also patronizingly calls her "Granny," "Grandma," or "Aunt," reinforcing racial stereotypes.

To survive in the hostile wasteland around her, Phoenix has had to rely on her wits. She has had to create and re-create herself to meet the expectations of others. Phoenix's constant journeying into her creative imagination and her repeated acts of love give meaning to her life. Alun Jones has observed this view of life in much of Welty's fiction: "The effort of living is [portrayed as] an act of imagination and, like the regeneration of the Ancient Mariner (which has often been interpreted as a poem about the workings of the creative imagination), must begin with an act of love" (26). Along the path, Phoenix talks to animals and uses her imagination to ease her difficulties. When she stops to rest after freeing herself from the thorn bush, Phoenix imagines a small boy offering a slice of marble cake to her. She had already been traveling for some time without eating. Such a treat would be "acceptable," she thinks. Phoenix's most daring use of her wits occurs when she meets the hunter. Having seen him drop a nickel, she must devise a way to get her hands on it. Phoenix must know hunters like to show off their dogs, so she diverts his attention to the stray black dog in a way that will send the hunter off after the stray. This done, she is free to pick up the nickel, a true windfall for her.

Although her exact age is unknown, Phoenix reveals that she was a former slave, too old at Reconstruction to be required to attend school. For her entire existence, she has had to speak different languages, choosing appropriate words and attitudes, especially for circumstances involving white people. She is fully aware that being "uppity" may lead to punishment. According to Forbes, literacy is not only reading and writing, it "is also a matter of relationships among people" (237). During Phoenix's life in the South, relational literacy could mean her very survival. Phoenix describes herself as "an old woman without an education," and it's true she didn't attend school, but careful examination of what Phoenix says, of the manner in which she says it, and even of her silences, reveals how literate she is. Her use of language—complicated, intricate, at times humorous—reveals a woman of color who refuses to be silenced by the society in which she lives. When a hunter finds Phoenix in a ditch and asks what she is doing there, she replies she's lying there on her back "like a June-bug waiting to be turned over." The hunter wants to know where Phoenix lives, but she replies noncommittally, "Way back yonder. . . . You can't even see it from here." Surely Phoenix knows where she lives and could have given the man a more exact location, but she chooses not to reveal too much. Likewise, her answer to the question about her age is vague and even playful. Is there "no telling" because she doesn't know her age or because she doesn't wish to reveal this about herself? When Phoenix comes to the dead cornfield, she says, "Now through the maze," a play on the word *maize*. On her journey, Phoenix continues to play with language. She imaginatively converses with animals and a scarecrow and cryptically repeats, "I walking in their sleep" when she passes abandoned cabins.

In Natchez, the doctor's office attendant greets Phoenix with the words, "A charity case, I suppose." Phoenix's reaction is to remain silent, even as the woman asks questions that affect Phoenix "as if a fly were bothering her." With her silence, Phoenix controls the situation and exasperates the brusque attendant by forcing her to pay attention to the black woman. Phoenix continues her silence, sitting "erect and motionless, just as if she were in armor," when the nurse comes in and questions her. Finally, "like an old woman begging a dignified forgiveness," Phoenix knows and tells the story the nurse and attendant want to hear and already believe: She is old, uneducated, and has a failing memory. Phoenix again takes control of the situation by speaking without being asked and talking about her grandson. This confirms that the nurse did not really want to know about Phoenix, as she quickly dismisses her with the medicine and the word *charity*. After hearing her story, the attendant, perhaps because "it's Christmas time," offers Phoenix a few pennies. Cleverly, Phoenix points out that "five pennies is a nickel" and receives a nickel from her. This nickel will do nothing to improve Phoenix's condition in life, but together with the nickel from the hunter, Phoenix can buy a small present for her grandson.

Until Phoenix tells her story in the doctor's office, we do not know the true nature of her journey. Up until this time, we, like the other characters, may have been carried along with the stereotypes the story seems to reinforce. At this point, however, readers begin to know and understand Phoenix as the person she is and to truly see the hopelessness of her situation. Charity has been shown to her in only the most grudging way, and with Phoenix and her grandson "the only two left in the world," it is clear there will be no one to take care of him when she is gone. Phoenix uses whatever power she has, primarily her use of language, in her veiled resistance to the social oppression she suffers. Phoenix, who on first reading corroborates stereotypes, is a layered character who challenges readers' acceptance of these stereotypes.

Welty's skillful use of irony underscores the story's critique of a racist society. Dean Bethea sees the title as a call to readers to avoid the worn path of societal oppression, especially in this case of Southern black women. This interpretation is sustained by the irony of the title. Saying that the path is worn because Phoenix has traveled it numerous times to obtain the soothing medicine for her grandson ignores the truth of the path: It is anything but worn. Instead of taking a road or established trail, Phoenix traverses a cold wasteland filled with thorn bushes. There she encounters a "maze" through a cornfield where "there was no path," an unfriendly black dog, a threatening hunter, and a log instead of a bridge across a creek. She must get down on her hands and knees and crawl through a barbed-wire fence. What readers infer from the title on first reading only invites us to return to examine it more closely and to consider that Welty's intention may have been to overturn our expectations and to ask us to look more deeply at the entire story.

Use of the third-person point of view allows Welty's narrator to remain objective, describing only the observable events without comment on their significance. Though technique conveys a sense of detachment, Welty is always in control of the story she tells and carefully selects the details she reveals. The apparent detachment of the narrator underscores the shared attitudes of a racist society, prompting the reader to examine these attitudes. Welty tells us in "Is Phoenix Jackson's Grandson Really Dead?" "A fiction writer's responsibility covers not only what he presents as the facts of a given story but what he chooses to stir up as their implications" (221). Welty's story has profound implications for a society that countenances discrimination.

"The Worn Path," like so many of Welty's works, "elicits expectations that it promptly defies" (Pollack 498). Welty asks us what kind of readers we are. And we in turn ask what Eudora Welty expects of us. Welty skillfully uses conventional symbols and allusions to lead us down the worn path of racism she knew so well as a Southerner. That we are so docilely led is reason enough to reexamine the story. Are we like the white characters in the story who superficially acknowledge Phoenix but never acknowledge her humanity? Or are we willing to question existing social injustices and our own acceptance of them? Welty firmly insisted that her writing was not political but relational. Although the racial realities may be unspoken or even veiled, any story about the relationships between blacks and whites in southern Mississippi in the first half of the twentieth century has the worn path of politics securely embedded in its telling.

WORKS CITED

Bethea, Dean. "Phoenix Has No Coat: Historicity, Eschatology, and Sins of Omission in Eudora's 'A Worn Path.'" *International Fiction Review.* 28.1–2 (January 2001): 32.

Brans, Jo. "Struggling Against the Plaid: An Interview with Eudora Welty," reprinted in *Listen to the Voices: Conversations with Contemporary Writers,* Southern Methodist University Press, 1988.

Cole, Hunter. "How to Read Eudora Welty." Originally published 24 July 2001 in the *Clarion-Ledger,* Jackson, Miss. Available at: http://www.textsandtech.org/orgs/ews/teaching /cole.php.

Daly, Saralyn R. "'A Worn Path' Retrod," in *Studies in Short Fiction,* Vol. 1, No. 2 (Winter 1964): 133–39.

Forbes, Cheryl. "African American Women: Voices of Literacy and Literate Voices" in *Courage of Conviction: Women's Words, Women's Wisdom,* ed. Linda A.M. Perry and Patricia Geist. Mountain View, Calif.: Mayfield Publishing Co., 1997.

Heilbrun, Carolyn G. *Writing a Woman's Life*. New York: Ballantine Books, 1988.

Isaacs, Neil D. "Life for Phoenix," in *Sewanee Review*, Vol. LXXI, No. 1. (Winter 1963): 75-81.

Jones, Alun. "The World of Love: The Fiction of Eudora Welty." *The Creative Present: Notes on Contemporary American Fiction*. Ed. Nona Balakian and Charles Simmons. New York: Doubleday, 1963. 25–37.

Orr, Elaine. "Unsettling Every Definition of Otherness: Another Reading of Eudora Welty's 'A Worn Path,'" in *South Atlantic Review*, Vol. 57, No. 2. (May 1992): 57–72.

Pollack, Harriet. "Words Between Strangers: On Welty, Her Style, and Her Audience," in *Mississippi Quarterly*, Vol. XXXIX; No. 4. (Fall 1986): 481–505.

Sykes, Dennis J. "Welty's 'The Worn Path'" *The Explicator*. 56:3. (Spring 1998): 151–153.

Trefman, Sara. "A Review of 'A Worn Path'" in *The Explicator*, Vol. XXIV, No. 6. (February 1966).

Vaschenko, Alexandr. "That Which the Whole World Knows: Functions of Folklore in Eudora Welty's Stories," in *The Southern Quarterly*, Vol. XXXII, No. 1. (Fall 1993): 9–15.

Welty, Eudora. "Is Phoenix Jackson's Grandson Really Dead?" *Critical Inquiry*, Vol. 1, No. 1. (September, 1974): 219–221.

Welty, Eudora. "The Worn Path" in *The Collected Stories of Eudora Welty*. New York: Harvest Books, 1982.

❧ *Acknowledgments* ❧

Blake, Kathleen. "Alice's Adventures in Wonderland." *Play, Games, and Sport: The Literary Works of Lewis Carroll.* Ithaca, N.Y.: Cornell UP, 1974. 108–31. Used by permission of the publisher, Cornell University Press.

Bone, Robert. "James Baldwin." *The Negro Novel in America.* Revised edition. New Haven, Conn.: Yale UP, 1965. 215–39. Copyright Yale University Press.

Cook, Albert. "The Man of Many Turns." *The Classic Line: A Study in Epic Poetry.* Bloomington, Ind.: Indiana University Press, 1966. 120–37. Copyright by Indiana University Press.

Glover, T.R. "Aeneas." *Virgil.* Seventh Edition. New York and London: Barnes & Noble, Methuen & Co., 1969 (First printed in 1904). 208–32.

Herst, Beth F. "*David Copperfield* and the Emergence of the Homeless Hero." *The Dickens Hero: Selfhood and Alienation in the Dickens World.* New York: St. Martin's Press, 1990. 43–66. Reproduced with permission of Palgrave Macmillan.

Ker, W.P. "Beowulf." *Epic and Romance: Essays on Medieval Literature.* London: Macmillan, 1908. 158–75.

Moler, Kenneth L. "Jane Austen's 'Patrician Hero.'" *Studies in English Literature, 1500–1900*, Vol. 7, No. 3, Restoration and Eighteenth Century. (Summer 1967). 491–508. Reproduced with permission.

Purtill, Richard L. "Hobbits and Heroism." *J.R.R. Tolkien: Myth, Morality, and Religion.* New York: Harper and Row, 1984. 45–58. Copyright by Richard L. Purtill. Used by permission.

Raleigh, Sir Walter Alexander. "Don Quixote." *Some Authors: A Collection of Literary Essays, 1896–1916.* Freeport, N.Y.: Books for Libraries Press, 1968 (first printed 1923). 27–40.

Index